THE
INVESTIGATION
OF
CRIME

BY
WILLIAM T. FORBES

PUBLISHING

New York

© 2008 by William T. Forbes

Published by Kaplan Publishing, a division of Kaplan, Inc.
1 Liberty Plaza, 24th Floor
New York, NY 10006

Printed in the United States of America

August 2008
10 9 8 7 6 5 4 3 2 1

ISBN-13: 978-1-4277-9725-4

Kaplan Publishing books are available at special quantity discounts to use for sales pro-motions, employee premiums, or educational purposes. Please email our Special Sales Department to order or for more information at kaplanpublishing@kaplan.com, or write to Kaplan Publishing, 1 Liberty Plaza, 24th Floor, New York, NY 10006.

DEDICATION

To my wife, Michelle, for standing beside me; my father, Bill Forbes, for guiding the path; my mother, Gwendolyn Gore, for supporting me; and my son, Tanner, for making everything worthwhile. The patience of my entire family, including Logan Gray and Raven Miller, has been much appreciated.

CONTENTS

ACKNOWLEDGMENTS

This book would not have been possible without the invaluable editing skills of Carole Grinlinton. I cannot thank her enough for her time and assistance. Also, Chief Fred Mills and the men and women of the Independence, Missouri, police department were of great assistance in this process.

PREFACE

The Investigation of Crime offers insights into the basic elements of criminal investigation. The process of investigating criminal activity is vast; it seems that crime is limited only by one's imagination. In this text, I have attempted to explore the common elements of the investigation of frequently encountered crime.

The first portion of the book explores the foundation of criminal investigation. Included in this section is a basic explanation of terms used throughout the text, an exploration of who investigates crime, and a discussion of some of the legal aspects of criminal investigation. The second section of the book examines procedures used in most criminal investigations, including the gathering of physical and testimonial evidence. The third section of the book explores procedures used to investigate specific types of crime. Each chapter in this section defines the crime and describes the unique challenges of investigating the crime and the strategies used to investigate it.

The field of criminal investigation is constantly changing based upon changes in the socioeconomic world, technology, and a variety of other factors. Approaches used to address crime may change, but the basic elements of criminal investigation, identified in this book, will most likely remain constant.

PART I

FOUNDATIONS OF CRIMINAL INVESTIGATION

CHAPTER 1

INTRODUCTION TO CRIMINAL INVESTIGATION

CHAPTER OBJECTIVES

By the end of this chapter, the reader will be able to do the following:

- Define the term *investigation.*

- Define the term *evidence.*

- Differentiate between physical and testimonial evidence.

- Identify the types of criminal investigation activities conducted by agencies at the three levels of government.

- Explain the progression from an initial police call for service to a follow-up investigation.

The Code of Hammurabi has been estimated as originating around 1700 BCE. These clay tablets prescribed both the laws under the king and the measures used to determine guilt. When conflicting accounts existed, a judge could order that the defendant jump into a swift river. If the accused drowned, the assumption was that the gods had levied punishment upon the individual. If the defendant survived the rough waters, the accuser would be executed (Roth 2005).

The Code of Hammurabi not only lists the earliest known laws but also the procedures for the earliest known investigations. Modern criminal justice professionals would cringe at the "evidence" used to convict someone under the Code, but the goal of this crude trial by ordeal was the same as the overall goal of a modern criminal investigation today. The goal of a criminal investigation is to determine the truth.

INVESTIGATION AND EVIDENCE

Investigation can be defined as the process of collecting and analyzing evidence in an attempt to determine facts. Investigations can be conducted for a variety of reasons. A parent may conduct an investigation to determine which child took a cookie from a jar. A news agency may conduct an investigation to reveal why gasoline prices are high. Police departments initiate investigations to determine who committed a murder.

The final example in the previous paragraph describes a criminal investigation. A criminal investigation focuses upon a crime that has been committed. Absent a crime, an investigation might be classified as a civil investigation (to determine how much child support must be paid by a parent, for instance) or an informative investigation (to explain an event for the curious, such as the formation of "crop circles" at a rural farm). The vast majority of investigations conducted by criminal justice agencies are criminal in nature. Occasionally, a police agency may conduct an investigation only to find that a crime has not been committed.

Scenario

Detective Martinez is assigned an auto theft case. The victim, Cathy Crawford, reports that her car was taken from her driveway by unknown persons sometime between 9:00 PM Thursday and 7:00 AM Friday. Detective Martinez researches the vehicle in question and discovers that Ms. Crawford had a loan on the vehicle through First National Bank. Detective Martinez calls the bank and discovers that Ms. Crawford had not paid her car loan for the previous six months, so First National obtained a court order to repossess the car. County Repossessions Inc. picked up the car at 1:00 AM on Friday morning, and the car was transferred to the custody of First National Bank. Detective Martinez promptly closed the case as it did not involve a criminal offense.

Traffic investigations may be civil, as opposed to criminal, investigations.

There are some cases when a police agency might conduct an investigation that is not criminal in nature. For instance, traffic accident investigations may or may not involve criminal offenses. Unless a traffic violation is involved, police duties are limited to collecting and transferring information between involved parties for later insurance claims. Often accident investigation reports are more important for civil court consideration than for criminal cases.

Evidence is defined as any purported fact included in an investigation. Evidence falls into two categories: real and testimonial. *Real or physical evidence* is tangible material of any type (Fisher 2003). Real evidence can be collected, handled, tested, and moved. This wide category includes the evidence most people think of when they imagine a crime scene. Physical evidence can be as small as a strand of DNA or as large as a tractor-trailer. Blood stains, handguns, physical injuries, and fingerprint impressions are all considered real or physical evidence.

The second category of evidence, *testimonial evidence,* is evidence derived from statements (Fisher 2003). Evidence of this type can be in the form of written or oral statements from victims, witnesses, suspects, or other parties involved in an investigation.

Testimonial evidence is derived from the statements of witnesses.

Scenario

Officer Craig is called to the scene of a domestic violence assault. The suspect has fled the scene. The victim reports that she was struck by the suspect in the arm with a tire iron. Officer Craig takes a written statement (testimonial evidence) from the victim. Officer Craig photographs the victim's injury (physical evidence) and collects the tire iron (physical evidence). Officer Craig places the physical evidence in the police department property room and submits the written statement as part of the report.

When conducting an investigation, each piece of evidence must be carefully evaluated. A weight is often assigned to the evidence based upon the perceived veracity, or value. One piece of evidence may be more useful in an investigation than another. DNA evidence that ties a suspect to a scene, for instance, is likely to be considered more valid than an eyewitness identification of the suspect gained from a distance of 50 yards. The following case study illustrates how evidence can vary significantly in value.

CASE STUDY

Walter Snyder was convicted of rape in Virginia in 1986. Snyder lived next door to the victim, who had seen him washing his car shortly after the offense and notified the police of the possibility that he was the suspect. Snyder's picture was placed in a lineup of photographs, but the victim was unable to select him as a suspect from the array of pictures.

Snyder returned to the police station later to pick up some personal items that had been recovered from him during the course of the investigation. The victim also responded to the police station to contact the detective in charge of the case and noticed Snyder. The victim then reported to the detective that she was certain Snyder was the man who raped her.

After some additional shoddy investigative work and weak testimonial evidence, Snyder was convicted of the rape and sentenced to 45 years in prison.

Snyder's family continued to pursue appeals to free him. After reading articles and seeing television programs about the promise of DNA testing, the family finally came into contact with attorney Peter Neufeld. Advances in DNA technology provided an opportunity for comparisons to be made between the collected samples from the case and Snyder's DNA. The tests revealed that there was not a match.

Over seven years after being incarcerated, Walter Snyder was released from prison on a governor's pardon (Dwyer, Neufeld, and Scheck 2000).

Evidence must be carefully considered, and investigators must avoid developing preconceived notions about what the truth appears to be. Testimonial evidence should not be considered "fact" but only another piece of the investigative puzzle.

Figure 1.1 illustrates the investigative process. Physical and testimonial evidence lays the groundwork for the process. This evidence is considered by a detective through investigation. The ultimate goal of the investigative process is to discover the truth. Each piece of evidence assists in determining the truth.

FIGURE 1-1: Relationship of evidence, via interpretation during investigation, to truth

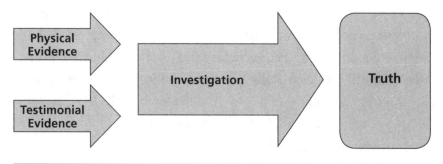

WHO INVESTIGATES CRIME?

Criminal investigations are conducted by a variety of entities. Three levels of government are involved in investigations: federal agencies nationwide, state-level criminal justice organizations, and local police departments. Private sector businesses and nonprofit organizations may also be involved in criminal investigations. Private involvement may be through a contract a government entity has with a business for investigative services, or private investigators may be hired directly by victims.

Federal Agencies

The federal government employs thousands of criminal justice professionals in agencies such as the Federal Bureau of Investigation (FBI); the Bureau of Alcohol, Tobacco, and Firearms (ATF); and the Drug Enforcement Agency (DEA). In addition to these investigative arms, nearly every federal government agency has an element that conducts criminal investigations. For example, the Department of Housing and Urban Development includes a division that investigates benefits fraud. The U.S. Postal Service employs inspectors to investigate a variety of crimes that can be committed via the mail.

Federal criminal justice agencies are restricted to investigating specific types of crimes. The mission of each agency is specified by the legislation that authorized that agency. Over time, these mandates have changed based upon the needs of the criminal justice system and in response to significant events. The U.S. Secret Service, for example, was created in 1865 in an effort to combat the growing issue of counterfeit currency (U.S. Secret Service n.d.). It was only after the assassination of President William McKinley that Congress formally requested that the agency direct resources toward presidential protection. The FBI has historically been involved in protecting the country from foreign aggression. After the September 11, 2001, terrorist attacks, Congress directed the FBI to focus more resources toward antiterrorism investigations as the lead law enforcement agency for the effort.

Federal criminal justice agencies investigate cases that relate specifically to federal law. Issues such as traffic enforcement and city ordinance violations are the purview of local departments. As a result, federal departments typically address higher-level crimes that may threaten the country as a

Depending upon the type of crime, federal agencies such as the FBI may be involved in the investigation.

whole. It is a surprise to many that federal agencies typically do not take a lead role in investigating important crimes such as murders; local or state agencies investigate such crimes, requesting federal assistance only when additional resources may be necessary.

State Agencies

At the state level, law enforcement is typically handled by highway patrol departments or the state police. State highway patrol agencies frequently handle investigations of crimes that fall within unincorporated areas outside of the jurisdictional boundaries of local (city and county) police departments. They also may address investigations of incidents that occur on state and interstate highways. For example, the mission of the Nevada State Highway Patrol is "to promote safety on Nevada Highways by providing law enforcement traffic services to the motoring public."

State criminal justice agencies are classified as either "state police" or "highway patrol" organizations.

State agency structures vary nationwide. Because highway patrol agencies typically investigate traffic-based crimes, many states have developed their own separate "bureaus of investigation." Crimes that fall outside of traffic offenses may be transferred to these bureaus. Within the state of Georgia, for example, "the Georgia Bureau of Investigation is an independent, statewide agency that provides assistance to the state's criminal justice system in the areas of criminal investigations, forensic laboratory services and computerized criminal justice information" (Georgia Bureau of Investigation, n.d.).

Local Agencies

The vast majority of criminal investigations in the United States are conducted by local police departments. The term *local* refers to agencies at the city and county level of government. The Department of Justice (2006b) reported the existence of 12,656 city police departments and 3,061 county sheriff agencies as of 2003. The total number of full-time employees for these departments numbered at over 900,000. In comparison, federal criminal justice agencies employed approximately 105,000 professionals in 2004 (Department of Justice 2006a).

Local police departments have the benefit of being close to the communities they serve. Their investigative activities can be tailored to the distinctive issues of their communities.

Local police agencies investigate the widest variety of crimes. A police department might be solving a vandalism one minute, a murder the next. Investigators in local agencies must be knowledgeable about how to approach this assortment of investigations. Only the larger police departments have the flexibility to create specialized units for specific crimes.

State and federal agencies in many cases have larger budgets than local police departments, and as a result they may have more resources available to aid in investigations. It is not uncommon for local criminal justice agencies to call upon state or federal departments for assistance.

If a question arises regarding a conflict of interest for a local police department, higher-level criminal justice agencies may be called upon. For example, if a crime is alleged to have been committed by a city manager during the course of her duties, the local police department may fear retribution by the manager or the chief of police might have a close relationship with the manager that would bias any investigation. In such cases, it is common to utilize a state or federal agency to alleviate these potential issues.

The Private Sector

In certain cases, businesses in the private sector may become involved in criminal investigations. Perhaps the most common example of this is the use of private crime laboratories for processing evidence. The processing of DNA in particular has become a heavy burden on government-run crime labs. In 2000, 45 percent of government crime labs reported contracting DNA testing out to private companies (Department of Justice 2002). Private organizations may also be used to process other evidence, such as audio and video recordings.

Nonprofit organizations may be used in investigative work. An example of nonprofit involvement is the use of child service centers to conduct "forensic interviews" of child crime victims. Forensic interviews utilize specially trained interviewers working in social services to reduce further trauma to a child in reliving a criminal event. The National Children's Advocacy Center (n.d.) states that "children are best able to communicate about personal experiences by allowing them to explain in their own words and communication style and by exploring their most salient memories about abuse incidents" (¶ 3). Forensic interviews conducted in a therapeutic environment by nonprofit-employed social workers can collect testimonial evidence needed for possible future prosecution.

In certain cases, a victim or victim's family may hire a private investigator to look into a criminal investigation. Professional investigators recognize the danger in interfering with an official investigation, and they will interact with police officials to avoid these circumstances. A private investigator who lacks experience and knowledge may permanently damage a case and prevent prosecution in the future by intruding into a formal investigation without coordinating with the police.

Cooperation

A trend in law enforcement is the cooperative investigation of crime between agencies at the same or different levels of government. A weakness of the criminal justice system in the United States is the divided effort that exists among local, state, and federal resources. Regional crime problems and issues such as terrorism (Oliver 2007) have increased the need for cooperation between agencies.

CASE STUDY

The High-Intensity Drug Trafficking Area (HIDTA) program is a good example of increasing cooperative investigations through the use of colocated task forces. One of the regional task forces funded by the federal government through the HIDTA initiative is the New England HIDTA Financial Task Force. This joint effort was created to address the growing issue of money laundering within the region (National Criminal Justice Reference Service n.d.). The task force includes representation from the federal level (the U.S. Customs Service and the Internal Revenue Service), state government (Massachusetts State Police), and a local agency (Boston Police Department). Each participant contributes unique benefits associated with their agency's resources and capabilities.

Within a police department, an investigation may be handled by a variety of personnel. A patrol officer may handle an investigation immediately after arrival at a call for service. Longer-term investigations may require referral to a specialized unit within the department.

Scenario

Officer Jenkins receives a call reporting larceny shoplifting at a local convenience store. The store owner has a 17-year-old subject in custody for taking eight packs of cigarettes from a counter display, concealing them within her shirt, and leaving the store without paying for the items. Officer Jenkins takes a statement from the store owner. He then recovers a store surveillance video that clearly shows the subject hiding the items and walking out. Officer Jenkins completes the entire investigation of this incident within minutes.

Scenario

Officer Jefferson responds to the scene of an armed robbery of a check-cashing facility. Two armed suspects entered, produced firearms, demanded cash, and left with approximately $2,500. Officer Jefferson orders the Crime Scene Unit and detectives from the Criminal Investigations Unit to assist with the scene. Crime scene technicians arrive and recover a surveillance video and dust doors and countertops for fingerprints (recovering seven latent prints). Detectives take statements from two employees who were present at the time of the robbery. Detectives also canvass the area and interview four employees of nearby businesses who observed a red sedan leaving the scene.

Two weeks later, the surveillance video is aired on local television news stations. An informant calls the police department with a possible suspect. A suspect is brought in, and his fingerprints match two of those left at the scene. The suspect gives a statement implicating a second individual who is also arrested. Overall, the investigation takes three months to complete.

As the above scenarios illustrate, one officer or several officers and civilians may be involved in an investigation. An investigation can take anywhere from minutes to years. Some investigations are never solved and remain perpetually open or inactive.

Although investigations may be conducted by such a wide variety of criminal justice entities, this text will focus primarily upon criminal investigations conducted at the local level.

POLICE RESPONSE AND INITIAL INVESTIGATION

A typical criminal investigation begins when the crime is reported to a police agency. In fact, the initial call may become evidence in the case. Callers reporting a crime are usually witnesses or victims, and

The 911 call taker may be the first witness to collect testimonial evidence in a criminal case.

the first interview is conducted by the police call taker or dispatcher. During major case investigations, detectives often refer to this initial call to compare it to later statements made by involved parties.

CASE STUDY

Near the California-Mexico border, a subject was arrested by the Federal Bureau of Investigation (2005) for "perpetrating a terrorist hoax and making false statements concerning an alleged plot to smuggle a nuclear warhead into the United States from Mexico" (¶ 1). The individual allegedly made a series of calls to the emergency 911 line from a cellular phone and advised the call taker that a warhead was being transported through a tunnel from Mexicali, Mexico, to Calexico, California. The caller advised that the device was to be delivered to a group of Chinese and Iraqi nationals. Fortunately, the call was a hoax. The call taker in this case became an important witness in a terrorist threat investigation.

After receipt of an emergency call, police officers are dispatched to the scene of a crime with details about the call. Officers begin observations on the way to the scene. If a subject has reportedly fled the scene, for instance, the officer will watch for the described vehicle or pedestrian on her way to the scene. Officers may also take note of the weather conditions, as they can influence the condition of physical evidence at an outdoor crime scene.

The highest priority for responding officers is safety, both of the officers themselves and of citizens in the area. An officer's actions are often influenced by safety concerns. For example, at crime scenes where a gun is present, it is a best practice for processing purposes to leave the gun in place. However, if numerous citizens are walking around the scene uncontrolled, the officer may retrieve the firearm due to safety concerns. The officer should make quick note of the position of the firearm and explain its positioning to investigators after the scene is secured.

As the officer considers safety, she is also observing as much as possible. The officer will usually attempt to obtain immediate information about a suspect. If the suspect is at the scene, that person is taken into custody as quickly as possible. If the suspect has fled the area, a description is broadcast, and attention is directed toward potential victims and witnesses.

If a victim is present and wounded, first aid is administered, and medical personnel are ordered. If a quick interview is feasible while still ensuring that the victim's medical needs are met, the responding officer may attempt to gather as much information as possible.

At a scene with multiple people walking about, it is important to detain as many potential witnesses as possible. Depending upon the size of the scene and the number of witnesses, a responding officer may order additional officers and resources to assist in controlling the scene.

Barrier tape is used to secure crime scene perimeters.

Once a scene is under control and safe, responding officers will focus upon *securing the scene* for further investigation. Securing a crime scene refers to the act of extracting all individuals who are not part of the investigating agency from the crime scene area and establishing a restricted zone. The crime scene boundaries are subsequently manned and/or defined with barriers, such as crime scene tape or police vehicles. Once a scene is under control, responding officers will focus upon securing the scene for further investigation.

After a scene is secured, investigators are typically ordered. Investigators are specialized detectives educated in various types of follow-up investigations. They have often received training in the interpretation of physical evidence and interviews and interrogations. These detectives focus on the collection of testimonial evidence and analyzing any physical evidence that is present.

Crime scene personnel are also ordered when available. Most mid- to large-sized police departments have a crime scene–processing element; some agencies without such a unit rely upon nearby larger or state-level jurisdictions. Crime scene technicians concentrate on the collection of physical evidence from the scene.

Most criminal investigations include the interviewing of a victim (if the victim is alive), the interviewing of witnesses, the collection of evidence, the analysis and processing of evidence, and an interview of potential suspects. Each of these steps will be detailed in later chapters.

FOLLOW-UP INVESTIGATION

Follow-up investigations proceed after a crime scene has been processed and released by police personnel. All of the evidence is analyzed for items that may tie a suspect to the scene. Witness statements are examined for clues as to who the suspect may be. Eventually, the investigator will attempt an interview with any identified suspect(s).

Once all evidence, both physical and testimonial, has been collected, documents describing the evidence and the steps in the investigation will be collected into a case file. The reports within the case file are then presented to a prosecuting attorney, who makes the ultimate decision on whether or not to file a criminal case against potential suspect(s).

SUMMARY

An investigation is an effort to discover facts. A criminal investigation involves some sort of criminal act. Evidence in an investigation can be classified according to two types: (1) real, or physical, evidence and (2) testimonial evidence.

Criminal investigations may be handled by different agencies at various levels of government, from the local to federal level. Private companies and nonprofit organizations also contribute to criminal investigations.

Investigations are conducted by employees at every level of a police department. The first responding officer immediately starts an investigation. Follow-up investigations are often handled by detectives trained in investigative techniques.

Key Terms

Criminal investigation: An examination of a purported criminal act in an attempt to discern the truth

Evidence: Any purported fact included in an investigation

Investigation: The process of collecting and analyzing evidence in an attempt to determine facts

Local police agency: A police department with city or county jurisdictional boundaries

Real or physical evidence: Tangible material of any type related to an investigation

Securing a scene: Extracting all noninvestigative personnel from the interior area of a crime scene and establishing a restricted area

Testimonial evidence: Evidence derived from the statements of those involved in an investigation

Discussion Questions

1. Which type of evidence do you feel is more important to an investigation: real (physical) evidence or testimonial evidence? Explain your response.

2. What are the benefits of handling investigations cooperatively between different agencies at different levels of government?

3. Safety has been identified as a top priority for police agencies responding to a crime scene. Name at least three safety concerns at a crime scene.

Exploration

1. Research a federal agency that is not typically known for its law enforcement activities. Find one that has an investigative arm. What type of cases does it investigate?

2. Watch a nonfictional police television program that follows patrol officers. Can you identify situations where it appears they are addressing safety issues before initiating any sort of investigation?

References

Department of Justice. 2002. *Survey of DNA crime laboratories, 2001.* Washington, DC: Bureau of Justice Statistics.

Department of Justice. 2006a. *Federal law enforcement officers, 2004.* Washington, DC: Bureau of Justice Statistics.

Department of Justice. 2006b. *Local police departments, 2003.* Washington, DC: Bureau of Justice Statistics.

Dwyer, Jim, Peter Neufeld, and Barry Scheck. 2000. *Actual innocence.* New York: Doubleday.

Federal Bureau of Investigation (FBI), San Diego Division. 2005. *Press release: Hoax bomber arrested,* October 15. Retrieved August 6, 2007, from http://sandiego.fbi.gov/pressrel/2005/sd101505.htm.

Fisher, Barry. 2003. *Techniques of crime scene investigation.* 7th ed. Boca Raton, FL: CRC Press.

Georgia Bureau of Investigation. n.d. *GBI Divisions.* Retrieved July 21, 2007, from www.state.ga.us/gbi/.

National Children's Advocacy Center. n.d. *Child forensic interview model.* Retrieved July 21, 2007, from www.nationalcac.org/professionals/model/forensic_interview.html.

National Criminal Justice Reference Service. n.d. *New England HIDTA.* Retrieved July 21, 2007, from www.ncjrs.gov/ondcppubs/publications/enforce/hidta2001/ne-fs.html.

Nevada Highway Patrol. n.d. *Mission statement.* Retrieved July 21, 2007, from nhp.nv.gov/.

Oliver, Willard. 2007. *Homeland security for policing.* Upper Saddle River, NJ: Pearson Education.

Roth, Mitchel. 2005. *Crime and punishment: A history of the criminal justice system.* Belmont, CA: Thomson-Wadsworth.

U.S. Secret Service. n.d. *Secret Service history.* Retrieved July 21, 2007, from www.secretservice.gov/history.shtml.

CHAPTER 2

INVESTIGATORS

CHAPTER OBJECTIVES

By the end of this chapter, the reader will be able to do the following:

- Explain why the structure of investigative units varies among police departments.

- Define the term *functional design* as it applies to investigative units and list the benefits and disadvantages of this approach.

- Define the term *geographical design* as it applies to investigative units and list the benefits and disadvantages of this approach.

- Classify crimes that fall under the category of *crimes against persons.*

- Classify crimes that fall under the category of *crimes against property.*

- Explain what the *Uniform Crime Reporting* and *National Incident-Based Reporting Systems* are.

CASE STUDY

With unsolved homicides stacking up at an alarming rate, the Charlotte-Mecklenberg, North Carolina, Police Department created a cold-case unit. The unit was initially staffed with two veteran homicide investigators. Additional assistance was obtained from the local office of the FBI, giving the investigators jurisdictional authority outside of

Mecklenberg County. Volunteers with prior law enforcement investigations experience were added to the unit in 2003 (Lord 2005, 2).

The unit reviews cases, looking for uninvestigated leads or instances where new technology (such as DNA) might help solve the case. As of 2005, 50 cases had been reviewed by the unit, resulting in the arrest of 12 offenders and the clearing of 11 cases (International Association of Chiefs of Police 2005, 2–3).

After police administrators in Charlotte-Mecklenberg determined the need for a cold case unit, other questions had to be answered to get the project off the ground. How should the unit be structured? What personnel should staff the unit? What elements of supervision would be needed? The answers to these questions are critical to ensure the success of investigative units.

STRUCTURE OF INVESTIGATIVE UNITS

Mid- to large-sized police departments usually have investigative units distinct from patrol or other operational divisions. The composition of these units varies. An assortment of factors determines how investigative units are structured within a police department, not the least of which is available manpower.

CASE STUDY

Investigative elements within the Los Angeles Police Department (LAPD) are scattered throughout several groups. The Detective Services Group houses the Robbery-Homicide, Commercial Crimes, Detective Support and Vice, and Juvenile Divisions. The Narcotics and Gang and Operations Support Divisions are housed under the Specialized Services Group. A distinct Criminal Gang Homicide Group falls under the command of the South Bureau of LAPD. Another investigative element, the Counter Terrorism and Criminal Intelligence Bureau, includes the Major Crime and Emergency Services

Divisions. Investigations are also conducted under the Internal Affairs Group (Los Angeles Police Department 2007).

In comparison, the staff of the Postville Police Department in Iowa includes a chief of police and three full-time officers. Four part-time officers also serve the city. While Postville does not have a formal investigations unit, some of its officers have been trained in follow-up criminal investigative work (City of Postville n.d.).

Larger police agencies have more investigative resources than smaller departments.

As you can see from case studies above, the population to be served and the number of officers available to serve the jurisdiction play an important role in determining how an investigative element is structured. Some agencies have seemingly limitless resources available to conduct an investigation; others are restricted and must rely upon ingenuity within existing personnel or assistance from other area police agencies.

Functional and Geographic Designs

For mid- to large-sized police departments with sufficient resources and manpower to staff an element of investigators, decisions must be made regarding how to structure the specialized units. There are two common ways to organize investigative units: functionally and geographically.

A *functional design* groups detectives according to the type of crime they investigate. For example, sex crimes detectives may be organized into a unit that focuses upon that type of crime, no matter where it happens within the city or jurisdiction. A sex crime detective would not be assigned another type of criminal case, such as an auto theft or burglary.

This type of organization brings certain benefits to investigative units. Detectives can concentrate their training and skill on their particular crime specialization. Certain crimes, such as narcotics and fraud, are quite complicated and require job-specific knowledge to ensure an effective investigation. Investigators working these types of cases benefit greatly from education and experience in this area. Additionally, when specialized investigators are grouped together, they can critique each other's work, collectively look at cases to determine the best approach, and work as a coordinated team to tackle a specific crime problem. For particularly complex crimes, the functional approach can be very effective.

There are some negatives to designing investigative units along functional lines. One downside to this approach is that in larger cities, functional detectives may not be able to familiarize themselves with the community well. When investigators accept cases citywide, trends and patterns in individual communities can become lost in the overall confusion of multiple crimes. Members of specialized investigative units can also find themselves alienated from other elements of the

Fraud investigators specialize in this field and develop the skills needed to analyze financial crimes.

agency. Detectives may become "experts" in their particular field and develop a belief that other officers aren't equipped to work on their types of cases. Patrol officers may be resentful of this attitude. This can create a communication block between the investigative units and other police divisions. The alienation issue can be resolved by ensuring that communication between the special units and other elements of the department is frequent and ongoing. Functional detectives should always be open to input from officers outside of their unit; the suggestions can be beneficial to the case and promote a sense of teamwork within the agency.

The second way to organize an investigative unit is along *geographical* boundaries. A geographically organized unit works any type of case, from vandalism to murder, that falls within the boundaries of the particular jurisdiction. The benefit of this type of organization is that it closely aligns with the concept of community policing. Community policing espouses a close working relationship between the police department and the citizens of a jurisdiction. If investigators are assigned a particular district within a city, they can become familiar with the residents of the area.

Scenario

Detective Chen is assigned to the northeastern quadrant of the city of Wise. Any follow-up investigation that is required for crimes that occurred in this section of Wise is assigned to Detective Chen. A burglary occurred in this area the previous week. A fingerprint was found at the scene; however, no other evidence of value was located. Detective Chen is familiar with the residents of his section of town. He is aware that a felon named Sonny James was recently released from prison for burglary crimes. Detective Chen requests that the fingerprint examiner compare James's prints with those found at the scene. The examiner finds a match between the two. This case was aided by Detective Chen's familiarity with the community.

A disadvantage of geographic organization is that when investigators are assigned a variety of cases, it can be difficult to become proficient in a certain type of criminal investigation. Detectives cannot concentrate on a specific field. As noted previously, some crimes require a detailed knowledge of a particular field to facilitate an effective investigation.

Departments may not have the ultimate ability to decide how to organize investigative elements. When manpower is scarce, training officers in a particular field and having them

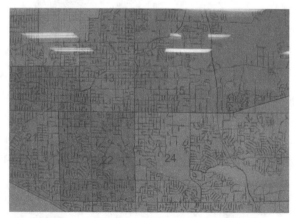

Investigations may be assigned to detectives according to geographical boundaries.

devote their abilities to that crime can be difficult. In smaller agencies, officers must often be varied in their capabilities.

It is important to note that the two types of organization are not mutually exclusive. In fact, many investigative units are organized along a mixture of these designs. In the New York Police Department, officers are assigned to specific units, such as homicide, but they are also allocated to segments of the city (boroughs). Smaller departments may have to cross-train their detectives, but the investigators can still specialize in two or three fields (rather than all crime types). For instance, one detective can work assaults, robberies, and homicides (violent crimes); another can work burglaries, larcenies, and auto thefts (property crimes).

INVESTIGATIVE UNIT SPECIALIZATIONS

In most large police departments, investigative units are broken down into groups of personnel (or individual detectives) who investigate specific types of crime according to functional designs. Special training provides detectives with an understanding of the intricacies of the crimes on which they will concentrate. It is common for police agencies to divide investigative responsibilities into two major categories of crime: *crimes against persons* and *crimes against property*.

Categories of Crime

A crimes-against-persons case is one in which a victim is subjected to bodily harm (or a threat of bodily harm). Examples of crimes against a person are robbery, homicide, and sexual assault. In each case, a human being is injured or is threatened with injury.

A crimes-against-property case is one in which the principal target of the offense is a tangible asset. While a human or organization is the ultimate victim, the person's property is the object of the crime. Examples of crimes against property include vandalism, burglary, larceny, and auto theft.

Crimes such as narcotics violations and prostitution do not neatly fit into persons or property crimes categories. It is common for police departments to establish a separate narcotics and vice unit to handle these cases, often referred to as "victimless crimes." The victim in such cases is considered to be the "state," but these crimes often relate to other criminal activity that includes persons and property offenses. The classifications of certain common crimes are listed in figure 2.1.

Crime Reporting Systems

The persons/property method of delineation of duties is closely tied to the Federal Bureau of Investigation's *Uniform Crime Reporting,* or UCR, system. UCR was developed in 1929 to establish defined methods for police agencies nationwide to report crime data. The FBI collects these reports and compiles an annual summary of crime trends. UCR focuses upon how agencies should classify offenses according to type. Within these definitions, UCR establishes methods for counting crimes-against-persons offenses and crimes-against-property incidents (Federal Bureau of Investigation 2004).

UCR was based upon rudimentary criminal incident counts available to most police departments in the early 1900s. Police departments now can gather data beyond the number of crimes committed, including offender characteristics, victim demographics, and other important facts. As technology and information-gathering capabilities increased, criminal justice professionals recognized the need for

FIGURE 2-1: Common crime classifications

CRIMES AGAINST PERSONS	CRIMES AGAINST PROPERTY	CRIMES AGAINST SOCIETY
Murder	Larceny	Prostitution
Robbery	Vandalism	Narcotics Offenses
Rape	Auto Theft	
Sexual Assault	Arson	
Assault	Forgery and Fraud	

more specific data about not only the crime types being committed but also more specific details of each offense.

Law enforcement is now shifting toward a new reporting system called the *National Incident-Based Reporting System,* or NIBRS. NIBRS can collect and report more detailed information about crimes in a certain area. NIBRS has added an additional category to persons and property crimes: *crimes against society.* Narcotics violations and prostitution fall under this new reporting group (FBI n.d.).

Investigative Specializations

Under the crimes-against-persons category, typical investigative specializations include homicide, robbery and assaults, sex crimes, and domestic violence.

Homicide investigations are quite complicated. Significant training is required for investigators to interpret physical evidence at homicide scenes, as the victim is not available for testimonial evidence.

Robbery crimes, while usually not as complex as other crimes, are often committed by repeat offenders using the same methods (*modus operandi,* or MO). Investigators may be able to solve multiple crimes based upon the recognition of an offender's MO.

A robbery crime is considered a crime against a person due to the threat or use of violence

Sex crimes are delicate matters. Victims are frequently initially reluctant to report such crimes. Victims are often even more hesitant to follow up with prosecution after the initial report. Trained investigators can use techniques to overcome these hurdles.

Photo courtesy of the Independence (Missouri) Police Department

Domestic violence cases offer special challenges to police agencies. Victims may not wish to prosecute an offender with whom they have a relationship. It is important to follow up on such cases, as they can become increasingly dangerous. Statistics from 2002 indicate that around 22 percent of murders committed in the United States were family violence murders, with 58 percent of the victims being female (Bureau of Justice Statistics 2005, 1). Specially trained detectives can break what is commonly referred to as the "cycle of violence" that perpetuates such violent relationships.

Specializations that fall under crimes against property include burglary and larceny, auto theft, fraud and forgery, and arson.

Burglary and larceny crimes are similar to robberies in that offenders often repeat their crimes. Knowledge of crime patterns and methods can help solve multiple offenses under this specialization.

Auto theft crimes require training in the interpretation of evidence. Because identifying serial numbers are often removed from stolen cars, detectives may be trained in methods to identify both cars and vehicle parts without these numbers. Complicated auto theft rings also present special challenges to police agencies.

Fraud and forgery cases include complex evaluations of bank account transactions. Such crimes can involve analyzing a pile of paperwork to build a case against an offender. Investigators require specialized instruction in these types of cases.

Finally, the interpretation of arson evidence is based upon principles of fire science. To the untrained eye, an arson scene can appear to be a mess of charred remains. Arson investigators can recognize points of origin and probable causes for a fire when developing a case.

Narcotics cases involve the use of specialized techniques aimed at targeting higher-level drug dealers. Vice operations targeting prostitution require similar tactics. The use of informants, undercover operations, and audio and visual surveillance technology are common in these investigations.

Each of these crime specialties and the techniques utilized in investigating them are detailed later in the text.

SUPERVISION

Depending upon the size of the investigative unit, levels of supervision must be established. The number of supervisors required varies from jurisdiction to jurisdiction. *Span of control* refers to the number of employees assigned to a supervisor. Each department will establish the appropriate span of control within investigative elements based upon its unique circumstances.

Investigative supervisors perform important day-to-day functions. Supervisors are responsible for assigning cases referred to the unit to specific detectives. The supervisor may give direction to the detective regarding how to proceed with the case. Investigators normally return completed case files to the supervisor, who reviews the completed work to ensure that the case has been sufficiently investigated.

A primary function of investigative supervisors is the assignment of cases to appropriate detectives.

Supervisors fulfill larger roles in major case investigations. Major investigations are cases that require follow-up by several detectives, based upon factors such as the seriousness of the offense and the number of investigative leads. Supervisors are responsible for tracking and assigning leads to investigators or investigative teams.

Above the supervisory level, an investigative unit is led by a command element. A commander, among other duties, oversees overall unit operation, policy and procedure guidelines, and budgeting. The unit commander serves as the spokesperson for the investigative unit with other commanders throughout a police department and with other criminal justice agencies.

SELECTION OF INVESTIGATIVE PERSONNEL

Police officer selection for agencies in the United States is a detailed process. Written tests are used to screen potential applicants for a basic knowledge of police work. Also, pre-employment psychological testing is suggested to determine the best candidates for police work.

Detectives are typically selected from an existing pool of police officers. Applicants for investigator positions have already been screened for suitability for basic police work. Beyond these basics, police executives look for an officer's proficiency in specific aspects of police work to determine the best candidates. Jetmore (2006) suggests selecting personnel with an excellent work ethic, a loyalty to the profession, and a good understanding of human behavior as investigators (27–28).

Effective investigators possess superior communication skills. A significant portion of a detective's work involves communicating with crime victims, witnesses, and suspects. An investigator must have the ability to "read" a particular situation and approach it in an appropriate manner. Victims and witnesses can be challenging to interview. Suspects do not always respond to interrogation techniques in the same way. A detective must be flexible in his communication styles to approach each situation appropriately.

CASE STUDY

Police in the Wichita, Kansas, area spent nearly two decades searching for the "Bind, Torture, and Kill" serial murderer who taunted them with letters hinting at clues. In February 2005, they finally developed a concrete suspect, Dennis Rader, by matching a floppy disk communication with a computer from Rader's church. Rader was brought in for questioning.

After being confronted with mounting evidence, he offered a full confession to Lt. Ken Landwehr, recalling details of the torture he had put his victims through. Rader admitted to slaying ten people, including two juveniles. Rader was tried and convicted and sentenced to ten life sentences (Wichita Police Department 2006, 4).

Many police officers would likely find it difficult to listen to such a tale without showing signs of disgust. The investigators in this particular case knew that a confession would add to the essential elements of a solid case. Therefore, they encouraged Rader to speak freely.

In addition to interacting with citizens, investigators are required to testify in court on a more frequent basis than officers assigned to other elements of a police department. Detectives must be able to articulate steps taken in an investigation in a professional manner. It is not uncommon for investigators to testify regarding a case that is several years old. Courtroom testimony will be discussed in Chapter 8.

An investigator must possess objectivity when approaching an investigation. In considering evidence, investigators must keep an open mind. Preconceived notions can lead an investigator down the wrong path. Cognitive biases are natural preconceived notions that develop in one's mind in the course of contemplating different theories, often causing the individual to disregard valid hypotheses without due consideration. An effective investigator will identify these biases and keep an open mind to consider all the alternatives presented. "By recognizing cognitive biases and employing strategies to counter their influence, law enforcement agencies can take steps to avoid investigative failures" (Rossmo 2006, 7).

Investigative work involves sorting through an assortment of evidence, both physical and testimonial. Police detectives must be organized to keep crucial evidence in order. Detectives typically carry an assortment of cases at any particular time. Rarely do investigators have the luxury of working on a single case at a time. Detectives must organize individual case files in a manner that gives them immediate access to a particular investigation at a moment's notice. A victim may call to determine the progress on her case. If the detective is not familiar with at least the basic facts of the investigation, the victim may sense that the officer is not well organized.

Police officers are trained to act quickly in many circumstances. Decisive action is often required to address emergency calls for service. However, investigations often require a different approach. Police detectives normally have time to think through how to manage a particular case. It is not uncommon for investigators to consider options as a group before agreeing upon how to proceed in a case. Some officers struggle with this adjustment.

An attention to detail is helpful in investigations. Detectives are required to write numerous police reports during the course of a case. These reports are written with the understanding that they will be submitted initially to the prosecuting attorney's office and will later traverse various channels of the criminal justice system. An officer who routinely leaves important details out of a report would likely struggle as a detective. Investigative reports need to be well written, comprehensive, and professional.

While the initial police hiring process considers honesty and integrity as important traits, they may be even more critical for investigators to possess. Detectives are often faced with ethical decisions in the course of their work. Investigators possess a unique degree of control over the direction a case can turn. A case can be cleared or remain perpetually unsolved based upon the decisions made by a detective.

CASE STUDY

A police officer in Delray Beach, Florida, was indicted for his involvement in a fraud scheme of a local fortune teller. The officer's codefendant defrauded victims of over $1 million from 1994 through 2002 by claiming she could cure their fatal diseases by praying over their money. The officer was assigned as the primary investigator over many of the cases. Instead of investigating the cases, he assisted the fortune teller in defrauding victims and laundering the proceeds (FBI, Miami Division 2005).

Selection of Investigative Supervisors

Supervisors in investigative assignments need to possess the same characteristics described above as important for investigators. Supervisors are often charged with overseeing large, complex cases involving multiple investigators and numerous leads. Such cases require careful organization and the thoughtful assignment of leads based upon the strengths of the detectives involved. "Personnel constraints and sound judgment dictate that investigators prioritize leads and pursue those with the most potential first" (Rothwell 2006, 23).

The selection of supervisors for investigative divisions can impact the success of the unit's operations. Previous experience as a detective is not absolutely necessary, but it does give an incoming supervisor a significant advantage. If a supervisor does not have previous investigative experience, it is essential that suitable training is afforded to her. An inexperienced supervisor may take longer to become familiar with the challenges associated with the position.

Effective investigative unit supervisors can maintain both an open mind and the ability to take decisive actions, employing each approach at the appropriate time. Line-level investigators often come up with creative approaches to investigations that can help crack the most difficult case. Supervisors should remain open to listening to this input. In some situations, detectives disagree about which direction an investigation should take. A strong supervisor will make a determination based upon the facts of the case in question and communicate this decision with certainty to ensure a focused investigation.

CASE ASSIGNMENT

Chapter 1 described the initial police response to calls for service. In most cases, police officers handle the call at the scene, and no further investigation is necessary. In fact, many calls for service do not involve any crime.

Detectives keep files of associated case reports to track the steps that have been performed in an investigation.

For any case requiring a follow-up investigation, an investigator is assigned to oversee the leads to be examined. The assigned detective may be referred to as a *lead (or primary) detective*.

Significant criminal events, such as homicides, warrant calling detectives to the scene of the crime. Responding investigators can view the evidence remaining at the scene and interview on-scene witnesses to obtain relatively fresh, accurate statements. At such scenes, the lead detective may be assigned from a choice of the responding personnel.

More commonly, uniformed police officers respond to calls for service and perform an initial, cursory investigation. For example, a citizen may call to report a burglary. A police officer will respond to the crime scene, gather facts from the victim, view any evidence remaining, and prepare a police report. If any clues regarding who the suspect may be exist, the case will be referred to the investigative unit for assignment to a detective and further follow-up. An investigator may not actually respond to the crime scene unless it is required during the course of her investigation.

Once a case is referred to the investigations unit, a supervisor will typically review the case. The supervisor may consider *solvability factors* in determining whether or not to assign the case. Solvability factors are characteristics of an investigation that contribute to the chance of successfully clearing the case. Examples of solvability factors include the following:

- A reliable witness
- A detailed suspect description
- A named suspect
- A suspect vehicle description

- Traceable property taken from the scene

- Usable physical evidence

- Limited opportunity for anyone other than the suspect to commit the crime (Iowa City Police Department 2001, 2–3).

The supervisor then decides which investigator to assign as a lead detective for the case. This decision may be based upon the special training the investigator possesses and the detective's current case load. The term *case load* refers to the number of cases a detective is currently assigned. The sheer number of cases is not the only consideration for an investigator's workload; the complexity of the cases assigned should also be considered.

Once a case is assigned, the primary detective works on the various leads. Once leads are exhausted, the investigator makes a determination (sometimes with supervisory assistance) whether there is sufficient evidence to present the case to a prosecuting attorney. If there is any doubt, the case is normally presented so the prosecutor can make a decision about whether or not to file a criminal case.

Agencies track the closing of cases according to UCR guidelines for reporting purposes. According to UCR, cases can be cleared by arrest or closed for exceptional circumstances (FBI 2004). Exceptionally cleared cases may be closed due to a variety of situations, such as the death of the offender, refusal of the victim to cooperate in prosecution, or the deferral of prosecution due to other pending cases against the suspect. Cases may also be inactivated if all leads have been exhausted and the case could not be solved. The case is considered inactive because it is not truly closed; theoretically, new leads could surface, and the case could be solved at a later time.

Once the case is complete and is closed or inactivated, the investigator will turn the completed work into the unit supervisor. The supervisor will review the case and either approve the closing of the case or refer the case back for additional work. The investigative process is outlined in figure 2.2.

FIGURE 2-2: The investigative process

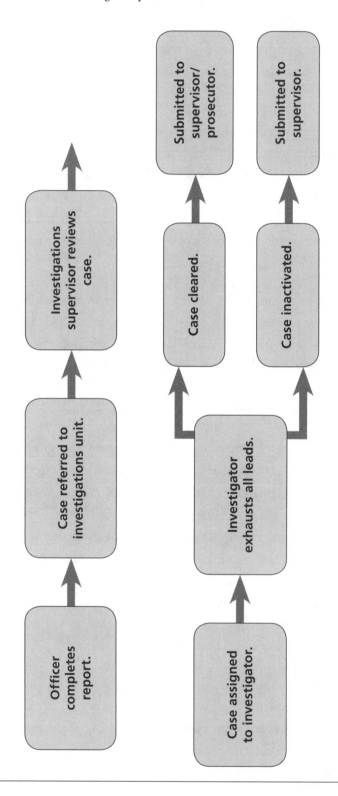

SUMMARY

Mid- to large-sized police agencies typically have investigative units that are distinct from other functions, such as patrol. The makeup of investigative units is determined by various factors, including the available manpower and resources a police agency has at its disposal.

Investigative divisions are arranged according to two different types of design: functional and geographical. Functional designs are based upon the types of cases investigated by a detective or group of detectives. Geographic designs divide work according to physical areas of a jurisdiction.

Crimes are organized by the categories of crimes against persons, crimes against property, and crimes against society. Investigative crime specializations are divided further by specific types of crimes, such as fraud, robbery, larceny, homicide, and others.

Investigators are selected from existing pools of experienced police officers. Communication, organization, attention to detail, integrity, and honesty are important elements to consider in the selection of investigative supervisors and personnel.

Cases are assigned to investigators by a unit supervisor. Once the case investigation is complete, a detective will return the case to a supervisor for review.

Key Terms

Case load: The relative workload of a particular investigator, based upon both the raw number of cases and the complexity of those cases

Crimes against persons: Crimes committed where the victim is subjected to actual or threatened bodily harm (e.g., robbery, murder, and rape)

Crimes against property: Crimes committed where the principle target of the offense is a tangible asset (e.g., burglary, larceny, and fraud)

Crimes against society: Crimes committed without a readily identifiable victim or where the victim is characterized as society as a whole (e.g., narcotics and prostitution)

Functional design: In police investigations, the assignment of cases according to a specific type of crime

Geographical design: In police investigations, the assignment of cases according to the physical area within a jurisdiction where the crime occurred

Lead (or primary) detective: The investigator assigned the chief responsibility for an investigation

National Incident-Based Reporting System (NIBRS): A system of reporting detailed statistical crime information for analysis within the criminal justice system, established to enhance the UCR system

Solvability factors: Characteristics of an investigation that contribute to the chance of successfully clearing the case

Span of control: The number of employees assigned to a supervisor

Uniform Crime Reporting (UCR): A system of reporting basic crime information to the Federal Bureau of Investigation

Discussion Questions

1. What are the benefits of assigning only one type of criminal case, such as a sex offense investigation, to a particular detective?

2. What skills are important for a street police officer to develop if that officer wishes to become an investigator?

3. What factors should be considered by a supervisor before assigning a case to a particular detective?

Exploration

1. Research the Internet and find an association of investigators for a specific type of crime, such as homicide, auto theft, fraud, etc.

2. Locate statistics from the FBI's Uniform Crime Report for a metropolitan area near where you live.

References

Bureau of Justice Statistics. 2005. *Family violence statistics.* Washington, DC: United States Department of Justice.

Federal Bureau of Investigation (FBI). n.d. *National Incident-Based Reporting System (NIBRS).* Retrieved July 24, 2007, from www .fbi.gov/ucr/faqs.htm.

Federal Bureau of Investigation (FBI). 2004. *Uniform Crime Reporting Handbook.* Clarksburg, WV: United States Department of Justice.

Federal Bureau of Investigation (FBI), Miami Division. 2006. *Press release: Delray Beach police officer and fortune teller indicted on corruption and fraud charges,* May 10. Retrieved August 9, 2007, from http://miami.fbi.gov/dojpressrel/pressrel06/mm20060510 .htm.

International Association of Chiefs of Police. 2005. *2005 IACP/ ChoicePoint Award for Excellence in Criminal Investigations.* Retrieved August 9, 2007, from www.theiacp.org/awards/ cpwinners2005.pdf.

Iowa City Police Department. 2001. *Investigative case screening process* (General order 91-07), February 12. Retrieved August 9, 2007, from www.icgov.org/policefiles/genorder39.pdf.

Jetmore, Larry. 2006. How to choose a detective. *Law Officer,* August. 26–28.

Lord, Vivian. 2005. Implementing a cold case homicide unit. *FBI Law Enforcement Bulletin* 74, no. 2 (February): 1–6.

Los Angeles Police Department. 2007. *Los Angeles police department organization chart.* August. Retrieved March 2, 2008, from the author's website at www.lapdonline.org/inside_the_lapd/content _basic_view/1063.

City of Postville. n.d. *Postville Police Department.* Retrieved July 22, 2007, from www.cityofpostville.com/ppd.html.

Rossmo, D. Kim. 2006. Criminal investigative failures. *FBI Law Enforcement Bulletin* 75, No. 9 (September): 1–8.

Rothwell, Gary. 2006. Notes for the occasional major case manager. *FBI Law Enforcement Bulletin* 75, no. 1 (January): 20–24.

Wichita Police Department. 2006. Lt. Landwehr honored by National Law Enforcement Officers Memorial Fund. *Wichita Police Department Monthly Report,* March. 4–5.

CHAPTER 3

LEGAL ASPECTS OF CRIMINAL INVESTIGATION

CHAPTER OBJECTIVES

By the end of this chapter, the reader will be able to do the following:

- Explain the components of the Fourth Amendment to the U.S. Constitution.

- Define the *exclusionary rule* as it relates to search and seizure in criminal investigations.

- Describe the concepts behind the *fruit of the poisonous tree doctrine.*

- List the steps involved in securing a *search warrant.*

- Describe the procedures involved in an *arrest.*

- Describe exceptions to the search warrant requirement, such as *plain view, abandoned property, open fields, special needs,* and *exigent circumstances.*

- Explain the warning of rights necessity defined under *Miranda v. Arizona* and the exceptions to this requirement.

- Express the need for ethical conduct in criminal investigations.

- Describe the findings of the *Brady v. Maryland* case as they relate to ethics in criminal justice.

CASE STUDY

A hotel manager calls police after he observes apparent drugs in a customer's room. The police respond and set up surveillance while other investigators begin to prepare a search warrant.

While waiting, surveillance officers observe two subjects enter the room with backpacks. Feeling an increased sense of urgency, the officers attempt contact with the suspects. First, they attempt a ruse by knocking on the door and claiming they are "room service" and "maintenance" for the hotel. When this fails, the officers knock more forcefully and announce that they are, in fact, the police.

After this announcement, rustling noises can be heard, followed by the flushing of a toilet. Sensing that valuable evidence is being destroyed, the officers make immediate entry into the room. Two subjects are taken into custody along with crack cocaine, a gun, and cash. It appears that two felons have been taken off of the streets.

The case proceeds through the court system until it reaches the Third Circuit Court of Appeals. The court consideres the circumstances of the search and determines that the officers did not follow proper procedures in obtaining the evidence. All of the seized evidence is thrown out, seriously damaging any possibility for prosecution (*United States v. Cole* 2006).

The above case illustrates how intertwined investigative procedures are with the legal system. Police officers must abide by legal rules or risk losing a case and seeing an offender walk free.

Criminal investigations are a component of a much larger criminal justice system. Investigations must comply with legal rules described in the Constitution and case decisions passed down by the Supreme Court.

Police officers must abide by search and seizure rules established by law when conducting investigative searches of residences.

Detectives must be well trained in how to conduct an investigation to comply with legal precedents and current laws.

Criminal lawyers attend years of schooling to understand case laws and the intricacies of the justice system. Conversely, most investigators have a much briefer legal educational background. Detectives often learn through on-the-job training and specific legal primer schooling. Investigators typically learn about how the system works through regular exposure to criminal proceedings, conferences with attorneys, and offering their own testimony.

This chapter examines some of the important aspects of the legal system that must be considered during investigative processes.

SEARCH AND SEIZURE

The basic element of any criminal investigation is evidence. Chapter 1 discussed both physical evidence (tangible evidence collected at crime scenes) and testimonial evidence (clues derived from statements of involved parties). In many cases, evidence is not readily available to investigators; that is, they must work to search for evidence and collect (or seize) it. The rules that govern this process are often referred to as *search and seizure* guidelines.

Fourth Amendment

In the 18th century, after the long battle for independence, the principle concern of the founders of the United States was an omnipotent federal government. Representatives in America sought to ensure individual rights for citizens in the newly formed country. Debates about these rights occurred long before the development of formalized policing in the country; however, these protections were established to protect citizens against oppression from any government agency. These rights were enumerated in the Bill of Rights and passed in 1781.

The *Fourth Amendment* to the Bill of Rights specifically addresses search and seizure law. These Fourth Amendment protections have stood the test of time and continue to regulate police investigative activities to this day. Each segment of the Fourth Amendment will be considered in the following sections as it relates to police search and seizure. The Fourth Amendment reads:

> The right of the people to be secure in their persons, houses, papers, and effects, against unreasonable searches and seizures, shall not be violated, and no Warrants shall issue, but upon probable cause, supported by Oath or affirmation, and particularly describing the place to be searched, and the persons or things to be seized.

The first portion of the Fourth Amendment, "the right of the people to be secure in their persons, houses, papers, and effects," describes what types of things are protected by the amendment. An individual himself is protected under the law. This protects a subject from being detained unlawfully. Also, a subject's home is protected from invasion by government officials. "Papers" include personal documents such as those of the 18th century, but this definition has developed to include modern-day information banks, such as computers.

The next section, "against unreasonable searches and seizures, shall not be violated," describes what the person and her property is protected from. A law enforcement officer (or other government official) may only search for evidence and seize that evidence if doing so on reasonable grounds. *Reasonableness* has been defined more clearly over time through court decisions; certain police actions have been declared reasonable under the circumstances.

The final section of the Fourth Amendment describes one reasonable method: "but upon probable cause, supported by Oath or affirmation, and particularly describing the place to be searched, and the persons or things to be seized." This element of the amendment specifically explains what is required for a warrant (a court authorization for a search and seizure). *Search warrants,* for instance, give the police the court's permission to search an individual's premises, person, or other property. *Arrest warrants* give officers authorization to seize someone and hold that person for court. Both warrants are to be based upon *probable cause,* or the reasonable belief that a person has committed a crime.

CASE STUDY

Police in Cleveland, Ohio, received information that a bombing suspect was hiding in the home of Dollree Mapp. Officers knocked on Mapp's door and demanded to search her home. After consulting with an attorney, Mapp refused to let them enter. A larger contingent of officers eventually forced entry into Mapp's home and waved a piece of paper at her claiming that it was a search warrant (it was not). The suspect was not found, but police did discover a stash of pornography and charged Mapp with possession of obscene material.

Mapp was convicted, but she appealed the case until it eventually reached the U.S. Supreme Court. The majority decision stated that the search was unreasonable. The evidence was deemed inadmissible (*Mapp v. Ohio* 1961).

The Exclusionary Rule

The *Mapp v. Ohio* case illustrates what is known as the *exclusionary rule.* This rule, first defined in *Weeks v. United States* (1914), excludes evidence from consideration at trial if it was obtained in an illegal manner. Weeks applied the exclusionary rule to federal government agencies; *Mapp v. Ohio* subsequently applied the rule to the state government officials (including local police officers).

Fruit of the Poisonous Tree Doctrine

Illegal seizures of property can ruin an entire investigation by compromising steps taken after the search. Under the *fruit of the poisonous tree doctrine,* any evidence obtained (even under legal circumstances) as a result of illegally obtained evidence is inadmissible in court (*Silverthorne Lumber Company v. United States* 1920). For example, a storage locker receipt may be found during an illegal search. Even if investigators are able to gain legal access to property within that locker, the evidence obtained from the locker may not be admitted in trial.

SEARCH WARRANTS

Mapp v. Ohio illustrates the importance of a proper search, preferably under the authority of a search warrant. To obtain a search warrant, an investigator must testify, under oath, to the reasons why he believes a subject has committed a crime. This is accomplished through the filing of a written *affidavit* describing the circumstances establishing probable cause (figure 3.1). Within this affidavit, the detective also specifies what he is requesting to search and what particular property

---

FIGURE 3-1: Search Warrant Affidavit

AFFIDAVIT/APPLICATION FOR SEARCH WARRANT

[STATE]
[COUNTY]

I, Detective Jones, affiant and applicant herein, being duly sworn, appears now before the undersigned Judge authorized to issue Warrants in criminal cases and makes this Affidavit and Application in support of the issuance of a Search Warrant, to search the following described person, place or thing:

101 South Main Street, [City], [County], [State], a single-family residence, the first house south of 1st Street on the east side of Main Street, with white siding, a gray shingled roof, with the numbers "101" affixed directly above an entrance door facing westward.

and to there search for and seize, photograph or copy, and make return thereof, according to law, the following property or things:

- Cocaine, a Schedule II Controlled Substance;

- Methamphetamine, a Schedule II Controlled substance;

- Heroin, a Schedule II Controlled Substance;

- Marijuana, a Schedule I Controlled Substance;

- Drug Paraphernalia;

- Any weapons;

- Currency in close proximity to narcotics;

- Drug Enforcement Unit buy money;

- Any papers, correspondence, or documents related to drug trafficking and/or the disposition of monies that are evidence of the proceeds from the illicit trafficking of drugs;

- Photographs, including still photos, negatives, videotapes, films, undeveloped film and the contents therein, slides, in particular photographs of coconspirators, of assets, and/or controlled dangerous substances;

- Indicia of occupancy, residency, ownership, management, and/or control of the premises described above including, but not limited to, utility and telephone bills, canceled envelopes, and keys

Affiant and Applicant being duly sworn deposes and states that he or she has Probable Cause to believe that the above listed property to be searched for and seized, photographed, or copied is now located upon said described person place or thing based upon the following facts, to wit:

On August 18, 2005, Officer Mike Smith was parked up the street from this residence writing a report about an unrelated police incident. He noticed that several cars were stopping at this house. The occupants would enter the house and stay for less than five minutes. During a 30-minute period, Officer Smith noticed five cars stop and leave in this fashion. He recognized from his experience that this type of activity is typically associated with a residence where narcotics are sold. Officer Smith is a 12-year veteran of the police department with 5 years in narcotics work.

On August 19, 2005, Officer Smith set up surveillance on the residence. He noticed a subject stop at the house five minutes after the surveillance was set up. The subject was a white male in a blue 1996 Pontiac Firebird. The vehicle's license plate, 662-XLS, had expired in December of 2004. The subject entered and exited the house within three minutes. Officer Smith followed the car a short distance to 2nd Avenue and Grand Boulevard and stopped the car for the expired license plate.

The driver of the car was contacted and identified himself as John Jones, date of birth 6-2-71, of Richmond, Missouri. Jones advised that his driver's license had been suspended. Per departmental policy, Officer Smith took Mr. Jones into custody for the violation and ordered a tow of his car. A search incident to Jones's arrest revealed a small bag of a white powdery substance, weighing approximately one-eighth of a gram. The substance tested positive for methamphetamine.

Jones was also booked for possession of methamphetamine and was later interviewed by Det. Johnson. Jones admitted to Johnson that he had purchased the methamphetamine from a Rick Wright at 101 South Main Street just prior to the car stop. He also advised that he frequently purchases narcotics there, including marijuana and cocaine.

Signed: Assistant Prosecutor

Signed: Detective
       Affiant and Applicant

he wishes to find and seize. For example, an investigator may want to search a person to seize a blood sample, a residence for drugs, or a car for stolen property.

The affidavit is only a request for a search warrant. A search warrant affidavit is reviewed by a judge, who approves or disapproves the request. If the affidavit is approved, the judge will sign and authorize the actual search warrant (figure 3.2). The search warrant is considered valid for specified period after it is signed, normally ten days.

SEARCH AND SEIZURE WITHOUT A WARRANT

Not all evidence is seized under a search warrant. The court recognized that certain exceptions exist where officers should be permitted to conduct a search and/or seize evidence without going through the steps to obtain a warrant.

FIGURE 3-2: Search Warrant

SEARCH WARRANT
[STATE] TO ANY PEACE OFFICER IN [STATE]

WHEREAS, on this 10th day of June 2008, Application for Issuance of a Search Warrant and Affidavit(s) in writing, duly verified by oath or affirmation, has been filed with the undersigned Judge of this Court, stated that heretofore the following described property is subject to seizure, to wit:

• Cocaine, a Schedule II Controlled Substance;

• Methamphetamine, a Schedule II Controlled substance;

• Heroin, a Schedule II Controlled Substance;

• Marijuana, a Schedule I Controlled Substance;

• Drug Paraphernalia;

• Any weapons;

• Currency in close proximity to narcotics;

- Drug Enforcement Unit buy money;

- Any papers, correspondence, or documents related to drug trafficking and/or the disposition of monies that are evidence of the proceeds from the illicit trafficking of drugs;

- Photographs, including still photos, negatives, videotapes, films, undeveloped film and the contents therein, slides, in particular photographs of coconspirators, of assets, and/or controlled dangerous substances;

- Indicia of occupancy, residency, ownership, management, and/or control of the premises described above including, but not limited to, utility and telephone bills, canceled envelopes, and keys

and it further appears that there is PROBABLE CAUSE to believe that said property subject to seizure is being kept or held in this county and state on the following person, place or thing, to wit:

101 South Main Street,[City], [County], [State], a single-family residence, the first house south of 1st Street on the east side of Main Street, with white siding, a gray shingled roof, with the numbers "101" affixed directly above an entrance door facing westward.

NOW THEREFORE, IN THE NAME OF [STATE], I Command that you search the person, place, or thing above described within 10 days after filing of the Application for issuance of this Warrant, by day or night, as soon as practicable, and to take with you, if need be, the power of your county, and, if said above described property, or any part thereof, be found on said person, place, or thing, that said property be seized or photographed, or copied and returned, or the photograph or copy, be brought to the Judge who issued the Warrant to be dealt with accordingly to law. Furthermore, entry into the residence may be made without knocking and embanking the presence of law enforcement and their purpose due to safety concerns enumerated in the affidavit of the search warrant. That you make a complete and accurate inventory of the property so taken by you in the presence of the person from whose possession the same is taken, if that be possible, and to give to such person a Receipt for such property, together with a copy of the Warrant, or, if no person can be found in possession of said property, leaving said Receipt and copy of said Warrant at the sight of the search. After execution of the Search Warrant, the Warrant with a Return thereon, signed by the officer making the search, shall be delivered to the Judge who issued the Warrant, together with an itemized Receipt for said property taken.

WITNESS my hand and the SEAL of this Court on this 10th day of June 2008 at the hour of 1:00 pm.

Signed: Judge

Consent to Search

Fourth Amendment rights can be surrendered. If, for example, the police request to enter a residence to search for evidence and the owner of the house agrees to a search, the person has temporarily waived her rights. Individuals may consent to a search of their property. Recognizing that the police could force a person to give such consent, the courts have stipulated through case law that such consent may not be coerced (*Bumper v. North Carolina* 1968). Investigators may utilize a *consent to search form* (figure 3.3) to help prove consent was given without coercion; however, verbal consent is all that is required.

Other methods of search and seizure without a warrant have also been recognized as reasonable under court decisions.

Expectation of Privacy

When considering whether or not a search warrant was necessary, the courts examine a person's *expectation of privacy* (*Katz v. United States* 1967). This refers to whether a subject can reasonably expect his surroundings to be free from external monitoring or intrusion. For example, one would expect that one's home would be free from others listening into conversations within the residence. In contrast,

---

FIGURE 3-3: Consent to Search

Consent to Search

I, _____, having been informed of my constitutional right not to have a search made of the premises hereinafter mentioned without a search warrant and of my right to refuse such consent to such a search, hereby authorize _____ of the police department to complete a search of the premises located at _____.
They are authorized to take from my premises any letters, papers, materials, contraband, or other property which they may desire. This written permission is being given by me voluntarily and without threats or promises of any kind.

Signed: _____

Witnessed: _____

Witnessed: _____

---

a person cannot expect that same degree of privacy when talking to someone on a public street corner.

When a person lacks a strong expectation of privacy, the police may be able to recover admissible evidence without a warrant. For example, if an individual calls the police and lets them into her home, she has given up a certain degree of privacy. While the police cannot necessarily rifle through the homeowner's belongings, if contraband (anything illegal to possess) is in "plain view" from where an officer is legally permitted to be, she may recover it without a warrant. This is considered the *plain view* exception to a search warrant.

Likewise, if a person *abandons property* in a public location, he has given up an expectation of privacy for that property. For example, if an individual is carrying a briefcase, he would expect the contents to be safe from intrusion from a government official who stops to question him. On the other hand, if the person drops the briefcase on the sidewalk and then walks away, he has abandoned the property, and the police may search the item without a warrant.

The *open fields doctrine* relates to the lack of an expectation of privacy. In *Hester v. United States* (1924), the U.S. Supreme Court advised that "conversations in the open would not be protected against being overheard for the expectation of privacy." Overhearing conversations relates to the collection of testimonial evidence. The open fields doctrine also relates to

Open fields possess less of an expectation of privacy for the owner of the property than, for example, homes.

physical evidence. Officers who were able to observe marijuana plants in a field from a path were able to recover the plants and charge the land owner based upon the open fields doctrine (*Oliver v. United States* 1984).

Other Exceptions

Other carefully defined exceptions to the search warrant requirement for evidence recovery exist. A *special needs exception* allows for warrantless searches under particular circumstances when safety interests supersede Fourth Amendment rights, such as searches in mass transit facilities like airports (*Ferguson v. City of Charleston* 2001). Officers with probable cause may search a car on a public street without a warrant in recognition of how easily evidence within the car can be moved (*Carroll v. United States* 1925). In the event of an emergency, defined as a "situation requiring swift action to prevent imminent danger to life or serious damage to property, or to forestall the imminent escape of a suspect, or destruction of evidence," the police may enter a dwelling, and evidence in plain view may be recovered (*People v. Ramey* 1976). This type of situation is referred to as the *exigent circumstances* exception to the search warrant requirement.

Fourth Amendment search and seizure law is dynamic. New cases arise from time to time that cause the courts to consider new issues. Also, prior decisions can always be reconsidered by the Supreme Court with more recent

The security of air travel has led to different search and seizure rules for airports, according to Supreme Court decisions.

cases and fresh interpretations. Although the basic rules of search and seizure have been presented here, a comprehensive study is beyond the scope of this text. Because search and seizure case law is a legal matter, investigators are encouraged to consult with a prosecuting attorney or government counsel when questions of reasonableness arise. Each case must be considered based upon its unique set of circumstances.

ARREST

The preceding examples describe searches and seizures for property. Search warrants can also authorize police agencies to search a dwelling for a person. The seizure of a person (an *arrest*), however, is authorized through the issuance of an arrest warrant. Arrests are also governed by the Fourth Amendment.

The courts have recognized that a warrant cannot be obtained prior to every arrest, and a warrant is not required in every arrest situation. When probable cause exists that a subject has committed a felony crime, an officer can make an arrest. Follow-up investigation is required after the arrest. While state laws vary, a detective generally is given 20 to 24 hours to complete an investigation and obtain an arrest warrant to continue to hold the subject. If the warrant cannot be obtained during this time, the subject must be released pending further investigation.

In other cases, a detective may be assigned a case where a subject has not yet been apprehended. Further investigation is required, and a case is developed. If sufficient probable cause exists, the investigator submits a file to a prosecuting attorney. After reviewing the case, the attorney may request a warrant from a judge for the suspect's arrest. Typically this arrest warrant is returned to the police agency, and officers begin the search for the suspect.

INTERROGATION

The questioning of a subject based upon the suspicion that she has committed a crime is considered an interrogation. The courts have specified procedures that should be undertaken prior to an interrogation.

CASE STUDY

In 1963, police in Phoenix, Arizona, arrested a suspected rapist and kidnapper, Ernesto Miranda. Miranda was questioned and confessed to raping a woman. The investigators then had Miranda write out his confession with a statement at the top of each sheet reading "this statement has been made voluntarily and of my own free will, with no threats, coercion or promises of immunity and with full knowledge of my legal rights, understanding any statement I make can and will be used against me."

Miranda's confession was the central piece of evidence for the prosecution in the subsequent rape trial. Miranda was convicted, but subsequent appeals took the case to the Supreme Court. The appeal issue was that Miranda had not been told by the investigators that he had a right to speak to an attorney prior to questioning. The Supreme Court reviewed the case, and a close majority (five to four) agreed that Miranda should have been informed of his right to an attorney. The confession was deemed inadmissible (*Miranda v. Arizona* 1966).

The Miranda case focused on the *Fifth Amendment* self-incrimination clause and the *Sixth Amendment* right to counsel. This case changed the way the police approach interviewing suspects. Prior to conducting an interrogation, officers must inform a person of his rights (to remain silent, to an attorney) and that his statements can be used against him, and the person must be asked if he understands his rights. To ensure uniformity, police departments utilize a waiver indicating that a person understands his rights and agrees to talk to the police (figure 3.4). Using a waiver removes some uncertainty as to whether a person understood his rights; however, it is not required. If an officer reads a person his rights verbally and asks for understanding, this fulfills the requirement.

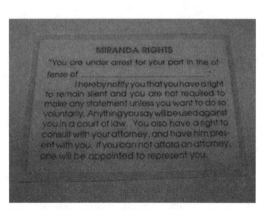

Many agencies issue reference cards with the warning of rights printed on them, to ensure that the warning is given uniformly after every arrest.

A common misconception is that the police must read a person her rights anytime they ask her about a possible crime. Miranda-based warnings are only required after a person has been taken into custody (during "custodial interrogations"). *Custodial interrogations* have been defined as "questioning initiated by law enforcement officers after a person has been taken into custody or otherwise deprived of his freedom of action in any significant way" (*Oregon v. Mathiason* 1977).

FIGURE 3-4: Warning of Rights

Warning of Rights

1. You have the right to remain silent and refuse to answer questions. Do you understand?

2. Anything you do say may be used against you in a court of law. Do you understand?

3. You have the right to consult an attorney before speaking to the police and to have an attorney present during questioning now or in the future. Do you understand?

4. If you cannot afford an attorney, one will be appointed for you before any questioning if you wish. Do you understand?

5. If you decide to answer questions now without an attorney present, you will still have the right to stop answering at any time until you talk to an attorney. Do you understand?

6. Knowing and understanding your rights as I have explained them to you, are you willing to answer my questions without an attorney present?

Signed: _____

Witnessed: _____

Witnessed: _____

Rights warnings are also not required if a person spontaneously begins to talk about a crime. Even after a person has been taken into custody, if a person starts to confess to a crime without being questioned, the police are not required to stop that person from talking until he understands his rights. Rights warnings are only applicable if questions are being asked. Recording such spontaneous confessions or taking detailed notes is a good idea.

If a question exists regarding whether or not a warning of rights is necessary, the best approach is to offer the warning or consult with a prosecuting attorney or government counsel. However, the courts have recognized that emergency circumstances do arise where the issuance of a warning of rights is not practical due to concerns for the safety of the general public.

CASE STUDY

Police in New York responded to the report of a rape. The victim told officers that the suspect had gone into a supermarket. Officers apprehended the suspect, Benjamin Quarles, near the back of the store. Quarles was wearing an empty shoulder holster at the time of his arrest.

The officers asked Quarles where the gun was without reading him his rights. Quarles directed them to some empty boxes where a loaded revolver was found and recovered. Quarles was then given his rights and answered some additional questions about the gun.

Quarles was charged with criminal possession of a weapon; however, the trial judge excluded Quarles's statement about the gun from being presented as evidence, because he was not read his rights per *Miranda v. Arizona*. The prosecution appealed, eventually reaching the Supreme Court. The Court reversed the decision and decided that when public safety is at risk, there is an exception to the warning of rights. The threat posed by a firearm left accessible to the general public was considered more important than enumerating Miranda rights to Quarles (*New York v. Quarles* 1984).

The Quarles case demonstrates the fluid nature of case law as it relates to criminal investigations. A solid criminal investigation is required for a successful prosecution; however, public safety is paramount.

ETHICS

CASE STUDY

In April 2001, the Federal Bureau of Investigation released a report detailing its investigation into the work of forensic chemist Dr. Joyce Gilchrist of the Oklahoma City, Oklahoma, police department. Investigators found that of eight reviewed cases, five contained erroneous statements by Dr. Gilchrist identifying potential suspects.

In one case, Jeffrey Pierce was convicted of a rape that occurred on May 8, 1985. Pierce's conviction was based largely upon the Gilchrist's scientific examination of physical evidence, even though testimonial evidence from witnesses countered the chemist's claims. A review of Dr. Gilchrist's work in this investigation revealed that a body hair comparison she claimed tied Pierce to the crime scene was flawed and that, in fact, none of the hairs matched in microscopic comparisons. Pierce's conviction was vacated on May 7, 2001 (*Pierce v. Gilchrist et al.* 2004).

Unethical work in investigations can lead to tragic results. The need for ethical behavior in criminal investigations, and more broadly law enforcement in general, cannot be denied. Ethics is promoted in law enforcement internally, through personnel rules and regulations and the self-governing of behavior through internal investigations within a police department, and externally through case law.

Brady v. Maryland

Dishonesty cannot be tolerated in law enforcement, from both ethical and legal standpoints. The landmark case *Brady v. Maryland* helped establish the importance of truthfulness in investigative work. In this case, the Maryland Court of Appeals ruled that the prosecution cannot withhold exculpatory evidence in a criminal case. Exculpatory evidence is any evidence that indicates that a defendant in a case did not commit a crime (*Brady v. Maryland* 1963).

Included in the definition of this *exculpatory evidence,* also known as "Brady material," is any information that speaks to the truthfulness of a witness in a case. For police officers, this includes any information about whether or not an officer has ever lied in her official police capacity. In other words, if an officer has a past history of dishonesty, this becomes germane to a criminal investigation. The officer's testimony can be tainted by any Brady material that exists within her official employment (or prior testimonial) record. Past dishonesty speaks to the officer's trustworthiness as a witness.

Unethical behavior is not only potentially damaging to innocent witnesses in a criminal case, but it can also be career ending (or worse) for an investigator. Proper close supervision of conduct in investigations can help avoid such situations. Agencies can also institute cross-checking of investigative work by having a supervisor from a different unit or even an outside agency conduct periodic audits of case work.

SUMMARY

Actions undertaken during a criminal investigation must abide by rules and regulations set forth through case law. The search for and seizure of physical evidence and the arrest of individuals must comply with the Fourth Amendment to the United States Constitution. A search warrant is required for the seizure of property undertaken without the consent of the owner, unless the seizure falls under carefully defined exceptions to the warrant requirement.

Arrests may be made without a warrant. However, a warrant must be obtained after further investigation, as a subject cannot be detained more than 20 to 24 hours (depending upon the state).

Interrogation procedures fall under regulations defined under the Fifth Amendment protection against self-incrimination and the Sixth Amendment right to representation by counsel. The *Miranda v. Arizona* decision helped define the warning of rights that must be given to suspects prior to questioning during a custodial interrogation. Certain exceptions apply; however, in most cases, the warnings must be given.

Ethical conduct in criminal investigations is necessary, not only due to internal expectations and controls but in accordance with prevailing case law. Dishonesty in a criminal case can end an investigator's career, as that person's value as a witness can be challenged in all future trials during testimony, according to *Brady v. Maryland*.

Key Terms

Abandoned property: Property that the owner or possessor has given up claim to through disposal

Affidavit (for search warrant): A request for a search warrant, specifying the place or person to be searched, the item(s) to be recovered, and the probable cause for the case

Arrest: The seizure of a person

Arrest warrant: A document authorized by a judge, allowing for the seizure of a person

Brady v. Maryland: Court case that defines the requirement for the prosecution in a criminal case to turn over any exculpatory evidence to the defense

Consent to search: A term describing a situation where an individual has voluntarily waived Fourth Amendment rights and has allowed officials to search a place under his control or his person

Custodial interrogation: The interview of a suspect after her freedom has been reasonably restricted

Exclusionary rule: A rule defined by case law that excludes the use of evidence obtained in an illegal manner from admission into a criminal trial

Exculpatory evidence: Any evidence in a criminal case that indicates a defendant did not commit a crime

Exigent circumstances: Emergency situations where intervention to ensure public safety overrides Fourth Amendment protections against unlawful searches and seizures

Expectation of privacy: The degree to which an individual can expect his surroundings to be free from external monitoring or intrusion

Fifth Amendment: The Bill of Rights Amendment that pertains to an individual's protection against self-incrimination

Fourth Amendment: The Bill of Rights Amendment that pertains to search and seizure of evidence and arrest

Fruit of the poisonous tree doctrine: Case law doctrine that dictates any evidence obtained as a result of illegally obtained evidence is excluded from admission into a criminal trial

Miranda v. Arizona: Criminal case that defined the standards under which an individual must be given a warning of Fifth and Sixth Amendment rights prior to a custodial interrogation

Open fields doctrine: Case law that dictates an individual does not have an expectation of privacy in an area reasonably accessible to view and open to others

Plain view doctrine: Case law directive that allows police officers to seize contraband that is in plain view of an area where they are legally allowed to be

Probable cause: A reasonable belief that a person has committed a crime

Public safety exception: An exception to the warning of rights requirement stipulated under *Miranda v. Arizona* allowing for the immediate questioning of a subject when public safety is at risk

Search and seizure: A term used to describe the prevailing case law establishing legal rules for the exploration for and collection of physical evidence or subjects for arrest

Search warrant: A document, authorized by a judge, allowing officials to search a specified person or place for specified items within a certain time period

Sixth Amendment: The Bill of Rights Amendment that pertains to an individual's right to representation by legal counsel

Special needs exception: An exception to the search warrant requirement that allows for search and seizure under specifically defined circumstances where public safety overrides Fourth Amendment protections (e.g., border crossings, transportation searches)

Discussion Questions

1. If an officer encounters a situation where it is not clear whether an exception to the search warrant requirement for search and seizure exists, should the officer proceed with the seizure or obtain a search warrant? Explain your response.

2. Describe an area or situation where you feel an individual has a high expectation of privacy. Also describe an area where an individual has a low expectation of privacy.

3. Why do you believe the courts have dictated that all individuals should be advised of their Fifth and Sixth Amendment rights prior to a custodial interrogation?

4. An officer lies in an internal investigation about whether or not he slept while on duty. Why would this fact be important for the defense in a criminal burglary trial to know?

Exploration

1. Watch a fictional detective or crime scene television program or movie. Identify scenes in which a search or seizure occurs. Try to determine if the investigators appear to be following proper Fourth Amendment guidelines.

2. Look for an instance of unethical police investigation conduct through Internet news sources. What steps might have been taken to avoid the improper conduct?

References

Brady v. Maryland. 373 U.S. 83. 1963.

Bumper v. North Carolina. 391 U.S. 543. 1968.

Carroll v. United States. 267 U.S. 132. 1925.

Ferguson v. City of Charleson. 532 U.S. 67. 2001.

Hester v. United States. 265 U.S. 57. 1924.

Katz v. United States. 369 U.S. 347. 1967.

Mapp v. Ohio. 367 U.S. 643. 1961.

Miranda v. Arizona. 384 U.S. 436. 1966.

New York v. Quarles. 467 U.S. 649. 1984.

Oliver v. United States. 466 U.S. 170. 1984.

Oregon v. Mathiason. 492 U.S. 492. 1977.

People v. Ramey. 545 P.2d 1333, 1341. Cal. 1976.

Pierce v. Gilchrist et al. 369 F .3d 1279 (10th Cir.). 2004.

Silverthorne Lumber Company v. United States. 251 U.S. 385. 1920.

United States v. Cole. 2006 WL 302243 (437 F .3d 361). 2006.

Weeks v. United States. 232 U.S. 383. 1914.

PART II

CRIMINAL INVESTIGATION PROCEDURES

CHAPTER 4

CRIME SCENE INVESTIGATION

CHAPTER OBJECTIVES

By the end of this chapter, the reader will be able to do the following:

- Define the terms *crime scene* and *crime scene investigation*.

- Differentiate between a *primary* and *secondary crime scene*.

- Describe the personnel who typically work in crime scene investigation jobs and the training and education required.

- Define the characteristics of *direct, circumstantial,* and *trace evidence*.

- Explain the concepts of *inner* and *outer perimeters* in crime scene security.

- Explain the principle of transference defined by Edmond Locard.

- Identify the steps undertaken to record a crime scene, including photography, videotaping, and sketching.

- List crime scene search methods.

- Explain the concept of "chain of custody."

- Describe methods utilized to locate and collect different types of evidence.

- Describe the operations of an evidence storage facility.

The introductory chapters of the text introduced the core component of a criminal investigation: evidence. To review, physical evidence includes any tangible item that helps to solve a case. Testimonial evidence is derived from the statements of individuals involved in an investigation. Neither type of evidence is more important than the other; the value of each type of evidence to a particular case depends upon the circumstances of that investigation. However, in many cases, victims and witnesses cannot identify a suspect, and potential offenders refuse to offer a statement confessing to the crime. In such cases, physical evidence is indispensable, as it may provide the sole basis for tying a suspect to a scene (see chapter 5).

A *crime scene* is any area where physical evidence in a case may be. A *primary crime scene* is where a crime occurred. A *secondary crime scene* is where evidence from the crime may be located, although the crime did not actually happen in that area. For example, a bank robber may flee a bank to his hotel room, where he is apprehended by the police. In this example, the bank is the primary scene, and the hotel room, where proceeds from the robbery are recovered, is a secondary scene. The systematic collection and interpretation of physical evidence at such scenes is referred to as *crime scene investigation.*

This chapter will examine the procedures involved in crime scene investigations, including the identification, collection, and storage of physical evidence. Chapter 5 will explore the value of commonly collected evidence in assisting in the identification of individuals involved in a criminal investigation.

CRIME SCENE PERSONNEL

Crime scene investigative duties may be performed by either sworn officers or civilian personnel within a police department. Some agencies do not have the resources for a dedicated crime scene investigations unit, so they either train uniformed officers or detectives in the required methods or call upon neighboring departments to assist. Crime scene–processing techniques are increasingly complex, and periodic retraining and practical experience is necessary to maintain skills in this area.

In large departments with dedicated crime scene units, it is usually necessary to train field officers in basic techniques despite the existence of specialized personnel. Crime scene units may not always be available to respond to the scenes of more minor incidents, such as property crimes (burglaries, auto thefts, etc.). Basic crime scene procedures, for example simple photography and fingerprinting, can be performed by almost every officer after minimal training.

Crime scene investigators are equipped with an assortment of tools to aid in scene processing. A typical crime scene response kit may contain a fingerprint kit, camera equipment, impression evidence (print) casting materials, measurement devices (tape measures, rules, yardsticks, GPS receiver), personal protective clothing for hazardous scenes, crime scene security tape, bags and containers for evidence, portable lighting, and a bullet trajectory kit. These items may be organized in a special response vehicle.

Agencies with crime scene response units may issue vehicles fully equipped with the tools needed to process a typical crime scene.

TYPES OF PHYSICAL EVIDENCE

Physical evidence can be divided further into more descriptive categories. *Direct evidence* refers to physical evidence that links a person to a crime scene. This type of evidence is valuable when a subject does not have a legitimate reason to have been at a crime scene. *Circumstantial evidence* requires that a person evaluating the evidence (such as a judge or jury) make a judgment to connect a person to the scene. It cannot be said with certainty that a person was at a crime scene based upon circumstantial evidence; however, multiple circumstantial indicators can help solidify a case in the jurors' minds.

Photo courtesy of the Independence (Missouri) Police Department

---

Scenario

Crime scene investigators respond to a murder scene and recover an apparent sample of blood from an exit door handle. A DNA profile of the blood reveals that it does not belong to the victim. Further tests are conducted, and a DNA match is made with a convicted sex offender who lives nearby. This direct evidence ties the offender to the crime scene.

Scenario

Police officers respond to an armed robbery scene where the suspect has just fled the area. While investigators at the scene are reviewing a surveillance videotape of the crime in progress, officers five blocks away have apprehended a subject running from the area. The person does not have a gun but does have a large sum of cash. The video unfortunately does not offer a clear view of the suspect's face; however, his clothing is visible. The apprehended subject's clothes match those of the offender in the video. The circumstantial video evidence does not link the suspect to the crime scene without question, but it does provide a strong suspicion that the police have found the offender. Further investigation is warranted.

Trace evidence is a broad category that refers to miniscule amounts of physical evidence. It is often difficult to identify trace evidence with the naked eye. Examples of trace evidence would be small fibers, human hair, or tiny slivers of glass.

CRIME SCENE SECURITY

In chapter 1, it was noted that responding officers first attend to the safety of everyone involved in a crime scene. After this step, the officers concentrate on securing the crime scene to protect evidence within the scene and continue to provide for the security of investigators in the area.

Two different zones are established when securing a crime scene: an inner and outer perimeter (figure 4.1). The *outer perimeter* is typically established first. The outer perimeter is a large zone that provides a buffer area between the outermost crime scene boundaries and any physical evidence. The outer perimeter serves to restrict noninvestigative personnel and citizens from entering the scene and deliberately or unintentionally contaminating physical evidence. Only investigators are allowed access into the outer perimeter. This perimeter may be defined with police personnel or material barriers, such as crime scene tape or vehicles. Because investigators cannot rely upon material barriers to prevent human intrusion, stations must be staffed to ensure firm security.

To prevent anyone from tampering with evidence, individuals from the media, witnesses, and public officials are not allowed entry into the outer perimeter. The more people who enter a crime scene, the greater

FIGURE 4-1: Inner and outer perimeters surrounding a residential crime scene

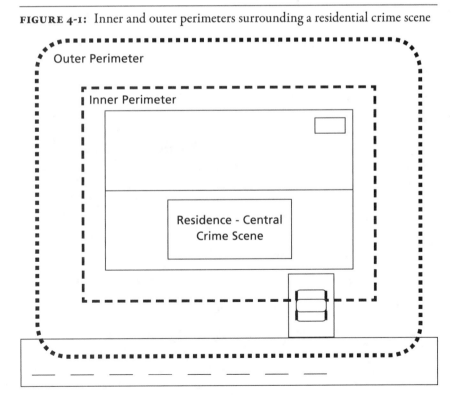

Outer Perimeter

Inner Perimeter

Residence - Central Crime Scene

the chance that they could contaminate the scene with fingerprints, bodily fluids, discarded trash, etc. French scientist Edmond Locard (1877–1966) was among the first to suggest formally that a human could leave and remove trace evidence from a crime scene without knowing it (Georgia Bureau of Investigation, Division of Forensic Sciences n.d.). Every effort should be extended to avoid this transference and contamination. A crime scene contamination log is created, listing everyone who has entered and exited the scene and when they did so. The purpose of the contamination log is to help explain any unintended contamination that has occurred (figure 4.2).

An *inner perimeter* is also established. The inner perimeter is completely surrounded by the outer perimeter. This area contains important pieces of physical evidence. If a body is discovered in a house, for instance, the outer perimeter may consist of the residence and the entire lawn surrounding the house, while the inner perimeter may be established as the actual dwelling or the room where the deceased is located. The reason for a distinct inner perimeter is to afford additional protection from intrusions. Distraught family members, for example, may attempt to reach a loved one by breaking through the

FIGURE 4-2: Contamination log for a crime scene

POSITION/NAME	AGENCY	TIME IN	TIME OUT
P.O. J. Collins	Newtown Police	0847	1044
Sgt. E. Wilson	Newtown Police	0849	1050
Capt. P. Gray	Newtown Police	0901	1048
EMT G. Waters	Ericson Ambulance	0848	0930
Paramedic Williams	Ericson Ambulance	0848	0930
FF J. Drew	Newtown Fire	0848	0928
Capt. L. Smith	Newtown Fire	0848	0928
Dr. C. Ford	Medical Examiner	0945	1130
Det. M. Collins	Newtown Police	0934	1130

outer perimeter. If they are stopped prior to gaining access to the inner perimeter, the chance for contamination is lessened.

Prior to searching and processing evidence within a crime scene, officers should consider the circumstances under which they gained access to the crime scene and whether or not they have a legal basis to seize property. Investigators may need to acquire a search warrant (described in chapter 3) to process a crime scene once any emergency conditions have been addressed.

RECORDING THE CRIME SCENE

From the moment the first officer enters a crime scene, it is forever altered by her presence. Based upon Locard's principle of contamination, any officer may inadvertently leave something at the scene and take something away. Whether it is a fiber from the officer's uniform or a shoeprint from a boot, the scene has been changed in some way. Because of this fact, every effort should be undertaken to record the crime scene as accurately as possible prior to any further unnecessary contamination.

Prior to processing any evidence, crime scene investigators gain an overall impression of the work to be done by conducting an initial "walk-through" assessment of the area (U.S. Department of Justice, Officer of Justice Programs, National Institute of Justice 2004, 26). After gaining a general understanding of the characteristics of the crime scene and some basic facts known about the crime, an investigator will typically photograph the scene in its existing state. Initial photos will be taken from a distance, with closer, more detailed pictures following. Longer-distance photos, which give the viewer a sense of where the crime scene is located, are referred to as *overalls*. The more detailed shots, which offer a closer examination of individual pieces of evidence, are referred to as *close-ups*.

For a photograph to be admissible as evidence in a court proceeding, it must be a fair and accurate representation of the actual scene (DOJ 2004, 33). In other words, items should not be moved or altered to present a better photograph; they must be documented as they were found.

Crime scene investigators will photograph a piece of physical evidence with a scale or rule included to give the viewer an impression of its size.

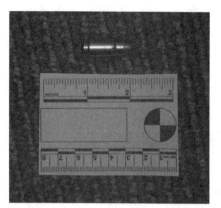

A photograph taken with a rule gives the viewer an indication of the size of the evidence.

A scale is an L-shaped ruler giving two dimensions of measure. A rule gives one dimension of measurement. Items photographed with a scale should also be photographed without the scale to show the piece of evidence as it was initially discovered, helping to ensure admissibility in court proceedings.

Prior to the development of digital photography, cost concerns factored into the decision of how many photos to take at a crime scene. Now, however, processing costs for digital photos are minimal, and prints may be produced selectively. (Some cases do not go to trial, and in other cases, a disk of images can be presented rather than prints.) Investigators record a description of each image and the image number in a written photographic log as they proceed.

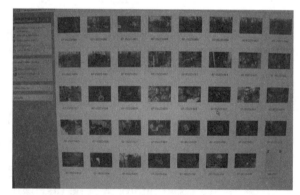

Digital photography has allowed for the storage of crime scene photographs in computerized databases.

Particular attention is devoted to photographing bloodstains at scenes of violent crime. Bloodstain pattern analysis involves applying scientific principles to determine a possible weapon type, a sequence of blows, and the approximate position of the offender. Photos of bloodstains can be useful to bloodstain pattern experts for interpretation (although visiting the scene itself is preferred).

A video may be taken of a crime scene to provide an additional reference for investigators and the court system. Videos should not replace photographs as a method to record a crime scene, however. Photos are preferred because they provide a more detailed view of particular elements of the crime scene, they are easier to distribute, they can be excluded from consideration in trial on an individual basis if found to be inadmissible, and they are easier for potential jurors to view. Videos are often taken without audio, which can distract viewers from viewing the crime scene (DOJ 2004, 34).

While videos and photographs provide a good representation of the crime scene, it may still be difficult for investigators, jurors, or other parties involved in the process to formulate mental pictures of where certain pieces of evidence are actually located within the scene. This can be clarified through a crime scene sketch. Crime scene sketches label where pieces of evidence are located within a perimeter. Crime scene sketches in the past were completed by hand; however, police agencies increasingly utilize computer programs to draw clearer, more precise sketches. A crime scene sketch is completed after the scene processing is complete based upon earlier measurements and rough sketches.

LOCATING AND IDENTIFYING EVIDENCE

Determining what evidence is important to collect and preserve within a crime scene can be challenging. The elements of the crime determine what is important to collect and what may be superfluous. Is a lead pipe at the scene of a homicide a weapon or simply a leftover piece of construction material? A crime scene investigator must consider the other physical evidence that is present and the testimonial evidence that detectives may have gathered.

Another difficulty is locating small pieces of evidence within a crime scene or finding a piece of evidence of any size in a large crime scene. While a typical crime scene might be a residence or small business, a scene can be as large as a five-acre field or one-square-mile wooded area. Crime scene searches must be carefully coordinated to ensure that all pertinent evidence is recovered.

Automobile searches may seem simple in scope; however, the various compartments and recesses present a challenge to investigators. If only one person searches a car, he must systematically cover each area, remembering to include the trunk and engine compartments. If two investigators are present, one can search the driver's side while the other searches the passenger side. Then each person can switch sides to double-check the other and ensure a thorough search.

Searches within a standard residential dwelling are conducted with an investigator assigned responsibility for an individual room. When the investigator is done with that room, she can switch rooms with another investigator, and each can ensure nothing was missed during the initial search.

Large-area searches present significant challenges. Police agencies must utilize the personnel available and ensure that a thorough examination of the area is conducted. Search patterns may be utilized to cover the area comprehensively. Two methods, the grid search and the strip search, are commonly employed (Federal Bureau of Investigation 2003).

The *grid search* divides a larger area into more defined smaller zones for individual investigators or groups of investigators to search carefully (figure 4.3). This pattern is useful in scenes where a large amount

FIGURE 4-3: Crime scene search patterns

Grid search pattern with zones of responsibility

Investigator A	Investigator B
Investigator C	Investigator D

Strip search pattern

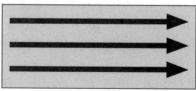

of evidence is scattered about (e.g. aircraft crashes). The location of each piece of evidence can be associated with an assigned grid for later mapping.

The *strip (or lane) search* involves a group of investigators walking an area in a uniform line with each individual having responsibility for the region within his path. When a piece of evidence is encountered, the line is stopped until the evidence is staked, recorded, collected, or otherwise addressed. The strip search can be reconducted perpendicular to the original path to verify the original results.

Whatever method is utilized to search a crime scene, a general rule is that investigators should take their time. Evidence can be overlooked if a crime scene search is conducted hastily. Prior to leaving a crime scene after searching for and collecting all evidence, it is a good to have a group "debriefing" meeting, where everyone discusses the investigation and makes certain nothing has been overlooked. It is very difficult, or impossible, to return to a crime scene later to reprocess it. Search warrants are only valid for one entry; once a scene is released, it cannot be re-searched without an additional warrant. The scene may have been tampered with or contaminated since it was left unsecured.

COLLECTION OF EVIDENCE

As evidence is located within a crime scene, careful procedures must be followed to provide investigators, and eventually jurors and other parties in the legal process, an accurate representation of the site. When a piece of evidence is collected, a chain of custody is started. The *chain of custody* refers to the steps an item takes from the point of collection until it reaches a court proceeding where it is considered as a trial exhibit.

Scenario

Crime Scene Technician Gonzalez responds to a reported burglary scene, where Officer Gray directs him to a screwdriver near the front entryway. The reporting party indicates that the screwdriver is not hers. Pry marks near the door lock indicate that the screwdriver may have been involved in the forced entry into the house.

Technician Gonzalez recovers the item, utilizing proper procedures to protect it for further processing. The item is placed in the police property and evidence room. A suspect is later caught and charged with burglary. Technician Gonzalez retrieves the screwdriver from the evidence room clerk and transports it to the prosecuting attorney so that it may be utilized as a court exhibit. Once the trial is completed, the screwdriver is returned to Gonzalez and retransported to the evidence room. The chain of custody for this item is reflected in figure 4.4.

Prior to moving a piece of evidence from its location in a crime scene, it must be documented. Photographs are taken of the item from a distance to record its context within the scene and up close for more detail (see "Recording the Crime Scene" above). Measurements of the item's location are taken from at least two fixed points for accuracy (a method called *triangulation*), and its location is included in reports and in later sketches drawn to approximate scale. Global Positioning System (GPS) coordinate measures to indicate evidence positioning are also used, particularly in large, outdoor crime scenes. As technology has developed, GPS equipment has become more readily available to police agencies. It is helpful if two investigators are utilized during evidence collection: one to perform the collection duties and the other to take notes and photos during the process.

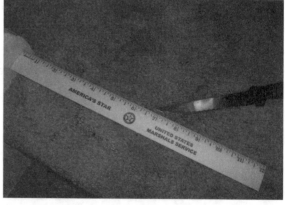

Photographs and measurements are taken of pieces of evidence prior to their collection.

FIGURE 4-4: Chain of custody report, showing the checkout and return of evidence for trial

NAME	DATE OUT	TIME OUT	DATE IN	TIME IN
Tech Gonzalez	N/A	N/A	3/4/08	1230
Tech Gonzalez	3/15/08	0830	N/A	N/A
Prosecutor Smith	3/15/08	0900	N/A	N/A
Tech Gonzalez	N/A	N/A	3/16/08	1530

Crime scene investigators must be able to identify evidence they collected at a crime scene later—sometimes years later—in court. To report that the evidence presented in court is the same evidence that was collected at the crime scene in question, the investigator will mark the packaging, or sometimes the item, with basic information. A police report number, the collecting person's initials, and the date of collection are standard markings on an evidence bag. Investigators also will staple and tape bags shut and initial the seals so they can testify that the evidence has not been tampered with since it was sealed at collection.

The method for collecting and packaging a piece of evidence varies, depending on the type of evidence. Most standard types of evidence (articles of clothing, tools, etc.) can be collected in either a plastic or paper bag and sealed with heat, staples, and/or tape. If fingerprints might be on an item,

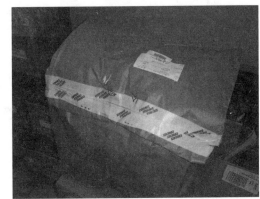

Evidence is packaged and clearly marked with the information about the collecting investigator and the case.

care should be taken to avoid damaging this potential evidence. Using gloves to pick up these items carefully can help avoid the destruction of prints. Methods that are unique to specific other types of evidence are addressed below. Other evidence collection and processing methods will be discussed in future chapters as they relate to specific crimes. Fingerprints and impression evidence (e.g., shoeprints and tool marks) are the focus of chapter 5.

Biological Evidence

Biological evidence, such as saliva, semen, blood, skin tissue, and bone, can often be located more readily through the use of alternate light sources, such as black lighting. Fluid evidence may be collected with a sterile cotton swab or gauze pad. Solid types of biological material are often collected in boxes or vials to protect them from contamination or further damage (DOJ 2004, 39). These materials should be handled with care due to the danger of disease; red biological hazard tape can be utilized to indicate that care in handling is necessary. Clothing soiled with wet biological stains is dried in a cabinet or at room temperature before placed in permanent packaging. Sealing biologically stained clothing in a plastic bag can degrade the sample for later testing purposes.

Trace Evidence

Trace evidence can be difficult to locate because by nature, it is extremely small. Alternate light sources may be helpful in finding small items. Another technique, called oblique lighting, helps to reveal trace evidence. Oblique lighting is accomplished by holding the lighting source (such as a flashlight) at an angle to the surface. Collection of trace evidence is achieved by gloved hands or the use of forceps or tweezers. Items collected in this manner can be sealed in a paper envelope. Multiple items, such as hairs and fibers, can be lifted with special adhesive-backed lifters similar to wide strips of invisible tape. Forensic vacuums with filters are also used to gather minute trace evidence (DOJ 2004, 40).

Narcotics

Illegal drugs are typically collected in standard packaging; however, the sensitive nature of narcotics requires careful handling. Drugs should be weighed (or counted in the case of pills) at each stage of the chain of custody. Some drugs, such as lysergic acid diethylamide (LSD), can be absorbed through the skin and thus should be handled with extreme caution. Using gloves or tweezers can help the investigator avoid such contact.

Glass and Paint Chips

Small fragments of glass or paint chips, often encountered in vehicle collision or burglary investigations, are gently collected and deposited in small boxes, sometimes with protective padding inside. Boxes protect these items from further damage, allowing for a possible fracture match at a later time.

Firearms

Guns present an obvious danger to each individual involved in the chain of custody. The smooth surfaces of many guns provide a good chance for latent fingerprint processing (see chapter 5). Handling a firearm by the checkered portions of the handgrips or stocks (where prints are less likely) lessens the possibility of damaging any prints that are present. Guns should never be picked up by placing a stick, pen, or other item in the barrel; the gun barrel often contains valuable evidence, and tampering with it can also be dangerous. Firearms must be unloaded by an officer or technician familiar with gun safety. During the unloading process, the recovering officer makes note of the number and position of loaded ammunition, as this information can be important to investigators. Guns are packaged in boxes as an additional safety measure.

Bullets and Shell Casings

A bullet is the actual projectile that is propelled out of a firearm during the shooting process (figure 4.5). A shell casing is the jacket that

FIGURE 4-5: Round of ammunition

Shell Casing   Bullet - Projectile holds the bullet, gunpowder, and a primer that ignites the powder and thrusts the bullet forward. Shell casings are expelled out of a semi-automatic pistol onto the ground or other surroundings. Shell casings in a revolver remain within the gun and must be manually ejected by the shooter.

Bullets are often collected from walls where they have come to a stop. Care must be taken not to damage the bullet, as striation marks on the bullet may be matched later to the gun barrel of a suspect weapon. The wall around the bullet hole is cut away, exposing the bullet for collection rather than prying it from the wall. Bullets may also be recovered from a variety of other locations, including from bodies by medical personnel. Bullets are placed in a small box along with cotton (or other soft materials) to prevent further scratching or other damage to help facilitate possible comparison. Bullets are often recovered in fragments, as their violent flight may cause breakup upon impact.

A trajectory kit is used to estimate the approximate flight path of a bullet. A trajectory kit consists of rods and string, or possibly laser lighting, to indicate a bullet's flight path based upon the angles of impact indicated by bullet holes. It is possible to estimate the position of the shooter with this method. Trajectory kits are used after bullets have been recovered to prevent damage or loss to imbedded bullets.

Shell casings may be compared to the firing weapon as well, based upon a variety of marks made during the firing process and the ejection of the casing. Shell casings are also boxed in cotton to prevent any damage. The forensic comparison of bullets and casings is explored further in chapter 5.

Computers

Evidence contained on computers and memory devices must be collected with caution to avoid accidental erasure or destruction. Criminals familiar with computers have been known to manipulate a system so that evidence disappears from its memory if the system is shut down through normal procedures. Evidence technicians can be trained in the correct handling of computer evidence by organizations such as the FBI. The typical preferred method is to unplug the computer rather than shut it down; however, each case must be considered individually. Care should be taken to avoid exposing computer memory equipment to magnetic sources, as they can erase saved material in some devices.

STORAGE OF PHYSICAL EVIDENCE

After evidence is collected, it is transported to a secure evidence facility. A facility must offer limited, controlled access to ensure that evidence is not tampered with in any fashion. An evidence room is staffed by sworn or civilian personnel who carefully log, catalog, and maintain the various items of evidence and property that come into the facility.

Most evidence can be safely stored at room temperature on shelving with location codes so the evidence officer can easily locate it. Refrigerators are maintained in evidence rooms for perishable items, such as blood. Many police departments maintain additional safes for storing particularly sensitive evidence, such as narcotics or cash.

Evidence may be stored in a locked area, accessible only to the evidence room staff, or turned over directly to on-duty personnel. Reports will indicate this transfer of custody. The evidence is maintained in the facility until it is needed for other purposes, such as forensic testing or for court exhibition. If it is released for any of these purposes, the individual checking the property out of the facility will sign a chain of custody form. Evidence may be returned to the evidence room at a later time. Periodic audits of evidence room property by random police supervisors help ensure the integrity of chain of custody procedures.

Evidence is stored in a secure facility until it is needed for trial.

Evidence may remain in a facility until all court proceedings related to the case are concluded and possibilities for appeals have been exhausted. For unsolved cases, evidence may be maintained for decades. Often a court order will be acquired authorizing the disposal of unnecessary evidence. Some property placed in an evidence room is merely "found" and not associated with a criminal case. Agencies maintain this type of property for a period of time according to established policy before disposing of it or auctioning it off.

SUMMARY

A crime scene is any location where physical evidence is located. A primary crime scene is where the actual crime occurred. A secondary crime scene is where evidence is located but where the crime was not committed. Crime scene investigators may be sworn officers, trained civilians, or investigators from an outside agency called in for assistance, depending upon an agency's available resources.

Direct evidence links a suspect to a crime. Circumstantial evidence requires a judgment to link a person to a crime. Trace evidence describes small evidence that may be difficult to see with the naked eye.

Crime scenes are protected with an outer perimeter, which provides a buffer zone around an inner perimeter; the inner perimeter contains the crucial physical evidence of a crime. Access is limited to individuals who have a legitimate reason to investigate the crime scene. Detailed logs are kept of everyone who enters and exits a crime scene and what time they did so.

Crime scenes are documented through photographs, videotaping, and sketching. Overall photographs give a more distant view of the scene to provide a viewer perspective on the setting. Close-up photos provide more detail.

Testimonial evidence provided to investigators can help determine what physical evidence is important to collect. The search of any crime scene must be systematic to avoid missing an essential piece of evidence. Two search methods are the line, or strip, search and the grid search.

A chain of custody begins when evidence is located and collected and ends when the evidence is released or destroyed. Prior to the moving of any evidence, it should be photographed and its location recorded through measurements. An investigator marks evidence to ensure she can testify in court that the evidence presented as an exhibit is the same evidence that was collected at the scene. Collection methods vary based upon the type of evidence. Evidence is carefully logged and tracked in a facility that provides limited access to police personnel.

Key Terms

Chain of custody: The trail a piece of evidence takes from discovery through court presentation and eventual release or destruction by evidence room personnel

Circumstantial evidence: Evidence that requires an individual to make an assumption to link an individual to a crime

Close-up photographs: Crime scene photos that provide a detailed view of individual pieces of evidence

Crime scene: Any area where physical evidence in a criminal investigation is located

Crime scene investigation: The systematic collection and interpretation of physical evidence in a criminal case

Direct evidence: Evidence that links an individual to a crime

Grid search: A method for locating evidence in which an area is divided into defined zones and responsibility is assigned to an individual or group to search that area

Inner perimeter: An area, surrounded by an outer perimeter, that contains physical evidence within a crime scene

Outer perimeter: An area, surrounding an inner perimeter, that offers a buffer zone separating noninvestigative personnel and the general public from physical evidence

Overall photographs: Photos taken from a distance that give the viewer a sense of the general setting of the crime scene

Primary crime scene: An area where a crime has occurred and evidence is located

Secondary crime scene: An area where evidence from a crime is located, although the actual initial crime did not occur in this area

Strip (or lane) search: A group method for locating evidence in which a uniform walking line of searchers proceeds with individuals responsible for checking their immediate areas as they progress

Trace evidence: Evidence that is very small, difficult to detect, or present in minute quantities

Triangulation: A method for measuring the location of a piece of evidence from two fixed points within a crime scene

Discussion Questions

1. What are the benefits of having trained civilian personnel who process crime scenes as their sole duty? What are the benefits of using sworn police officers to process scenes in addition to other standard police duties (if any)?

2. What are some ways in which an investigator can unintentionally contaminate a crime scene?

3. Why is it a good idea to have a debriefing meeting of all investigators at a crime scene prior to their leaving that scene?

4. Explain why a chain of custody is important.

Exploration

1. Watch a televised court case or read about a court case in a news report and attempt to identify direct and circumstantial evidence.

2. Examine photo or video news coverage of crime scenes and identify what might be an inner or outer perimeter.

3. Visit a professional crime scene investigator's association website and review developing issues and trends in the field.

References

Federal Bureau of Investigation (FBI). 2003. *Handbook of forensic services: Crime scene search.* Retrieved August 16, 2007, from www .fbi.gov/hq/lab/handbook/intro16.htm.

Georgia Bureau of Investigation, Division of Forensic Sciences. n.d. *Trace evidence.* Retrieved August 15, 2007, from http://dofs.gbi .georgia.gov/00/channel_title/0,2094,75166109_75730766,00 .html.

U.S. Department of Justice (DOJ), Officer of Justice Programs, National Institute of Justice. 2004. *Crime scene investigation: A reference for law enforcement training.* Washington, DC: U.S. Department of Justice. Available at www.ncjrs.gov/pdffiles1/ nij/200160.pdf.

CHAPTER 5

IDENTIFICATION

CHAPTER OBJECTIVES

By the end of this chapter, the reader will be able to do the following:

- Describe the difference between *class* and *individual characteristics* as they pertain to physical evidence comparisons.

- Explain the physical evidence comparison process.

- Describe the characteristics of fingerprints impressions.

- List the three types of fingerprint patterns.

- Describe what *deoxyribonucleic acid* (DNA) is and why it is important in criminal investigations.

- Explain why care is important in the collection of biological materials (potential sources of DNA).

- Identify the parts of a firearm and a round of ammunition involved in a bullet-firing process.

- Explain how *rifling* is important in recovered bullet evidence.

- Describe the databases AFIS, CODIS, and IBIS.

- Explain the importance of the comparison of impression, soil, and building-material evidence in criminal investigations.

- Describe recommended procedures to be used in an eye-witness identification.

Physical evidence presents value to a criminal investigation for several reasons. Physical evidence may indicate a motive for the crime (e.g., a few bills strewn on the floor in a business where a homicide occurred may indicate a robbery). It may help explain the sequence of events of a crime (e.g., at a burglary scene where the suspect cut his hand while breaking into the residence, his movements can be tracked by blood trails throughout the scene). Perhaps the most important benefit of physical evidence is its ability to tie a suspect to the scene of a crime through the process of identification.

CASE STUDY

On July 29, 2000, a five-year-old girl named Iriana DeJesus was kidnapped from her home in Philadelphia. An intensive search was conducted, but Iriana was not found. Her body was discovered August 3, 2000. Iriana had been strangled to death.

A DNA sample was collected from the body, and tests revealed that the sample did not belong to Iriana. The DNA profile was entered in a national database of unknown profiles. Seven years later, on March 22, 2007, investigators in Philadelphia were notified that a positive link had been established between the unknown profile and the profile of a convicted felon from Arizona (Federal Bureau of Investigation, Philadelphia Division 2007, 1).

Cases such as the one above illustrate how valuable physical evidence can be in the absence of any other investigative information. These investigations rely heavily upon physical evidence to indicate a conclusive match to a suspect. In other cases, a witness may be available to make this match. Investigations with witnesses offer detectives an opportunity to collect testimonial evidence to track down a suspect. This chapter will first explore identification through physical evidence, then identification through victim and witness testimony.

CLASS AND INDIVIDUAL CHARACTERISTICS

Physical evidence collected at a crime scene is compared to a specimen with a known origin to determine if a match exists. Various factors determine whether or not a match can be made with certainty or if the evidence resembles the comparison specimen to a degree. Not all evidence can categorically tie an individual to a scene. However, there is value in evidence that compares favorably, even if not conclusively, with a comparison sample; it provides circumstantial evidence for the case.

Assorted types of evidence can be matched under two different dimensions. Some evidence can be matched under *class characteristics*. Other evidence exhibits *individual characteristics* that offer a more exact comparison. Class characteristics can narrow down a piece of evidence to a specific comparison group. Individual characteristics can restrict the comparison even further, matching it to a single source. The DNA case study at the beginning of the chapter demonstrated evidence with individual characteristics.

CONTROLS AND COMPARISON

Identification of evidence is accomplished by comparing the collected evidence with a control specimen. A *control sample* is one with a known source. Collected physical evidence, on the other hand, may come from an unknown source. Comparing the known to an unknown either creates a match or not.

Control samples are taken from individuals with legitimate access to a crime scene to eliminate them from consideration as suspects. For example, a homeowner's fingerprints are taken to exclude him from comparisons to prints collected at a burglary scene. Samples collected for this purpose are called *elimination samples*.

Comparison of evidence takes place in a crime laboratory. Each piece of evidence is inspected, often by a specialist trained in examining that particular type of material. Specialists include those who examine blood, trace evidence examiners, firearms examiners, forensic botanists (for plants and soil), and glass specialists, to name a few. Each examiner compares the control and the collected evidence and makes one of three determinations: a match was made, the collected evidence demonstrated similarities to the control sample, or no similarities could be found (inconclusive).

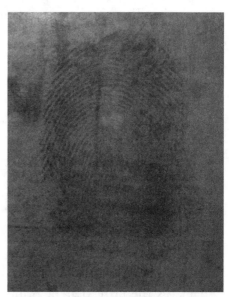

Comparisons made in the field cannot be trusted as scientifically valuable. Crime scene technicians may make observations and educated guesses about whether or not a match or similarity exists; however, this is not conclusive enough upon which to base an investigation. For example, a pry mark on a door frame may be visually compared to a screwdriver recovered from an individual, but the results

Evidence, such as a fingerprint, is collected from a crime scene for later comparison in the crime lab.

of this examination are suspect. A number of screwdrivers probably compare favorably to the pry mark. Microscopic examination is far more conclusive than assessment with the naked eye.

The process of identification utilizing different types of common evidence will now be explored.

FINGERPRINTS

Fingerprinting for identification has been in use since 1902. The New York Civil Service Commission fingerprinted applicants at this time to ensure someone else did not take the civil service exam for them:

> The New York state prison system began to use fingerprints for the identification of criminals in 1903. In 1904 the fingerprint system accelerated

when the United States Penitentiary at Leavenworth, Kansas, and the St. Louis, Missouri, Police Department both established fingerprint bureaus." (FBI n.d., "History").

Friction ridges are the raised areas of skin on an individual's fingers. The friction ridges of each finger help a person pick up and manipulate items. These ridges form distinct patterns. Everyone has a different friction ridge pattern; no two individuals have identical patterns. Fingerprints are classified according to pattern types. The three patterns are arches, loops, and whirls (FBI n.d.).

Fingerprints may be discovered at crime scenes in one of three forms. *Latent fingerprints* are those that are not visible to the naked eye but present when developed through the application of powders or chemicals. These fingerprints are most often collected by applying the powder or chemical, photographing the resulting print(s), and recovering them with clear-tape lifts. A photograph is taken before collecting with tape in case something happens during the tape-lifting process that damages the print. Latent prints are created through the exposure of finger ridge patterns to natural oils and contaminants; uncontaminated fingers do not leave prints.

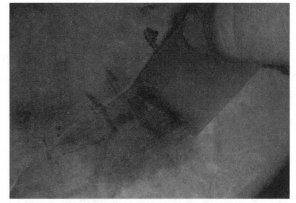

Patent prints are observable without the need for further development. Fingers that have been exposed to a visible contaminant, such as blood,

The standard method for collecting latent fingerprints is development with powder and lifting with clear tape.

may leave a discernable pattern for the investigator. Photographs are taken of such prints. Collection may be facilitated with clear-tape lifts in some instances, or if possible, the entire item may be retained.

Plastic prints are those that are left in malleable substances, such as clay, soil, or even peanut butter. These prints are also visible to the naked eye. After photographing a plastic print, an investigator may collect it by making a cast with special materials. It may be preferable to collect the entire item if possible.

Once these fingerprints are collected, a fingerprint examiner in the crime lab compares the collected print to a suspect's print to determine if a match exists, if there is no match, or if there is not enough detail in the collected print to make a determination. Fingerprint examiners look for specific points within the patterns that match. The more points that can be matched, the more positive the identification.

It is helpful to the examiner if a specific suspect is in mind to compare the print to. Police departments take fingerprints of individuals who are booked after an arrest. The examiner can search these fingerprint records and compare the collected example to the control fingerprint. The *Automated Fingerprint Identification System* (AFIS) is a computer database of fingerprints of individuals who have been arrested in the past. If no suspect exists, it is possible through computer technology to compare fingerprints electronically to those stored within this database. The computer will report close matches based upon identified points of similarity (National Science and Technology Council 2006, 2). A fingerprint examiner must always check to determine if there is a conclusive match based upon the computer reports.

Feet and palms also leave prints due to friction ridges. Footprints are not collected as a matter of routine during arrest booking procedures, so a database of comparable footprints does not exist as it does with fingerprints. If a suspect is known, however, a footprint impression can be collected and compared to those recovered as physical evidence (using procedures similar to those for fingerprints).

DEOXYRIBONUCLEIC ACID (DNA) AND BIOLOGICAL EVIDENCE

Deoxyribonucleic acid, or DNA, is contained in virtually every cell of the human body. The DNA in every cell in a person's body is the same; that is, DNA in a man's blood is the same as the DNA in his skins cells and semen. An individual's DNA is distinct from others' DNA, with the exception of identical twins (National Institute of Justice n.d.). This makes evidence with DNA valuable in the process of identification.

DNA may be collected from samples of various biological fluids and tissues, including sweat, skin, blood, hair, tissue, mucus, vaginal and rectal cells, and semen. Anything that comes into contact with these bodily materials may be a source of DNA evidence. For example, weapons, hats, cigarettes, envelopes, bite marks, and toothpicks may all provide DNA samples for investigators (NIJ n.d.). For this reason, these types of items are frequently collected for further evaluation.

The usefulness of a DNA sample to compare to a control sample depends upon several factors. DNA can degrade over time due to environmental conditions. Heat and sunlight may break down a sample. Moisture and mold can cause deterioration. Bacteria might affect DNA samples as well. All of these issues can reduce the ability of forensic scientists to create a DNA profile from the sample. However, in some cases, a sample that was several years old has revealed a profile, so samples should be collected at all times with the belief that a comparison is possible (NIJ n.d.).

Care should be used when collecting evidence that potentially contains a DNA sample. Concerns about contamination and disease exist because this evidence is a biological material. Investigators can easily contaminate a sample with their own DNA or cross-contaminate it with DNA from other evidence if proper procedures are not followed. Evidence with a possible DNA profile, such as blood, can carry potential blood-borne infections, such as human immunodeficiency virus (HIV) or the hepatitis B virus (HBV). The Centers for Disease Control (2005) recommend using "universal precautions," including wearing gloves, protective clothing, and masks to avoid exposure to these infections. These precautions can also help avoid contamination issues.

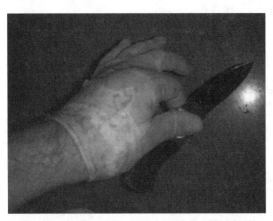

Latex gloves are used in the collection of evidence to avoid contamination and meet suggested "universal precautions."

A catalog of DNA profiles, similar to the AFIS system for fingerprint evidence, has been collected in the *Combined DNA Index System,* or CODIS. Samples are collected from offenders convicted of certain crimes, and the profiles are entered into the computerized database. The known control samples are compared to evidentiary samples collected from unsolved cases to determine if a match exists (NIJ n.d.).

CASE STUDY

In 1996, Gerald Parker—then in a California prison on a parole violation stemming from a 1980 sentence for raping a child—was charged with the rapes and murders of five women between December 1978 and October 1979 and the murder of a fetus during a rape in 1980. (NIJ 1999, 1)

Parker's DNA had been entered into California's computerized DNA database, revealing a match between his known control profile and these unsolved cases. In one of these newly solved cases, a subject had already been convicted and had served 16 years in prison. The wrongly convicted man, Kevin Green, was released based upon this new evidence (NIJ 1999).

FIREARMS

It is possible to match recovered components of fired ammunition to a firearm and determine a match. This is accomplished through microscopic examination of the recovered bullet or cartridge casing and the comparison of it to the barrel and other parts of the questioned gun. A piece of ammunition consists of two primary parts: the bullet and the cartridge casings. The *bullet* is the element of the ammunition that actually exits the firearm and strikes the target. The *cartridge casing* contains primer and gunpowder that help propel the bullet forward. Cartridge casings are either ejected from a firearm automatically or retained until ejected manually by the shooter; depending upon the particular gun.

The *barrel* of a firearm is the chamber a fired bullet travels down before exiting a gun. Generally, a longer barrel helps improve accuracy. Accuracy is also assisted through *rifling,* helical grooves cut into the barrel of a firearm during the production process. Rifling places a spin on the bullet in the firing process, thus improving accuracy. Rifling is present in most common firearms, with the exception of smoothbore weapons, such as shotguns. Each weapon has unique imperfections in its rifling. These rifling characteristics, including the imperfections, are transferred as striation impressions onto fired bullets. The result is that fired bullets can be matched with barrels (Schehl 2000, 1).

The barrel of a firearm is rifled to improve accuracy; this also allows for the comparison of recovered bullets to the firearm.

A semi-automatic or automatic firearm is one that ejects cartridge casings and mechanically reloads ammunition into a firing position after every shot. A revolver has a spinning cylinder that places a new round of ammunition into the firing position after every shot but retains the spent cartridge casings. Cartridge casings may not be present at every crime scene, depending upon the weapon fired. Also, a shooter may easily retrieve cartridge casings from the ground and take them with her. Identifying marks may be present on expended cartridge casings, giving forensic scientists the ability to match casings to a particular firearm.

During the firing process, a firing pin within the firearm strikes a primer in the rear of a cartridge. This ignites gunpowder within the cartridge, propelling the bullet forward. The firing pin leaves a mark on the primer, which can be compared microscopically to control sample casings that have been fired through the firearm in question. When cartridge casings are extracted and ejected from a firearm, this action also leaves gouge impressions that may be compared under a microscope. These marks on the cartridge casings can potentially allow a match between the expended casing and a firearm (Schehl 2000, 2).

AFIS provides a comparison database for fingerprints, and CODIS does the same for DNA. For firearms, the *Integrated Ballistic Identification System* (IBIS) collects images of bullets and casings for comparison. IBIS is administered by the Federal Bureau of Investigation. Expended ammunition components from unknown cases can be entered and compared to known specimens (Missouri State Highway Patrol 2002).

When a firearm is discharged, various elements are expelled into the air from the ignition of cartridge gunpowder. Some of these elements may attach to the shooter's hand and arm. A gunshot residue analysis examines an adhesive lift from a person's hand to determine if gunpowder elements are present, indicating that he may have fired a weapon recently. The lifts must be collected within five hours of a shot's being fired (Wade 2003). It should be noted that gunshot residue tests may not provide conclusive results, because materials similar to residue may be acquired from sources other than a gunshot.

IMPRESSION EVIDENCE

Impression evidence is a broad category that describes any sort of item that leaves a comparable impression at a crime scene. Common examples include shoeprints and tire tread impressions. Similar to fingerprints, impressions can be latent, patent, or plastic.

Impression evidence comparisons are based upon examining the collected sample and the known control and looking for unique imperfections for a match. Imperfections develop through use as well as during the manufacturing process. For example, the sole of a shoe may be cut by a rock while walking. This imperfection may be reflected in a shoeprint left in soil at a crime scene. An examiner will look for this unique

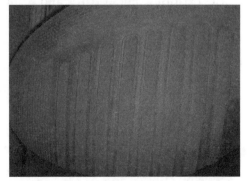

Shoes leave distinctive prints at crime scenes that may be compared to the original source.

imperfection in the control source (the shoe) and the collected impression to determine a match.

Tool Marks

Imperfections may not be visible to the naked eye. This may be the case in impressions made by tools, or "tool marks." A common tool mark at a crime scene is a screwdriver pry mark gouge on a window sill caused during a forced entry. A crime scene investigator may collect a portion of the wooden window frame, keeping the mark intact. A comparison may be made between the wood and a collected screwdriver itself, or a sample impression may be made in similar wood by the examiner. Such examinations are made through a comparison microscope, which displays images side by side to reveal similarities or differences.

The method for collecting impression evidence depends upon how the evidence is presented. Latent or patent shoe, tire, or similar prints are collected through methods similar to those for fingerprint collection. Photographs are taken of the print, and the print is lifted with a large, special lifter. A comparison print can be made on large sheets of paper with ink. Plastic prints may be collected through casting. The standard material to use in a casting is dental stone.

SOIL

Soils can be compared with control samples to determine if similarities exist in "color, texture, and composition" (Wade 2003, 119). Soils may be collected from a suspect's clothing, vehicle, weapon, or other areas for comparison. A control sample may be recovered from the actual crime scene (e.g., where the victim's body lies). A soil sample is not as conclusive an indicator to tie a subject to a scene as a fingerprint or DNA sample, but it can provide circumstantial, class evidence to help solidify a case.

Soil samples are collected around the actual crime scene (without disturbing other evidence) and from likely entrance and escape routes

(Wade 2003). Samples are microscopically compared to the evidence collected from the suspect in a laboratory setting to check for similarities. Soil comparisons reveal class characteristics. Results can indicate similar tendencies, but it cannot be categorically concluded that a certain soil came from a particular scene.

BUILDING MATERIALS

Certain building materials, including wood, glass, and paint, can provide some clues for identification. Materials such as these can be found relative to crimes such as burglary and robbery and at vehicle accident scenes. During violent property damage, it is common for such debris to attach to a suspect or her vehicle. Comparisons can be made to the damage left at a scene. Whether or not a class or individual characteristic can be identified depends upon the particular item of evidence.

Materials can reveal class characteristics through a variety of tests administered depending upon the type of evidence. Paint samples may contain similar properties when compared. However, similar paint is often present in multiple locations (e.g., car manufacturers paint multiple vehicles the same color, house paint is sold in bulk, etc.). A wood type, such as oak, can be identified, but again, the use of this wood is common. Glass properties vary based upon the manufacturing process, so it is possible to state that two samples are similar. Class characteristic evidence can be important in establishing a circumstantial connection.

It is possible in certain instances to establish individual characteristics that tie two material samples together. This is accomplished through "breakage comparison." This method compares the edges of two samples where they have broken apart after an impact. Breakage comparison among small samples can be accomplished through microscopic examination. If a unique fit between the broken pieces can be sufficiently established, an individual match can be made (Wade 2003).

VICTIM OR WITNESS IDENTIFICATION

A suspect in an investigation may be identified not only through physical evidence but the testimony of victims and witnesses. Just as specific procedures must be followed in the collection and processing of physical evidence, certain steps should be followed to ensure that an identification by a victim or witness is accurate. It is possible for a victim or witness to forget a suspect's features and falsely identify a subject.

CASE STUDY

William Gregory was sentenced to 70 years in prison for the rape of two women in 1993. Gregory lived in the same apartment complex as the two victims. One victim reported having seen Gregory in the complex at various times. One victim picked Gregory out of a photographic lineup and expressed certainty that he was the suspect. Although hairs were found at the scene, DNA technology at the time could not create a profile from this type of evidence.

Gregory served seven years in prison before aid from the Innocence Project, a group of attorneys dedicated to exonerating the falsely accused through DNA evidence, secured a review of the case. Technology had advanced to the point where a comparison could now be made between Gregory's control DNA sample and the hairs collected from the crimes. A new test revealed no match between the two, and Gregory was released from prison (Lowe 2006, 16).

Cases such as the one above illustrate the fact that eyewitness identification can be incorrect. The National Institute of Justice, however, advises that "the vast majority of eyewitness identifications are accurate and provide trustworthy evidence for the trier of fact" (2003, v). Investigators can avoid such tragic cases when they understand the dangers of erroneous identification and follow procedures to reduce such possibilities.

Identification may be quite simple in many cases, as the victim or witnesses may know the suspect well. In domestic violence cases, it is likely the victim has detailed information about the suspect. In other cases, witnesses or victims may know basic identifying characteristics of the suspect, such as his first name or the neighborhood where he lives.

Cases where the suspect is completely unknown present more difficulties. An investigation may reveal clues about the subject's identity. A detective can use these clues to attempt to establish who the suspect is. For example, a license plate from a getaway car will reveal a registered owner. This does not conclusively reveal the suspect; a witness or suspect must identify the perpetrator to solidify an identification.

Face-to-face identifications of individual suspects are only recommended if a suspect is apprehended quickly after a crime has occurred. If a significant amount of time has passed between the occurrence of the crime and the development of a suspect, a formal procedure should be followed to avoid leading a witness into a mistaken identification. This procedure involves displaying a *lineup,* or a choice of several potential suspects for the witness to choose from. A lineup may be presented live or through video or photographs.

Whether photos, a video, or a live presentation is used, particular steps can be taken to ensure that the investigator does not intentionally or inadvertently lead a witness into the identification of a particular person. Witnesses or victims should always view a lineup separately so one does not influence the other's decision. The witness should be advised that the suspect may or may not be in the lineup; the witness should not feel compelled to choose anyone from the choices presented. Witnesses are told that excluding innocent people is as important as unearthing a suspect. The lineup procedure should be documented with a report that indicates the date and time, the names of the individuals included in the lineup, and what choice the witness made (including whether the witness indicated that none of the subjects was the suspect). This document is signed by the witness.

The actual lineup should be preserved for court consideration (retain photos, videotape live lineups, and maintain videos shown to witnesses) (NIJ 1999).

At least five "filler" subjects (those who are not of the alleged suspect) should be used for a lineup, offering the witness a number of choices. The subjects chosen for a lineup should have physical characteristics similar to those of the suspect as described by the witness. If photographs are used, they should be in the same format (e.g., all black-and-white or all color), so no particular photo stands out from another (NIJ 1999).

The most common method of displaying a lineup is with the use of photographs. A benefit of using photographic lineups is that photos of the potential suspect(s) may be readily available through mug shots taken after the subject was arrested for previous crimes or from a source of driver's license photos. A video or live lineup may be preferred when possible, as the subjects can be asked to speak and their voices may be recognizable. Also, three-dimensional representations of the subjects are likely more recognizable than two dimensional pictures.

SUMMARY

The identification of suspects in a criminal case can be accomplished through an evaluation of both physical and testimonial evidence. Physical evidence can be compared to control samples to reveal either class or individual characteristics. Types of evidence that are useful for comparison include fingerprints, DNA, firearms, impression evidence, soil, and building materials.

Witnesses may be available to identify a suspect through testimonial evidence. A lineup of potential suspects is often used to identify a possible perpetrator. A lineup may use photographs, video, or live subjects. Specific procedures are followed in a lineup to avoid the possibility of a mistaken identification.

Key Terms

Automated Fingerprint Identification System (AFIS): A database of fingerprints used for comparison to fingerprints collected as physical evidence in criminal cases

Barrel (firearm): The portion of a firearm through which a bullet travels during the firing process

Bullet: The portion of a round of ammunition that is expelled forward from a firearm during the firing process

Cartridge casing: The portion of a round of ammunition that contains primers and powders, which force the attached bullet to propel forward during the firing process

Class characteristic: An attribute of a piece of physical evidence that can link that evidence to a group or category source

Combined DNA Index System (CODIS): A database of unknown DNA samples collected as evidence in cases for comparison to control samples collected from known offenders

Control sample: A known example of a material to compare to a collected piece of physical evidence for a possible characteristic match

Deoxyribonucleic acid (DNA): A biological material present in many cells of the human body that is useful in forensic comparisons due to highly individualized characteristic patterns

Elimination sample: A control sample collected with the purpose of excluding from comparison evidence matching a known person who is not considered a suspect (e.g., a homeowner's fingerprints from comparison to fingerprints collected at a burglary scene)

Friction ridges: The elevated, patterned portions of a finger, palm, or foot that may leave an impression or print on a surface

Integrated Ballistic Identification System (IBIS): A database of known and unknown bullets and cartridge casings collected as physical evidence, allowing for forensic comparison

Latent fingerprint: A fingerprint not observable with the naked eye that is developed using powders or chemicals prior to collection

Lineup: A collection of live subjects, photographs of subjects, or a video of subjects used to show to eyewitnesses of a crime for possible suspect identification

Individual characteristic: An attribute of a piece of physical evidence that can link that evidence to a specific source

Patent fingerprint: A fingerprint that is left on a surface that is visible due to the subject's finger being contaminated with a substance

Plastic fingerprint: A fingerprint that is left as an impression in a malleable substance (e.g., clay)

Rifling: Helical grooves cut into a firearm barrel to increase accuracy by placing a spin on a fired bullet

Discussion Questions

1. Which of the three computerized databases for evidence comparison mentioned in this chapter (AFIS, CODIS, and IBIS) do you believe is likely used most frequently in criminal investigations? Why do you believe this is so?

2. Describe three possible reasons why fingerprints may not be present at a crime scene.

3. What might an investigator do that would unintentionally influence a witness into making a mistaken identification during a lineup procedure?

Exploration

1. Explore the FBI's website about CODIS, www.fbi.gov/hq/lab/html/codis1.htm, and review why it is helpful in investigations.

2. Search the Internet for cases involving the "Innocence Project," a group of legal professionals dedicated to freeing wrongfully convicted felons. Find a case where a person was mistakenly identified

by a victim or witness and later freed due to scientific evidence. Were recommended lineup protocols broken in this case?

References

Centers for Disease Control and Prevention (CDC). 2005. *Universal precautions for prevention and transmission of HIV and other bloodborne infections,* March 1. Retrieved August 22, 2007, from www.cdc.gov/ncidod/dhqp/bp_universal_precautions.html.

Federal Bureau of Investigation (FBI). n.d. *Fingerprint identification.* Retrieved August 21, 2007, from www.fbi.gov/hq/cjisd/ident.pdf.

Federal Bureau of Investigation (FBI), Philadelphia Division. 2007. Press release regarding Alexis Flores, June 2. Retrieved August 20, 2007, from http://philadelphia.fbi.gov/pressrel/2007/ph060207.htm.

Lowe, Melanie. 2006. What went wrong? A closer look at wrongful conviction in Kentucky (part I). *The Advocate* 28, no. 4 (July): 16–18.

Missouri State Highway Patrol. 2002. NIBIN system replaces drugfire. *Under the Scope* 2, no. 2.

National Institute of Justice (NIJ). n.d. *What every law enforcement officer should know about DNA evidence.* Washington, DC: Department of Justice.

National Institute of Justice (NIJ). 1999. *Eyewitness evidence: A guide for law enforcement.* Washington, DC: U.S. Department of Justice.

National Institute of Justice (NIJ). 2003. *Eyewitness evidence: A trainer's manual for law enforcement.* Washington, DC: U.S. Department of Justice.

National Science and Technology Council. 2006. *Fingerprint recognition,* August 7. Washington, DC: Miles.

Schehl, Sally. 2000. *Forensic science communications: Firearms and toolmarks in the FBI laboratory*, April. Washington, DC: Federal Bureau of Investigation, Forensic Science Research Unit.

Wade, Coleen (ed.). 2003. *Handbook of forensic services.* Quantico, VA: Federal Bureau of Investigation.

CHAPTER 6

INTERVIEWS AND INTERROGATIONS

CHAPTER OBJECTIVES

By the end of this chapter, the reader will be able to do the following:

- Define the goal of an *interview* or an *interrogation*.

- Explain the difference between an interview and an interrogation.

- Describe steps that are taken by investigators prior to initiating an interview to help ensure it is successful.

- Explain how questions should be phrased to gain information.

- List reasons why juveniles must be approached differently in an interview.

- Explain why interrogations should be held in a controlled environment.

- Describe the crucial elements of Fifth Amendment rights warnings that are given to subjects prior to interrogations.

- Explain how *nonverbal cues* are used to help determine deception in an interrogation and the role of *kinesics* in the interrogation process.

- Describe the process of corroboration and why it is important.

The statements of those who witnessed or were involved in a crime are important elements of an investigation, to help determine what happened. Even in cases where physical evidence solidly points to a particular suspect, the accounts of those who were present can help clarify the sequence of events. Important questions can be answered through testimonial evidence gathered through interviews and interrogations.

CASE STUDY

During the years 1989 and 1990, seven men were found murdered not far from Florida highways. A woman named Aileen Wuornos became a suspect after she pawned a gun belonging to one of the victims and was seen driving his car. A confidant of Wuornos's, Tyria Moore, cooperated with police and led them to evidence that tied Wuornos to other victims (*Wuornos v. Florida* 1996).

Wuornos was later apprehended and brought in for questioning. Wuornos indicated that she wished to confess to the crimes, even after she consulted with an attorney, to clear her confidant of any involvement (Reynolds 1992). Although Wuornos agreed to confess, the investigators were able to elicit details from her that indicated premeditation and helped deny her later claims of self-defense. Wuornos told investigators that she killed the men because they could turn her in for prostitution and she thought they would not pay her (*Wuornos v Florida* 1996).

The confession of Wuornos and the statements of her confidant, Moore, played a vital role in solving multiple murders. Quality interview and interrogation work is important in the investigative process and for subsequent legal proceedings.

INTERVIEWS VERSUS INTERROGATIONS

The goal of both an interview and an interrogation is to ascertain the true recollections of the subject being questioned. Subjects who are not believed to be suspects in a crime are queried through *interviews*. An interview is less adversarial than an interrogation. This is not to imply that the subject of an interview will not be reluctant to

offer information; an investigator may have to employ certain tactics to uncover information that an interviewee is withholding for a variety of reasons. The subjects of interviews may include witnesses or victims of crimes. Individuals who possess intelligence information for law enforcement may also be interviewed (see chapter 7).

An *interrogation* is usually more confrontational than an interview, as the subject is thought to be concealing details of his involvement as a suspect in a crime. The objective of an interrogation is not to obtain a confession (an

Testimonial evidence is gathered through witness interviews; investigators must master the ability to gather this information.

admission of criminal involvement), as the investigator must bear in mind that the subject of the interrogation may be innocent. The strength of the belief that the interviewee is a suspect is based upon the investigation up to that point, an evaluation of previous evidence, and statements made during the interrogation.

INTERVIEWS

The approach an investigator may use in an interview depends upon a variety of factors. The type of crime, the characteristics of the victim, the setting of the interview, and the information already known about the crime all play a role in determining the methods that will be used. An interview may also change course as it progresses. The witness may become hesitant to give information to the investigator or become a suspect instead of a witness. For this reason, the investigator must remain flexible in her approach. Interviews are dynamic, based upon the interaction between the investigator and the subject.

While the investigator must remain adaptable to the situation as it presents itself, it is also advisable to implement a semistructured approach to most interviews. Using a structured method helps to ensure that the investigator gains as much factual information as she can. A structured interview also helps to avoid *interview contamination*. This "occurs when investigators impede or negatively influence the interview process, thereby causing the subject to provide inaccurate information" (Sandoval 2003, 2). If questions are posed in different ways, the subject of the interview may answer the question differently.

Scenario

Detective Martin requests that store owner Melissa Sanders respond to the police station to offer a statement as the victim of an employee theft (embezzlement) of $75. During the course of the interview, Detective Martin tells Mrs. Sanders that "these cases usually don't go far in court." Detective Martin then asks, "Do you want to prosecute anyone for this?" while shaking his head back and forth (no). Mrs. Sanders feels that the detective is indicating that the case is minor and he doesn't wish to pursue it any further. Although she feels strongly about prosecuting such cases to avoid more employee larcenies in the future, Mrs. Sanders tells Detective Martin that she doesn't wish to prosecute.

Prior to conducting an interview, an investigator considers how to best proceed based upon the circumstances. In many cases, the subject of the interview is under a great deal of stress as he is faced with reliving a criminal event. As such, the interviewer should consider how to reduce this anxiety as much as possible. Consideration may be given to the characteristics of the victim, the location of the interview, how to initiate the process, and the questions to be asked. Interviews should never be conducted in a group setting, as each person may influence the account of others. An exception would be an emergency when information is needed immediately, such as when a suspect is fleeing the area.

The emergency nature of some situations makes interviews more difficult.

Individuals vary widely in how they react to a criminal event. The spectrum ranges from a person who views crime as they would any other event in life to one who lapses into a state of shock. The investigator evaluates the individual's state of mind and approaches her accordingly. The more stress a person exhibits, the more time the interviewer may have to devote to calming her. For example, a domestic violence victim may require extensive reassurance due to the fact that she possesses a relationship with the suspect and may have concern for both herself and the family. A passerby who notices shoplifting in progress is more likely to be calm, as fears of retribution by the suspect are low.

Interviews conducted in a quiet, secure police facility may put the victim or witness at ease. Large, open rooms may calm the interviewee. If a subject is interviewed close to the crime scene, he may fear a continuation of the criminal event or that others are listening in on the conversation. In other cases, the interviewee may be apprehensive of going to a police facility based upon past experiences or accounts he has heard from others, so a "field interview" is more desirable. In either situation, the setting must be free from distraction.

The investigator can reduce tension in the interviewee during the introduction. A detective offers the subject his credentials as an investigator at the outset and may advise the person of the reason for the interview. The interviewer may wish to start the conversation by talking about subject matter not related to the actual crime. This helps build a rapport with the individual. Rapport building reduces apprehension in the interviewee and creates a natural flow of discussion (Simons and Boetig 2007).

Open- and Closed-Ended Questions

Questions are selected to avoid contamination and to encourage free-flowing communication from the subject. To help initiate conversation, *open-ended questions* are preferable. These types of questions cannot be answered with a yes or no but require a narrative explanation. The subject is forced to offer a more descriptive account of events. An example of an open-ended inquiry is "Tell me what happened from the beginning." *Closed-ended questions,* which can be answered with short affirmative or negative responses, may be used for clarification purposes (Simons and Boetig 2007). For example, the investigator may ask "You said the suspect was wearing a red shirt. Are you certain of that?"

Approach

Certain strategies may be employed to help the subject remember the events or provide more detail. One method is to ask the same question repeatedly but change its phrasing each time. The interviewee may reveal new details when asked in a different way. Additionally, if the subject's story changes drastically, this may indicate that the person is not being truthful. Another approach is to ask the individual to recount the event in reverse order, starting from the end and working backwards. This causes the subject to look at the occurrence in a different way and may reveal new facts.

Juveniles

Juvenile interviewees are given special consideration. Juveniles are particularly sensitive to witnessing criminal events. Depending upon the age of the victim or witness, the interviewer may consider interviewing the child with her parents present. A juvenile may feel compelled to please the interviewer and adjust her responses accordingly. Because children are particularly susceptible to interview contamination, it is particularly important for the interviewer to tell a juvenile interviewee that it is acceptable to say that she does not know the answer to a question or to correct the interviewer. It is also suggested to offer the young person practice open-ended questions to prepare her for what to expect in the interview (National Institutes of Health, National Institute of Child Health and Human Development 2000).

AREA CANVASS

An *area canvass* is a search for witnesses in the vicinity of a crime scene who may have observed a crime. While in many cases, witnesses may present themselves to investigators, at other times, the police must seek them out from bystanders. A common example of an area canvass is a door-to-door search for witnesses in a neighborhood. "The canvass should extend far enough to encompass any reasonable expectation of useful information from witnesses, and investigators should make as many attempts as necessary to contact them" (Rothwell 2006, 22). As each individual is contacted, an interview is conducted. If no one answers the door, the investigator makes note of this so the house can be rechecked later. When a witness is found, the investigator will review the information he has and decide whether to interview him at the residence or have him respond to a police facility for an interview.

When witnesses are not visibly present at a crime scene, a canvass of the neighborhood may reveal someone who observed the crime.

INTERROGATIONS

An interrogation differs from an interview, as it is likely the subject will deliberately attempt to withhold information because she may be a party to the crime. As a result, interrogations are inherently more confrontational from the outset. This does not mean that the investigator should approach the subject in a challenging manner, as this may only serve to increase the subject's resolve to hold back what she knows. Rather than being a heated verbal clash, an interrogation is usually a calm, complicated, cerebral process with the ultimate goal of getting the subject to reveal information.

An interview room provides a more controlled setting for investigators to gain information.

While interviews may be conducted in the field or at a police station, very rarely would an interrogation be conducted outside of a controlled setting (such as a police interview room). It is important during an interrogation for the investigator to control the environmental conditions and to avoid outside interferences. Something as minor as a noise can distract the subject and derail a rapport that has been established. Interview rooms are arranged to be soundproof and to put the subject in a physical position where he must engage in communication (verbal or nonverbal) with the interviewer.

Fifth Amendment (Miranda) Rights

One distinct difference between an interview and an interrogation is that a person may need to be given a warning of her rights according to the Fifth Amendment before an interrogation commences (see chapter 3). If a subject is in custody (reasonably deprived of freedom) prior to an interrogation, he must be given "Miranda warnings." Investigators give these rights in the same way each time so they can later testify to the exact wording utilized. A written waiver is used to show proof that these rights were offered to the subject, he understood his rights, and he agreed to speak with the investigator after considering his rights.

The courts have been clear in their interpretation of a proper rights warning. Miranda rights should not be minimized to the point where components of the warnings are left out. It is vital that four explicit elements are relayed to each subject: "the right to remain silent; that any statements may be used against them; the right to have an attorney present during questioning; and that an attorney will be appointed if he cannot afford one" (Hoover 2005, 26). Further, the investigator must be able to prove that the subject waived his rights knowingly, intelligently, and voluntarily.

Approach

The approach utilized during each interrogation will depend upon the interviewee and the subject crime, much as in an interview. An investigator more usually attempts to establish a rapport with a subject instead of becoming confrontational with them. Often the investigator attempts to develop a theme surrounding the interrogation to reduce the person's anxiety about confessing to the crime (Boetig 2005). In developing this theme, the initial stages of the interview may be more of monologue by the investigator than an interactive dialogue with the subject. The detective is laying the groundwork to allow the interviewee an easier route to offer admissions to participating in a crime.

Scenario

Detective Martinez questions a subject who has allegedly been breaking into automobiles and stealing car stereos. A witness has identified this person in a photographic lineup. The man has been brought in for questioning about ten car larcenies that have occurred in an eight-block radius over the last 30 days. Detective Martinez gives the subject a warning of his rights according to the Fifth Amendment, and the subject agrees to speak about the matter. Detective Martinez proceeds with the interrogation.

Prior to asking specific questions about the crime, Detective Martinez tells the man a story about how often individuals do things they wouldn't normally due because of circumstances in their life. Detective Martinez explains that sometimes people fall upon hard economic times and feel they have to resort to theft to get them through a rough period.

Detective Martinez has established a theme of the interview that is less accusatory and more sympathetic to the man's circumstances. Detective Martinez has paved a path for the subject to take that will help to preserve his dignity, while still admitting to the crime.

Kinesics

During the course of the interrogation, an investigator will watch for cues that indicate whether or not the subject is being deceptive. These signs may be verbal statements or *nonverbal* behaviors that the subject displays when certain questions are asked. For example, an investigator may know for a fact that a person was at the scene of a store robbery based upon a review of surveillance video taken at the time. If the interviewee indicates that she was not present, deception may be revealed through verbal cues. The investigator might also notice that whenever the subject denies being present, she shifts her eyes to the left. This could be a nonverbal indicator of deception for this and subsequent questions asked by the investigator.

Kinesics is the study of body language as part of the communication process. Investigators examining nonverbal behavior are applying principles of kinesics in their interviews. It is important to note that body language is not universal. People react differently under certain circumstances. Nonverbal communication indicators are considered on an individual basis, as factors such as age, culture, and experiences play a role in determining a person's reaction to questioning. For example, it is not uncommon for persons from Asian cultures to avoid eye contact with persons of authority (including police officers) as a sign of respect (Shusta, Levine, Wong, Olson, and Harris 2008, 158). For others, this could be an indication of deception.

Coercion

A difference exists between subtle pressure to admit to involvement in a crime and coercion. An investigator may develop the impression that the interviewee is not being truthful and may apply more direct and vigorous questioning techniques. Compelling a subject to reveal the truth based upon solid indications of false behavior is distinct from using heavy-handed approaches when doubt exists. Techniques such as physical abuse, torture, or presenting false evidence violate the due process clause of the Constitution and will make any confession inadmissible in court (*Brown v. Mississippi* 1936).

Admissions and Confessions

If the subject reveals involvement in a crime, it may be through an admission or a confession. An admission includes statements that involve the individual in the criminal act, although he may not implicate himself as the perpetrator or accept complete responsibility. For example, during an interview of an auto theft suspect, he may reveal that he was a passenger in the stolen car (explaining fingerprints that may be present within the vehicle) but deny committing the actual theft. A confession implicates the person as a perpetrator of the crime and satisfies the elements required to prove a violation of the law.

Juveniles

As in an interview, an interrogation of a juvenile often must be conducted under special conditions. Regulations for the interrogation of a child vary from state to state, but usually the presence of a guardian or a representative of the juvenile justice system is required. Additional protections are afforded juveniles because of the ease with which their statements can become contaminated.

CORROBORATING INFORMATION

An important step after an interview or interrogation is to attempt to corroborate the information that has been given to the investigator. Once the information is given to the detective in the form of a statement, further investigation can ascertain if the subject was truthful. Corroboration is helpful for the continuing investigation. When the statements are evaluated later in court, the person's statement will be weighed in terms of her believability as a witness.

A basic step to verify information given in a statement is to take particular sections of the testimony and investigate them. For example, if a person claims he was with another individual, the investigator would seek out that individual and interview her to see if the two accounts match. Corroboration can also be accomplished by comparing statements with physical evidence. Bloodstains, footprints, and fingerprints may be evaluated in comparison with a suspect's statements.

Another method used to verify information is through statement analysis. Investigators use *statement analysis* to "examine words, independent of case facts, to detect deception" (Adams 1996, 12). Specific verbiage is examined to determine if the individual has used wording that strays from a normal, truthful answer. Investigators also look for any information that the suspect may have omitted from her statement. For example, the suspect may unintentionally switch simple pronouns (e.g., changing *I* to *we*) to distance herself from the crime. Adams (1996) offers two examples, the first demonstrating a truthful statement and the second indicating possible deception:

> 1. "I met four friends at the movie theater, watched a movie, then stopped to get something to eat with them. We had a few drinks at the bar on the way home. I stayed until just after midnight. I drove home..."

> 2. "We all met at the movie theater, watched a movie, then stopped to get something to eat. We had a few drinks at the bar on the way home. We stayed until just after midnight. We each drove home..." (14).

Statement analysis is based upon the premise that individuals subconsciously select the words they use and attempt to minimize their involvement if they feel guilt.

Lie Detection Devices

The goal of an interview or an interrogation is to collect facts that are useful to the case. Part of discerning what is factual involves eliminating what is fiction. Throughout history, investigators have sought to develop mechanical means to determine lies from the truth. Two instruments have been commonly used as mechanical deception detectors: the polygraph and the *computer voice stress analysis* instrument (CVSA).

The polygraph machine was developed through various incarnations in the late 1800s and early 1900s. Leonarde Keeler was instrumental in experimenting with an instrument developed specifically for police investigative applications. Keeler initially worked with police departments in California in testing the polygraph as an investigative tool (Segrave 2004). Prior to questioning, the interviewee is outfitted with devices designed to measure physical reactions. During the polygraph examination, the investigator asks a series of questions, while a written record of physiological reactions to the questions is recorded. Three specific reactions are measured: cardio-sphygmograph changes (pulse rate, pulse wave amplitude, blood pressure), pneumograph changes (respiration or breathing), and galvanograph changes (sweat glands) (Harrelson 1998). The examiner evaluates the record of readings from the instrument after the interview in an effort to determine if the subject is being truthful or deceptive.

Polygraph machines, now aided by computer interpretation, may be used to corroborate information.

CVSA instruments are similar in concept to polygraphs, but they attempt to measure stress in the subject's vocal cords while the subject responds to questions. The person's answers are recorded and processed by a computer program. The examiner again reads a report and evaluates responses, offering a judgment of the interviewee's truthfulness or deception. CVSAs became popular in law enforcement, as manufacturers claimed they were more accurate, required less training to operate, were less invasive (had less apparatus to hook up), were less expensive, and produced reports that could be evaluated more quickly than those of a polygraph (Damphousse, Pointon, Upchurch, and Moore 2007).

A significant issue is that polygraphs and CVSA instruments are generally not admissible in court proceedings as evidence of a defendant's deception in a criminal trial (U.S. Department of Justice 1997). Lie detection devices are not accurate beyond any doubt. Because of their inadmissibility, these instruments are limited in their usefulness in an investigation. In cases where it is unclear after significant investigation whether or not a subject is being deceptive, these instruments may be helpful in giving the investigator additional information to help make a determination. Lie detection results can also be helpful in the interrogation process in convincing a subject to tell the truth.

SUMMARY

The collection of testimonial evidence may be as important or more important than the collection of physical evidence in a criminal case. Investigators collect testimonial evidence through interviews and interrogations. Interviews may be of victims, witnesses, or anyone with information about criminal activity. Interrogations typically are conducted with individuals who have direct involvement in a crime.

The approach used in an interview or an interrogation depends upon a variety of factors. A controlled, quiet environment is favored. Investigators avoid contaminating the answers of interviewees with leading questions. Open- and closed-ended questions are used, depending upon the information being sought. Juveniles are interviewed carefully because they are particularly susceptible to contamination.

An area canvass is a special type of interview method where a particular zone around a crime scene is searched for potential witnesses.

Interrogations usually require that an individual be given Fifth Amendment (Miranda) rights prior to questioning. Investigators look for signs of truth or deception through statement analysis, kinesics or body language interpretation, and corroboration of the information given. The use of coercion in an interrogation causes any resulting admission or confession to be inadmissible in court.

Commonly used lie detection instruments include the polygraph and the computer voice stress analysis (CVSA) instrument. Both are used as tools only, as they are not admissible as evidence for the prosecution in court because they are not completely accurate.

Key Terms

Area canvass: A search of a particular area for witnesses to a crime

Closed-ended question: A question that is answerable with yes or no

Computer voice stress analysis (CVSA): An instrument that measures vocal cord patterns in an effort to discern truth from deception during an interview

Interrogation: In an investigation, a communication between an investigator and a subject where the investigator has reason to believe the subject has been involved in a crime

Interview: In an investigation, a communication between an investigator and a subject with the goal of gaining information

Interview contamination: Phrasing that leads a subject to respond in a certain way, thus influencing answers to questions

Kinesics: The study of body language as the part of the communication process

Nonverbal cues: Nonlinguistic (kinesic) body movement indicators during communication that may reveal whether a person is being truthful or deceptive

Open-ended questions: A question that requires a narrative explanation and cannot be answered with a simple yes or no.

Statement analysis: The process of examining the specific words used by an individual to answer questions during an interview or interrogation to unearth signs of truth or deception.

Discussion Questions

1. What factors are considered by the investigator during an interrogation in determining whether an individual may be a suspect?

2. What actions might an investigator take that could accidentally contaminate an interview?

3. What factors does an investigator take into account prior to an interview to make sure it is successful in gaining information?

4. What are some methods that can be used to help an individual recall an event?

5. Explain why it is preferable for interrogations to be conducted in a controlled environment.

Exploration

1. Look for articles on kinesic interviewing techniques and review what methods are used to interpret nonverbal communication.

2. Visit the website for the American Polygraph Association and review its code of ethics. What safeguards do you see in the code to protect interviewees?

References

Adams, Susan. 1996. Statement analysis: What do suspects' words really reveal? *FBI Law Enforcement Bulletin* 65, no. 10 (October): 12–20.

Boetig, Brian. 2005. Reducing a guilty suspect's resistance to confessing. *FBI Law Enforcement Bulletin* 74, no. 8 (August): 13–19.

Brown v. Mississippi. 297 U.S. 278. 1936.

Damphouse, Kelly, Laura Pointon, Deidra Upchurch, and Rebecca Moore. 2007. *Assessing the validity of voice stress analysis tools in a jail setting,* March 31. Rockville, MD: National Criminal Justice Reference Service.

Harrelson, Leonard. 1998. *Lie test: Deception, truth, and the polygraph.* Fort Wayne, IN: Jonas Publishing.

Hoover, Lucy. 2005. The Supreme Court brings an end to the "end run" around Miranda. *FBI Law Enforcement Bulletin* 74, no. 6 (June): 26–32.

National Institutes of Health, National Institute of Child Health and Human Development (NICHD). 2000. *NIH news alert: NICHD researchers improve techniques for interviewing child abuse victims,* June 27. Retrieved September 2, 2007, from www .nichd.nih.gov/news/releases/interviewing.cfm.

Reynolds, Michael. 1992. *Dead ends.* New York: St. Martin's.

Rothwell, Gary. 2006. Notes for the occasional major case manager. *FBI Law Enforcement Bulletin* 75, no. 1 (January): 20–24.

Sandoval, Vincent. 2003. Strategies to avoid interview contamination. *FBI Law Enforcement Bulletin* 72, no. 10 (October): 1–12.

Segrave, Kerry. 2004. *Lie detectors: A social history.* Jefferson, NC: McFarland & Company.

Shusta, Robert, Deena Levine, Herbert Wong, Aaron Olson, and Philip Harris. 2008. *Multicultural Law Enforcement.* Upper Saddle Ridge, NJ: Pearson Prentice Hall.

Simons, Andre, and Brian Boetig. 2007. The structured investigative interview. *FBI Law Enforcement Bulletin* 76, no. 6 (June): 9–20.

U.S. Department of Justice (DOJ). 1997. *United States Attorneys' manual: Title 9 criminal; Polygraphs—Introduction at trial,* October. Retrieved September 26, 2007, from www.usdoj.gov/usao/eousa/foia_reading_room/usam/title9/crm00262.htm.

Wuornos v. Florida. 81 Fla. 498. 1996.

CHAPTER 7

INTELLIGENCE, UNDERCOVER OPERATIONS, AND INFORMANTS

CHAPTER OBJECTIVES

By the end of this chapter, the reader will be able to do the following:

- Describe issues that complicate the police/informant relationship.

- List the common motivations for individuals to become investigative informants.

- Describe the procedures involved in utilizing informants.

- Explain the benefits of undercover investigative work.

- Define *entrapment*.

- Describe the elements of an undercover investigative operation.

- Define the purpose of criminal intelligence.

Most investigative activity is reactive in nature; that is, the police respond to a crime that has already occurred and handle the investigation after the fact. However, criminal justice agencies also conduct proactive investigations to deter future crimes or disrupt ongoing criminal operations. Proactive investigations are accomplished through gathering intelligence; using informants; and operating in a secret, undercover capacity. The goal of each of these techniques is to unearth the truth about criminal activity, including who the participants are, what they are doing, where they are performing crimes, and how they are committing their crimes.

CASE STUDY

> In the spring of 2006, an Afghan national working for the DEA in an undercover capacity infiltrated a heroin trafficking organization operating in Afghanistan. The undercover, posing as a heroin transporter who could bring heroin to the United States and the United Kingdom, met with two members of the organization and received a heroin sample for delivery to New York. (Mulvey 2007, ¶ 1)

A business relationship was built between the undercover informant and the Nigerian sources of supply. Fifteen kilograms of heroin intended for delivery to the United States and the United Kingdom were intercepted as a result. Recorded conversations about drug transactions were used in trial to implicate the two drug traffickers (Mulvey 2007).

It is possible that the shipment of narcotics in the above case study could have been seized by law enforcement by some other means; however, proving the extent of the involvement of these two suspects would have been much more difficult without the physical and testimonial evidence collected in the undercover operation. Investigators might have struggled to infiltrate the organization and disrupt its activities without the use of the informant. This case illustrates the value of proactive investigative operations.

INFORMANTS

The previous chapters described the value of testimonial evidence in investigating crimes that have already occurred. Testimonial evidence is also important in preventing current and future criminal activities. This testimonial evidence is acquired from *informants* who have been developed through a variety of means. These sources may have access to criminal elements that are difficult for a law enforcement official to gain.

The police-informant relationship is unique. A trust must be developed; however, that trust can never been completely certain. The informant may be distrustful of the police. In most cases, from the investigator's point of view, the fact that the informant associates with criminals puts the informant himself in question. An investigator must be mindful of the frequency with which an informant may violate this trust, putting a criminal case or the criminal justice professional herself in jeopardy.

CASE STUDY

FBI agent John Connolly, Jr. was sentenced in September 2002 to ten years in prison for racketeering, obstruction of justice, and making false statements to investigators—all stemming from his handling of two FBI informants, James J. "Whitey" Bulger and Stephen J. "The Rifleman" Flemmi, leaders of South Boston's Winter Hill Gang. (U.S. Department of Justice, Office of the Inspector General 2005, "Case Study 1")

Agent Connolly had developed a close relationship with the informants, fueled by the valuable investigative information the two were providing about the La Cosa Nostra criminal enterprise. Violating the ethical standards of the criminal justice system, Agent Connolly

filed false reports of information purportedly provided to them by the informants, ignored evidence that the informants were extorting others, caused the submission of false and misleading applications for electronic surveillance, and disclosed other confidential law enforcement information to them. (DOJ 2005, "Case Study 1").

While police officers cannot constantly control the behavior of informants, they must maintain ethical behavior themselves. Improper actions on the part of the informant must be dealt with legally and may result in the termination of the police-informant relationship.

Informant Motivations

Individuals become informants for a variety of motivations. These should be considered by the agency utilizing the informant in determining his trustworthiness. Common motivations include revenge, eliminating competitive criminal enterprises, monetary compensation, consideration in a criminal case, altruism, an affection for law enforcement, and "eccentric thrill seeking" (Internal Revenue Service n.d.). A vengeful spouse who wishes to turn in her significant other for drug dealing may be acceptable to use as an informant under controlled conditions. Con-

versely, it may not be wise to utilize a drug dealer who wishes to get rid of a rival peddler, as the informant's own criminal dealings cannot be ignored.

Some informants present themselves to a police agency as available sources of information; others are cultivated through other means. A per-

An informant, such as a drug dealer, may work to rid himself of competition in criminal activities. Investigators can't ignore an informant's criminal behavior.

son who has a fondness or excitement for law enforcement may voluntarily call an investigator to offer information. Others find themselves in a difficult position and seek work as an informant to get out of the situation. An individual in need of money may seek to be paid for information by a criminal justice agency. Those who are facing minor criminal charges may offer their services as informants for consideration by a judge in lessening punishment. It is important to note that a police officer cannot guarantee an individual that a criminal case will be dismissed or that a sentence will be reduced due to informant work. An investigator cannot give immunity to an informant for past or future offenses. This decision can only be made by a judge. However, magistrates often take such deeds into consideration in arriving at their decisions in recognition of the value of informants in the investigative process.

Restricted Informants

Some categories of informants cannot be used without following special guidelines. Juveniles typically are not used without the permission of a parent or guardian (Virginia Department of Criminal Justice Services 1999) or under the direction of a juvenile court official. Even in situations where these circumstances are met, careful consideration should be given to utilizing a juvenile informant due to the fact that such work can be dangerous. Individuals who are on probation or parole also receive special consideration. Technically, these individuals are under the supervision of the court system, so authorization to use them in an informant capacity is sought from the relevant magistrate (DOJ 2002).

Juveniles cannot be utilized as informants without special permission from parents and juvenile justice authorities.

Informant Management

When an informant is utilized by an investigator, that individual essentially becomes an extension of the police agency while acting in an informant capacity. The actions the informant takes reflect upon the agency that sponsors her. The agency therefore assumes a degree of liability for the conduct of the informant. For this reason, it is important to establish control mechanisms to manage the informant. These controls start with the initial screening process. An evaluation of the potential informant's background is conducted to establish her reliability. If she has ever been an informant before, her prior record is checked to ascertain her trustworthiness. A periodic review of active informants is conducted by investigative supervisors to ensure that they still meet suitable standards to work for the agency. For example, if it is discovered that an individual has resumed criminal activity (e.g., she has warrants for her arrest), she may be deactivated as an informant.

When an individual agrees to become an informant, an investigator fills out a series of forms to create a permanent informant file. The exact number and types of forms vary by agency. Typically, the informant file includes a release of liability, an agreement to follow certain procedures, a debrief interview report, a criminal history record, and a validation record of informant reliability. If an informant strays from the instructions given to him during an operation, the agreements protect the agency from the consequences. A *debriefing* relates what types of information the individual has about ongoing criminal activities. A *validation report* indicates when the information given by the informant is dependable and when it is not. This record is important in establishing documentation to show the trustworthiness of the informant, which is important for court purposes for later cases.

Corroboration is the process of determining whether an informant is offering honest information. Prior to utilizing the informant in an undercover capacity, the investigator may attempt to verify information the source has given about past or current minor crimes. This may establish the reliability of the informant's information. Each success or failure is documented in the validation record. If an investigator uses the informant's information to apply for a search warrant, the court will consider the source's past record of reliability in weighing the value of the information.

Informant records must remain confidential, unless the release of information is required for court purposes. The investigator should not reveal to others that the informant is working with law enforcement. Likewise, the informant should not discuss her work with acquaintances. Because information may have to be revealed eventually in court, a complete confidentiality guarantee cannot be extended to the informant; however, every effort can be made to keep the working relationship classified before that time.

UNDERCOVER OPERATIONS

Informants are extremely helpful in proactive investigations. However, the actions of an informant can never be completely controlled, and liability concerns exist as a result. Ideally, a law enforcement officer can be used in the same capacity of infiltrating criminal organizations and gathering information for use in criminal trials. Investigators working in an undercover capacity can avoid the issue of controlling an informant's actions while still proactively deterring crime.

The benefits of undercover work are many, but the work is also dangerous. Police officers acting secretively to associate with strangers with criminal ties place themselves in harm's way if their true objectives are revealed. As with the use of informants, operations involving undercover work require that procedures are followed carefully to ensure safety and success. Undercover investigations are not an individual undertaking; they require the coordination of groups of officers working different assignments to achieve the same goal.

CASE STUDY

On October 30, 1990, Syracuse, New York, police investigator Wallie Howard was working for a local drug enforcement task force.

> Officer Howard was shot during an undercover operation when drug traffickers from Brooklyn, New York, attempted to rob him of $42,000 he had for the purchase of two kilograms of cocaine. He was 31 years of age at the time of his death. (Drug Enforcement Administration n.d.)

An award is presented annually to a Syracuse police officer in honor of Investigator Howard's legacy and bravery.

Characteristics of a Successful Undercover Officer

A successful undercover officer must possess distinctive qualities. All investigators develop an understanding of the specific type of crime in which they specialize. However, undercover officers employ additional special skills. An undercover investigator must have courage and good judgment and be able to act a part to fit in with a criminal element (Fuller 1998). Some officers struggle to adapt to this new role, which requires that they temporarily abandon elements of the behavior that is expected of a police professional.

Management of Undercover Operations

Undercover operations are closely controlled by multiple levels of supervision. Oversight helps to lessen the hazards associated with this type of work. Each plan for face-to-face interaction is approved through a chain of command. The ultimate consideration is given to the safety of the undercover officer. The investigators who are closest to the operation may inadvertently emphasize furthering the investigation over the safety of those involved due to their enthusiasm to build a case against the criminal elements. Other potential concerns for supervisors of an undercover investigation are the risk of liability, the possibility of invading a person's privacy, ethical matters, and the risk that an undercover officer may participate in illegal activity (DOJ 1992).

Entrapment

Undercover investigations are used to disrupt operating criminal enterprises. An undercover operation should not entice an innocent person to participate a criminal act when that person normally would not. *Entrapment* is the term used to describe when a government agent intentionally or unintentionally plants the idea to commit a crime in an individual's mind. The criminal thought must originate with the offender, not an undercover officer.

Undercover Operations and Personnel

Two types of officers are used in undercover investigations. The undercover investigator is the actor who actually interacts with the target group, attempting to gain intelligence about criminal activities. Because such contacts are extremely dangerous, the undercover officer is accompanied by another group of investigators, who work behind the scenes to ensure the officer's safety. The *surveillance group* monitors the operation from a close distance, prepared to react if the undercover officer is placed in danger. The surveillance group may also collect notes about conversations between the undercover officer and the target subjects, the activities of the criminal enterprise, and details of the associates involved with the group.

An undercover investigator must somehow interject himself into a group of offenders to initiate a proactive investigation. The officer may accomplish this by introducing himself "cold" to a member of the criminal enterprise and slowly building a relationship to generate trust. An investigator may also be introduced to the group by an informant, developed through means described previously, who is already trusted.

Every effort is made to avoid placing the undercover investigator in a position where she must participate in criminal activity to avoid detection. For instance, a police official cannot assault or harm another person, except in defense of herself or others. Interacting with criminal elements but avoiding participation in actual crimes is a delicate challenge.

The primary objective of an undercover operation is to gain firsthand information about criminal activities. An undercover officer can accomplish this by recording audio and video evidence of criminal operations and observing crimes in progress. A typical crime targeted through undercover investigation is the distribution of narcotics. It is important to note that violent crimes, such as robbery and assault, cannot be allowed to proceed and thus are not suitable for investigation through undercover operations. A common undercover approach is to purchase contraband, such as narcotics and stolen property, implicating the subject in these crimes. In other cases, the undercover officer may be the subject selling contraband or illegal services, such as imitation narcotics, fake stolen property, or the promise of sexual services.

The surveillance team is always present during any face-to-face dealings the undercover officer has with the criminal group or its members. A constant concern is that the undercover officer will be exposed, placing him in immediate danger. The surveillance team is trained in responding immediately to any type of distress signal by the undercover officer and extracting him from the situation. Additionally, the team can alert the undercover officer to potential dangers, such as additional unknown subjects arriving in the area during a drug exchange.

In addition to providing safety coverage for the undercover officer, the surveillance team also monitors the activities of the officer as she proceeds via audio or video transmitters or through the use of binoculars or scopes. Conversations are recorded for investigative purposes and for later presentation in court. The surveillance team also listens for signals of distress. If the interaction is conducted in an open environment, the team may videotape the proceedings for the same purpose. Recording undercover operations also avoids accusations that the police acted unethically, entrapped the subject, or committed a crime themselves during the course of the investigation.

Monitoring equipment is used to monitor the activities of undercover officers to develop evidence and assure the officer's safety.

The surveillance team also collects intelligence during the operation, recording information such as license plate numbers, names, and descriptions of subjects and their vehicles. The surveillance team may follow individuals to determine where they or their associates live or where contraband may be located. Moving surveillance operations are conducted with multiple investigators or vehicles to avoid detection.

Surveillance Operations

Some investigations may be conducted with the surveillance team only, particularly where it is not possible to develop a relationship with the criminal enterprise and the undercover officer. These investigations are based upon the collection of intelligence in conjunction with other information to secure probable cause for search and arrest warrants. Surveillance operations may be conducted with officers and vehicles that fit in, appearance-wise, with the demographic makeup of the area. Advances in technology have made sophisticated audio and visual monitoring instruments available to law enforcement to assist in these operations. Surveillance camera systems have shown great promise in providing video evidence of crime.

CASE STUDY

"In mid-2005, the Baltimore Police Department, in partnership with the City of Baltimore, began the installation and use of video cameras on the streets of Baltimore. The function of the cameras is two-fold: deterrence and detection of crime." The camera systems in Baltimore operate in all lighting conditions in full color. The cameras are recorded and monitored 24 hours per day by police employees and volunteers. "In areas where the cameras were installed, a 17 percent reduction in violent crime was achieved" (Baltimore Police Department 2006, 10).

INTELLIGENCE

Police departments collect a vast amount of information about criminal activity. This information comes from reports of crime from victims, informants, undercover operations, direct observations from field officers, information passed from other agencies, and a variety of other sources. This information becomes a part of an immense pool of data that develops into criminal intelligence.

The purpose of a criminal intelligence program is to investigate crime proactively through the analysis of data. Intelligence can indicate solutions to past crimes, signs of current criminal trends, and answers to future issues facing the criminal justice agency. The mere collection of criminal information is of very little help to a police agency. The gathered data must be analyzed by trained investigators to identify vital statistics and information, which in turn are passed on to other investigators and field police personnel.

Intelligence can be the key to a proactive response to crime by providing decision makers the information needed to deploy police resources for maximum effectiveness. This approach has been coined "intelligence-led policing" (Carter 2005, 2). Intelligence-led policing combines the intelligence efforts of law enforcement agencies to address crime concerns that cross jurisdictional boundaries, such as terrorism. Information and statistics can be analyzed to identify important trends before crime occurs.

Carter (2005) identified two types of intelligence. *Tactical intelligence* is the analysis of information to prevent crime from happening. "This includes gaining or developing information

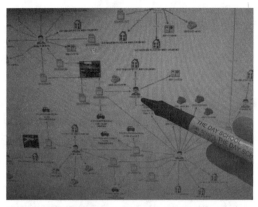

Intelligence analysts explore the activities of criminal organizations in an attempt to disrupt their activities.

related to threats of terrorism or crime and using this information to apprehend offenders, harden targets, or employ strategies that will eliminate or mitigate the threat" (Carter, 2). *Strategic intelligence* is focused on developing response strategies to organize resources in the most effective manner.

Intelligence Databases

What type of information is stored in a criminal intelligence database? Law enforcement can store criminal intelligence information if there is some connection to a crime. However, a criminal intelligence database cannot be used to store certain demographic information that does not relate to crime, such as an individual's religion, the library books he has read, or his involvement with noncriminal organizations. Collecting such information is a violation of a person's civil liberties. The laws regarding criminal intelligence programs are specified under federal regulation 28 CFR Part 23.

Analysis of Intelligence

Information is analyzed through a variety of means. Advancements in technology have led to the increased use of computer programs to sift massive amounts of data for targeted information for study. For example, an analyst may be charged with locating information about a particular person who has been involved in recent crimes. Computer software can search every report taken in the last five years for the person's name and forward these reports to the investigator. Human review of the data can help further analyze this information to determine what is important and what is not.

Criminal intelligence information is collected and analyzed, but the final report product determines the value of these prior steps. Intelligence analysis must be communicated effectively to interested parties to be of use. How the analysis is presented depends upon the purpose of the report. Information may be evaluated by investigators for a specific purpose ordered by organizational decision makers. The report will seek to address the questions of those decision makers by providing answers based upon statistical data and qualitative information. Other reports may be produced on a regular basis (e.g., monthly or quarterly) to distribute to investigators and field officers. Officers may adapt their investigative approaches based upon the information in these reports.

Scenario

Investigator Hassan has noticed a dramatic increase in vehicle thefts citywide. To investigate this matter further, she works with intelligence investigators within her department to see if a pattern has emerged of a) where the thefts are happening and b) where the stolen cars are being found. A targeted analysis is performed, and it is discovered that 70 percent of all stolen cars are being recovered within a five-square-block section of the city. Investigator Hassan then looks for individuals who live in and near that section of the city who have a past record of auto thefts to compare fingerprint records with physical evidence recovered from recently located stolen cars.

The intelligence investigators also provide their monthly crime analysis reports to Investigator Hassan. Included in the report is a list of the make and model of every car stolen in the last month. Investigator Hassan notices that a specific type of domestic sedan is frequently listed, so she asks uniformed officers to keep an eye out for these vehicles on the roadway. If this type of vehicle is observed, the officers check the car's license plate to ascertain if it is stolen.

SUMMARY

Investigators use informants to infiltrate and disrupt criminal operations. Individuals become informants for a variety of reasons. The investigators decide carefully whether or not a person is suitable to use as an informant based upon that person's motivation, his background, and other factors. Informant-based investigations are carefully controlled to reduce liability and ensure that the investigation remains proper and legal.

Undercover officer–based investigations are similar to informant-based investigations, but they are more easily controlled from a law enforcement point of view. Undercover operations are inherently dangerous and must be approached with considerable caution. Each operation involves both an undercover operative and a surveillance team to protect that officer. The steps of the investigation are recorded to provide evidence for court purposes. In some cases, an investigation is based entirely upon the collection of evidence through surveillance.

Police departments collect a variety of information through the course of their day-to-day duties. Police intelligence is derived from the analysis of this data and the reporting of findings to end-user investigators. Tactical intelligence is used to prevent crime from happening. Strategic intelligence is used to deploy resources to combat crime effectively.

Key Terms

Debriefing report: A written record of the criminal activity an informant has related to an investigator

Entrapment: A legal finding that investigators lead an individual to commit a crime when he otherwise would not have done so (the criminal thought must originate with the individual)

Informant: An individual who reports criminal activity to a law enforcement official

Strategic intelligence: The collection and interpretation of criminal information for the purpose of allocating law enforcement personnel and resources

Surveillance group: A team of undercover investigators utilized to protect an undercover officer and record intelligence information during undercover operations

Tactical intelligence: The collection and interpretation of criminal information for the purpose of preventing crime

Validation report: A written record of whether information given to an investigator by an informant could be corroborated or not

Discussion Questions

1. What types of behavior would be considered unethical in a police-informant relationship?

2. Explain why it is important to have established controls over the behavior of informants. What are some of these controls?

3. Why is the process of corroboration important in using an informant?

4. List some reasons why undercover operations should be closely supervised.

5. Which type of intelligence do you feel is more important for day-to-day law enforcement operations: tactical or strategic? Why do you think so?

Exploration

1. Research the police corruption exposed in the late 1960s and early 1970s by New York Police Detective Frank Serpico. What controls seemed to be missing from police interactions with informants?

References

Baltimore Police Department. 2006. *Annual report.* Baltimore, MD.

Carter, David. 2005. The law enforcement intelligence function. *FBI Law Enforcement Bulletin* 74, no. 6 (June): 1–8.

Drug Enforcement Administration. n.d. *Wall of honor list: Wallie Howard Jr.* Retrieved September 8, 2007, from www.usdoj.gov/ dea/agency/10bios.htm#howard.

Fuller, Charlie. 1998. *The art of undercover.* Youngsville, NC: Law Enforcement Associates.

Internal Revenue Service. n.d. *Internal revenue manual: Criminal investigation: Investigative techniques: Sources of information.* Retrieved September 7, 2007, from www.irs.gov/irm/part9/ch04s02 .html.

Mulvey, Eric. 2007. *News release: Two Nigerian drug traffickers convicted on heroin conspiracy charges,* June 14. Retrieved September 3, 2007, from the U.S. Drug Enforcement Administration website www.usdoj.gov/dea/pubs/states/newsrel/nyc061407.html.

U.S. Department of Justice (DOJ). 1992. *Undercover and sensitive operations unit: Attorney General's guidelines on FBI undercover operations,* November 13. Retrieved September 8, 2007, from www.usdoj.gov/ag/readingroom/undercover.htm.

U.S. Department of Justice (DOJ). 2002. *The Attorney General's guidelines regarding the use of confidential informants,* May 30. Retrieved September 7, 2007, from www.usdoj.gov/olp/dojguidelines .pdf.

U.S. Department of Justice (DOJ), Office of the Inspector General. 2005. *Special report: The Federal Bureau of Investigation's compliance with the Attorney General's investigative guidelines (redacted): The Attorney General's guidelines regarding the use of confidential informants,* September. Retrieved September 7, 2007, from www. usdoj.gov/oig/special/0509/chapter3.htm.

Virginia Department of Criminal Justice Services. 1999. *Sample directives: Informants* (General order 2-11), July 1. Retrieved September 7, 2007, from www.dcjs.virginia.gov/cple/sampleDirectives/manual/pdf/2-11.pdf.

CHAPTER 8

REPORTING AND COURT PROCEEDINGS

CHAPTER OBJECTIVES

By the end of this chapter, the reader will be able to do the following:

- Describe how a police report progresses through the criminal justice system.

- Explain the importance of using proper, uncomplicated wording in writing investigative reports.

- Describe the typical format of an investigative report.

- List and describe the types of investigative reports.

- Describe the procedures used in courtroom testimony.

- List the types of legal proceedings in which investigators must testify.

The actions a detective takes during an investigation determine his degree of success in uncovering the truth. An important part of accomplishing that goal is not only accumulating and examining physical and testimonial evidence but also documenting these efforts. An investigator must be able to reflect upon the actions that were taken during the course of an investigation. Investigative reports record the events of the investigation and how they unfolded. Investigators utilize these reports to help them remember events during courtroom testimony. The story of the investigation must be accurately related to the judge and jury so a determination of guilt or innocence can be made.

POLICE REPORTING

By viewing how a police report travels through the legal system, one can see how important a written record of a criminal investigation is within the legal process (figure 8.1). Police reports are routine but vital products of everyday police activities. Experienced investigators understand the importance of minor details in police reports right down to individual words. Inexperienced officers may not appreciate these aspects of investigative work until their written words are challenged strongly in court.

FIGURE 8-I: The various stages a police report takes through the criminal justice system

Officer: Writes police report.

Supervisor: Reviews written police report.

Investigations Supervisor: Reviews report.

Investigator: Reviews report for case file.

Prosecutor: Reviews report for criminal case.

Defense Attorney: Reviews report for trial.

Judge/Jury: Reads report in trial.

Corrections: Reviews report as intelligence.

Probation/Parole: Considers report for offender profile.

Many people are accustomed to writing essays or reports and submitting them to one individual for review. Conversely, a police report is preserved for posterity and is considered by a wide variety of persons during the course of an investigation and the subsequent trial. A report may be reviewed by department supervisors, attorneys, judges, probation and parole officers, a random sampling of citizens selected by juries, and possibly the media (further exposing the writing to the masses).

Police reports essentially become legal documents and are often subjected to careful scrutiny. A report documents how each step of an investigation unfolded. It must be accurate and coincide with how the investigator testifies later in court. In addition to criminal cases, civil lawsuits brought against police departments and individual officers for actions taken during an investigation can cause a critical evaluation of official documents. Police reports can be an important defense in these suits (Nelson 2002). Investigative reports are crafted carefully because of their potential significance.

Police reports become legal documents referred to during court proceedings.

Writing Style

Each report varies based upon the circumstances involved in the activity that the report describes. However, basic rules apply to all investigative reports. One essential standard for reports is that they must be grammatically correct. Misspelled words, run-on and fragmented sentences, incorrect pronouns, and other errors in basic grammar can cause confusion and give a defense attorney an opportunity to cast doubt upon the sequence of events as they are described. To avoid such issues, police agencies are placing more emphasis upon the writing abilities of officers, including requiring a minimum educational writing level (City of Salem Police Department n.d.).

Reports should be written to be understood clearly by not only police officers but also citizens who may serve upon a jury. Dees (2003) suggests using plain English within a report. Police jargon should be avoided, as many jurors will not understand what these terms mean. Police reports may be evaluated carefully during the course of a jury deliberation in a trial. Using long, multisyllabic words and a flowery writing style may only serve to confuse the reader, who may then miss important points.

Scenario

Officer Gray submits a report to his supervisor that reads as follows:

> On September 20 at 0900 hours this reporting officer received a call from the telecommunicator at police headquarters via the radio. She advised that I should respond to 1123 Hickory on the report of a domestic disturbance. Upon my arrival I contacted a female party who lived at the house in question. She stated that a male who was present in the house, her husband, had struck her in the face during an argument with an open hand. I observed apparent swelling and redness underneath her right ocular area on the upper portion of her cheek. I took the male subject into custody for the apparent violation.

The supervisor suggested to Officer Gray that he use less complicated phrasing in his reports. After some review, the wording of the report was changed to the following:

> On September 20 at 0900 hours I was dispatched to 1123 Hickory for a domestic disturbance call. Upon my arrival I contacted the female victim. She stated that her husband had slapped her in the face with an open hand. I observed swelling and redness on her cheek below her right eye. I arrested the husband for assault.

Using less complicated diction in an investigative report, as in the second example in the above scenario, paints a clearer picture for the reader about how events played out.

Format

Investigative reports typically follow the same basic structure. Similar to a novel, reports contain an introduction, a body, and a conclusion. Reports are easy to follow when they are delivered in chronological order, beginning when the officer was contacted about the crime and progressing based upon the investigator's activities. In the introduction, the date and time of contact is reported, followed by the time investigators arrived at the scene. After-arrival observations are then noted. What did the scene look like to the officer? Who was present? What were the environmental conditions of the scene?

The body of the report addresses the work that was done by the officer. The investigator lists whom she contacted and what was related by each party. A fellow officer may brief the investigator about basic facts of the crime. The investigator may contact a victim or witness at the scene. Whatever action the investigator takes, she lists it in preliminary notes to be transferred later into a formal report.

The conclusion of the report denotes the final actions of the officer. If an arrest was made, this fact may be noted along with information about the charges. If a suspect was not arrested but was identified, the officer denotes this and suggests that the case remain open for follow-up investigation. If a report is taken only for informational purposes, the investigator may state that it is forwarded for review by intelligence analysts.

Types of Reports

Many different types of reports may be written during the course of an investigation. Certain reports are more common than others, including statements, lead reports, and case closures.

Statements

A statement report is taken when a victim, witness, or suspect is interviewed. Some statement reports are summaries of what the interviewee related to the investigator, while others are word-for-word accounts of what was said. Whichever format a statement is written in, it must report what was said without any embellishment or revision. Filling in gaps within a story with assumptions can change the facts and harm the investigation.

A verbatim account statement is typically written in a controlled environment where interruptions can be held to a minimum. Word-for-word accounts of what is related to the investigator are written, typed, or dictated in a structured format. The introductory section includes information about who is offering the statement, who is taking the statement, what it is in regard to, and when and where the statement is being recorded (figure 8.2). An introduction may also offer a disclaimer that the statement was given voluntarily by the interviewee without duress. The body of the verbatim statement may be completed in a question-and-answer format, where the interviewee answers ques-

---

FIGURE 8-2: Example of a statement form

Case #: 08-93921

This is the statement of Michael Bell. This statement is being given at the James City Police Department by Detective Eric Ross on April 25, 2008, at 5:00 PM. This statement is being given voluntarily and of my own free will. I have not been promised anything in exchange for my statement.

Q. Did you witness a robbery at 1122 Smith this evening?
A. Yes. I was in the convenience store when a white male wearing a stocking cap walked in with a gun.

Q. What did he do?
A. He put the gun in the clerk's face and said, "Give me all your money!" The clerk handed it over, and the man ran out the front door. He ran north, but I didn't see where he went after that. I was scared.

Q. Can you describe the man further?
A. He was wearing a gray jacket, about six feet tall, slender, blue jeans, white tennis shoes. I can't remember anything else.

Q. Is there anything you would like to add to this statement?
A. No. That is all I can recall.

My signature to this statement indicates that it is true to the best of my recollection.

Signed: Michael Bell
Witnessed: Det. Eric Ross

---

tions posed by the investigator. An alternative method is to have the victim relate the facts he knows about the case in a narrative form. In either case, the interviewee is given a chance to read the statement, correct any errors or inconsistencies, and initial his responses. The state-

Witnesses offer or write statements to describe the testimonial evidence they can give in court.

ment is concluded with an open-ended question, such as "Do you have anything else you would like to add about this incident?" The interviewee then signs the statement, indicating that it is accurate.

Lead Report

Another report that an investigator frequently completes is a lead report. In major cases, an investigative supervisor follows leads that develop, tracks them by number, and assigns them to specific investigators. The most important leads are assigned first. A detective may be issued a brief report or card with the lead and lead number listed along with the facts and circumstances behind that information. The officer maintains that lead until it has been fully investigated. A report is written giving the lead number in the introduction. The body of the report indicates the steps that were taken to pursue the lead. The conclusion either requests that the lead be closed or that another lead be assigned based upon information that was developed in investigating the lead (figure 8.3).

Major cases with numerous leads present significant challenges to investigators. It is not uncommon for a murder investigation to generate hundreds of pages of police reports. Because of this complication, an officer may be assigned with the specific task of organizing and tracking the reports as they come in. A "table of contents" of reports assembled in chronological order may be developed to help investigators locate a certain report more easily.

FIGURE 8-3: Example of a lead report

Case #: 08-44310
Lead #: 17

On May 14, 2008, I was given lead #17 in reference to the homicide case involving the victim Clarence Howard. The lead was in regards to a tip given by an anonymous citizen. The tipster advised that Charity Green may have witnessed the incident, as she was present at the hotel room during a drug transaction with other, unknown parties. The citizen stated that Green could be found at 2233 Gulf Bay Road.

Detective Rogers and I responded to the address and made contact with Melissa Jones. Ms. Jones stated that she is a friend of Green's but she had not seen Green for over three months. Ms. Jones had no idea where Green could be located but said that Green often hangs out with Roger Michaels, who lives at 3299 Clifton Avenue.

This lead has been investigated and can be classified as closed. A request is made to issue a new lead to check the residence of 3299 Clifton Avenue for Green and Michaels.

Case Closure Report

Relatively minor cases are assigned to one investigator, who may pursue every lead involved with that case. During the course of such a case, the detective will record the various investigatory steps taken in reports. When the case is complete, the final report is written as a request to the investigator's supervisor to close or inactivate the case. A case might be closed if the suspect was charged with a crime or it was discovered that the incident was unfounded. It may be left as inactive if the investigation failed to identify a suspect. The investigative supervisor will review the reports in the case file and consider whether to support the detective's recommendations or return the case for further investigation.

COURTROOM TESTIMONY

If a criminal investigation reveals that a suspect has committed an offense, the next step is to charge and prosecute that individual. Each case report is transferred from the hands of a police agency to a prosecuting attorney. From that point, the reports become legal documents in the case against the individual in question. During legal proceedings in a criminal case, the investigator must relate, verbally through testimony, her involvement in an investigation. The detective will rely upon the reports that she prepared previously, but rarely is her testimony limited to reading these reports. Verbal testimony requires further preparation and skill.

An investigator's testimony in a criminal case must accurately reflect the events as they previously developed. The testifying officer should not embellish her account or diverge from the facts of the case. Investigators should not compare their testimony and adjust their description of the events based upon the recollections of others. In many cases, testimony is recorded, and attorneys and jurors will compare what was said in court to what was initially reported. An investigator's narrative should remain factual for ethical reasons as well. Finally, a statement that is proven to be false impeaches the investigator's entire testimony, effectively eliminating her from consideration as a witness in the case at hand. The investigator's testimony in future cases may be called into question as well. Prior to giving testimony, each witness in a case must give an oath declaring that the information she will divulge is true and accurate.

Types of Legal Proceedings

Investigators may give testimony within several different legal proceedings. These environments include grand jury hearings, depositions, criminal trials, and civil cases.

Grand Jury

The grand jury...does not determine guilt or innocence, but only whether there is probable cause to believe that a crime was committed and that a specific person or persons committed it. If the grand jury finds probable cause to exist, then it will return a written statement of the charges called an "indictment." (U.S. Courts n.d.)

A grand jury is composed of citizens who may question witnesses presented by government attorneys. The accused does not present witnesses, because the grand jury hearing is not a criminal trial; it is an evaluation of the merits of the evidence to determine whether or not to proceed for trial. A detective may be called to present evidence gained in the criminal investigation to the jurors and answer questions they may have.

Deposition

In preparation for a trial, attorneys may take depositions from witnesses involved in the case. A deposition is part of the "discovery" in a trial, or the initial examination by the attorneys of the evidence that will be used by both sides in a criminal case. During a deposition, attorneys are allowed to question witnesses for the opposing side to "determine the credibility of all witnesses and to evaluate what type of impact the witness would make on a jury" (North Dakota Office of Management and Budget, Risk Management Division n.d., 1). Depositions are attended by attorneys for both sides of the case and a court reporter. A judge and jury are not present at the deposition; however, recorded statements may be presented as evidence later in the trial.

Criminal Trials

Courtroom testimony is also offered during the criminal trial. After the witness is sworn in, the attorney who called the witness establishes the party's identity through some introductory questions. The witness' professional background may be explored to establish his credibility to testify in the case.

Scenario

Sergeant James Washington is called to the stand to testify in a murder trial. Prior to exploring Sergeant Washington's testimony, the prosecuting attorney asks him some introductory questions. "Sir, will you please state your name and occupation for the jury?" she asks. Sergeant Washington responds with his name and advises that he works for the criminal investigations unit of his police agency. The prosecutor then requests that he share his experience as a police officer. Sergeant Washington states, "I've been a police officer for 25 years; 10 of those have been working criminal investigations. I have worked as a supervisor for over 75 murder investigations."

Direct examination occurs when an attorney questions a witness that he has called. For instance, a prosecutor may call a police officer to describe a crime scene upon her arrival. The opposing attorney may then question the same witness during cross-examination. In the previous example, the defense attorney would have an opportunity to ask the officer questions about the scene as well. Each attorney is afforded a second chance to question the witness during "redirect" and "recross" questioning (Federal Judicial Center n.d.).

Civil Trials

In addition to testifying in criminal trials, police officers may have occasion to testify in civil trials. Subpoenas may be issued for an investigator to appear in a lawsuit, divorce trial, custody battle, protection order hearing, or landlord-tenant dispute. The methods of examination are no different than they are in criminal cases. In such cases, the officer is not testifying for the state but merely as a representative of a public agency subpoenaed by one party in the case.

Preparation

To offer testimony successfully, an investigator must prepare. It is not uncommon for years to pass before a case goes to trial. During this time, the officer may forget some of the details that occurred during the course of the investigation. Offering testimony is often not an everyday task for investigators, so officers may also need reminders of proper testimony methods. Finally, because each case has unique characteristics and is presented in court differently, the detective may benefit from insight about what to expect during the trial.

An investigator will refresh her memory of the case by reviewing the reports and physical and testimonial evidence involved. The case reports, described earlier in the chapter, will describe the particulars of the investigation for reference. Viewing the physical evidence in a case can increase the investigator's recollection of the incident. Surveillance or crime scene videos or photographs can be particularly helpful. The statements of witnesses and suspects are important to review as well.

Police investigators typically testify on behalf of the prosecution. The prosecutor usually meets with the officer to prepare him for appearing at a legal proceeding. A prosecutor is an impartial party in the criminal trial and as such should never direct the testimony of the investigator. The attorney can advise the officer of what to expect in the trial and remind him of proper testimony practices. The investigator can take this information and prepare for the trial by reviewing elements of the case about which he expects to be asked.

A professional demeanor is required to deliver testimony most effectively in a courtroom setting. The judge and jury are influenced by both the verbal communication and the nonverbal cues that the testifying subject offers (Navarro 2004). A juror may subconsciously evaluate the investigator's facial expressions, body posture, where he places his hands, and his eye movements during testimony. "Displays of indifference, disgust, antipathy, displeasure, or arrogance interfere with a jury's perception either on the stand or at the prosecutor's table" (Navarro 2004, 28). The tone of voice used by the officer can impact how the investigator is perceived.

The goal of the person testifying is to remove assessments about his personal appearance, demeanor, or other physical characteristics and move the jury's observations to the words communicated through testimony. The jury should be considering the story the investigator has to tell instead of his physical and nonverbal attributes. Meeting this goal starts before entering the courtroom. The type of clothing the officer wears should be considered. It may be desirable to wear a police uniform; if not, business attire is required. It is appropriate for the investigator to ask the prosecutor if he has a preference before the trial. A conservative business suit may help move the jury's concentration away from factors that are irrelevant to the testimony.

The investigator's dress should be professional during court proceedings; typically a uniform or business suit is worn.

The jury may also be influenced by the language used by the person testifying. The investigator should deliver her testimony in clear, uncomplicated words. Common, simple language will avoid confusing the jurors. Police vernacular and acronyms should be avoided. Additionally, there is no place in a courtroom for any slang or derogatory or offensive words. The testimony should be given in a loud enough tone for the judge, jury, attorneys, and court reporters to hear.

Other tips to assure effective testimony are as follows:

- *Avoid words such as* "'never,' 'always,' 'definitely,' 'without a doubt,' *or* 'absolutely'" (North Dakota Office of Management and Budget n.d., 2). Such words indicate a certainty that can be challenged with "what if" scenarios by the opposing counsel. Investigators must be cautious not to limit themselves with absolute statements when other words could explain a situation.

- *Do not expound upon the information that was asked for.* In other words, if the lawyer asks a question, the investigator should answer it as directly as possible without offering superfluous facts. For example, the defense attorney may ask why a particular witness was questioned. The investigator may answer, "I was given the assignment to interview this person by my supervisor," instead of, "My supervisor told me to, and once we started talking, it became obvious that they had a lot of information. They told me that they had witnessed this crime firsthand and had witnessed many other crimes in their neighborhood." It is the attorney's job to ask follow-up questions for clarification.

- *Maintain an even demeanor.* An attorney may attempt to discredit the officer as a witness by making him lose his temper with sensitive questions or by raising her own tone of voice. The investigator should testify in a calm and collected manner to be respected by the jurors. An attorney may also interrupt the person testifying. The best tactic is to wait for the interruption to end and then courteously answer the question.

- *Request clarification when necessary.* The attorney may either deliberately or mistakenly ask a question that is not clear. Instead of guessing what was intended by the question, the investigator should ask if the lawyer can rephrase or restate the question. If the question is about a particular report or exhibit (piece of evidence), it is appropriate to request to refer to that report or exhibit.

- *Take time to respond.* By waiting a few seconds to answer the question, the officer can accomplish two objectives. First, she can take time to consider carefully what was asked and formulate her response. Second, it gives the opposing attorney time to object to the question. If the attorney feels that the question violates rules of evidence, he may ask that the question not be answered. The judge will either sustain (approve) or overrule (deny) the objection. If an objection is made, the investigator should wait until she is directed either to answer the original question or for a new question to be asked.

- *Only testify according to the appropriate expertise.* An investigator may be asked a question that is outside his knowledge or experience. For example, an attorney may ask about a scientific principle associated with a particular piece of physical evidence. It is appropriate to say, "I don't know." A more qualified witness, such as a crime lab technician, can be called later to clarify such issues.

SUMMARY

Criminal investigative reports are important records of each step of an investigation. Reports become legal documents as a case progresses through the trial process. Reports are typically written with an introduction, body, and conclusion. Simple language should be used to keep reports uncomplicated for their various readers. Statements, lead reports, and case closures are common types of investigative reports.

Investigators testify in court based upon information contained in their investigative reports. Investigators may have to testify in grand jury hearings, depositions, and criminal and civil trials. Investigators must remain cognizant of their appearance and demeanor during testimony so the jury concentrates on their statements rather than other factors.

Key Terms

Case closure report: A written record of the disposition of a criminal investigation prepared by the investigator

Deposition: A hearing where attorneys for the prosecution and the defense in a criminal trial can query witnesses as part of the discovery process

Grand jury hearing: A court proceeding where a group of jurors determines whether or not probable cause exists to proceed with a criminal case

Lead report: A written record of the actions taken by a criminal investigator in response to an assigned investigative lead

Statement: A written record of testimonial evidence from a witness to a crime

Discussion Questions

1. Why are simple words and phrases favored in investigative reports and courtroom testimony?

2. Explain why investigative reports and courtroom testimony are closely related in the investigative process.

Exploration

1. Watch a televised court case on a news program or attend a live trial. Do the witnesses seem to be following the recommendations offered in this chapter?

References

City of Salem Police Department. n.d. *Lateral entry police officer.* Retrieved September 10, 2007, from www.cityofsalem.net/departments/police/lateralentry.htm.

Dees, Tim. 2003, December. Report writing aids. *Law and Order* 51, no. 12 (December): 18–20.

Federal Judicial Center. n.d. *Presentation of evidence.* Retrieved September 14, 2007, from: www.fjc.gov/federal/courts.nsf/autoframe?OpenForm&nav=menu4a&page=/federal/courts.nsf/page/D2138ACEC3810A7C8525682400789E9E?opendocument.

Nelson, Kurt. 2002. Patrol: The police report in the officer's arsenal. *Law and Order* 50, no. 9 (September): 226–228.

Navarro, Joe. 2004. Testifying in the theater of the courtroom. *FBI Law Enforcement Bulletin* 72, no. 9 (September): 26-30.

North Dakota Office of Management and Budget, Risk Management Division. n.d. *Preparation for testifying guidelines.* Retrieved September 14, 2007, from www.nd.gov/risk/publications/docs/preparation-for-testifying-guidelines.pdf.

U.S. Courts. n.d. *Handbook for federal grand jurors.* Washington, DC: U.S. Courts Administrative Office.

PART III

CRIME-SPECIFIC TECHNIQUES

CHAPTER 9

ROBBERY, BURGLARY, LARCENY, AND MOTOR VEHICLE THEFT

CHAPTER OBJECTIVES

By the end of this chapter, the reader will be able to do the following:

- Define the crime of robbery.
- List the types of robbery.
- Describe approaches used to investigative to robbery.
- Define the term *modus operandi*.
- Define the crime of *burglary*.
- List the types of burglary.
- Define the term *burglar's tools*.
- Describe methods used to investigate burglary.
- List typical motivations for burglary.
- Define the crime of *larceny*.
- List the types of larceny crimes.
- List typical motivations for larceny.
- Describe methods used to investigate larceny.
- Define the crime of *motor vehicle theft*.
- List typical motivations for motor vehicle theft.
- Describe methods used to investigate motor vehicle theft.

Theft cases such as burglary, larceny, and the stealing of motor vehicles may not be as serious as other crimes, such as homicide. However, these crimes are far more prevalent. Nationwide in recent years, there have been over 80 times more burglaries, over 60 times more robberies, and 250 times more larcenies than murders (Federal Bureau of Investigation 2006). Investigators spend countless hours investigating these cases.

Robberies are similar to theft cases in that they involve the motivation to steal. A robbery includes the added dimension of a threat or act of violence. A robbery can potentially lead to harm or death to the victims or witnesses. Investigative resources are thus heavily dedicated toward stopping serial robbers from continuing their crimes.

ROBBERY

Robbery is defined as "the taking or attempting to take anything of value from the care, custody, or control of a person or persons by force or threat of force or violence and/or by putting the victim in fear" (FBI 2004, 21). The difference between robberies and other types of thefts is the use or threat of violence. Without this forceful act, the theft is classified as one of the other crimes described in this chapter. The introduction of violence can change a crime's classification. For example, a larceny shoplift could become a robbery if the suspect uses force to overcome an attempted apprehension.

Types of Robbery

Robberies can further be classified according to the target of the offense. Robberies can occur in a *residence,* either due to a confrontation between a homeowner and suspect during what starts as a burglary or because a suspect forcibly enters a dwelling with the intent to use force. *Commercial robberies* occur frequently at establishments such as banks, convenience stores, and fast-food restaurants. Open-air, or *street robberies,* occur on street corners, in parking lots, or in any openly public environment. A *carjacking* is a robbery where a vehicle is the property in question and force, such as the threatened use of a firearm, is used to overcome resistance.

Investigation

A robbery investigation begins with taking statements from victims and witnesses. In burglaries, larcenies, and auto thefts, there may or may not be a witness to interview, but because of the confrontation that occurs in a robbery, a witness is always available unless he has been seriously injured. An identification by the witness may be possible but is often hampered when the suspect disguises his face from view. An area canvass for potential witnesses can be beneficial in some cases. An area witness may have seen a secreted getaway vehicle or be able to describe the suspect's direction of flight.

During the interview of the victim, it is important to ask exactly how the suspect(s) carried out the crime. The words that the suspect used during the crime, whether or not a weapon was presented or if the use of a weapon was merely threatened, and the physical movements of the suspect during the robbery may become significant factors in the investigation. Robbery suspects often repeat their crimes, and if a particular tactic has been successful in the past, it may be replicated. The repetitive method a criminal uses is termed her *modus operandi* (MO for short), which is Latin for "method of operation." If a suspect is caught in a robbery, it may be possible to tie her to previous cases based upon her prior MO.

An examination of any physical evidence is also important. A robbery scene is checked for fingerprints or any trace evidence the suspect may have left behind. Video and audio surveillance is often available in many commercial robberies. Businesses that are frequent targets for robberies typically install surveillance equip-

Surveillance cameras may provide video evidence to assist in the identification of individuals involved in robberies.

ment as a deterrent and to aid in the investigative process. The investigator may be able to identify the suspect based upon video evidence. Videos may be released to media outlets to show to the general public in an effort to generate investigative tips about the suspect's identity.

CASE STUDY

A convenience store in Fresno, California, was robbed by two subjects; one was armed with a large handgun. A clerk was tied up during the robbery, while a second store employee was forced to turn over money from the cash register. The entire incident was captured on the store's video surveillance system.

Lacking solid leads, the Fresno Police Department released video of the robbery to local media outlets. "After the video was shown, a citizen called Crime Stoppers and provided Street Violence Bureau Detectives with information regarding the identity of the suspects" (City of Fresno 2007, ¶ 3). A subject with an extensive, violent criminal past was later arrested and charged based upon the information.

Another method used to identify robbery suspects is tracking the property that was taken. Some businesses and institutions pass bills that have had the serial numbers recorded. If these bills are located, the individual in possession of them may be the suspect or perhaps connected to the suspect. Exploding dye packs are often used by banks to mark the stolen cash or the suspect with brightly colored ink.

False Robbery

In some situations, a false robbery may be reported. An employee may have stolen funds from the business and attempt to cover up the theft by reporting a bogus crime. The investigator must be conscious of subtle indicators that the crime may not have actually happened. The reporting party may have inconsistencies in repeated versions of the story, certain details may have been left out, or the reported events may simply not seem plausible. Suspicion may also be raised if a surveillance system that is present inexplicably has malfunctioned during the robbery. The background of the employee reporting the crime may be considered in making a determination about the veracity of the account.

BURGLARY

Burglary is defined as "the unlawful entry of a structure to commit a felony or a theft" (FBI 2004, 28). There are two elements to this definition. The first element is the entry into a structure, which would include houses, commercial businesses, offices, or other buildings, without permission from an owner or representative. The second part of the definition is the commission of a crime. Typically, this involves the theft of something within the residence; however, it could include any type of crime. For instance, if a subject breaks into a structure and commits vandalism, this would also fit into the definition of a burglary.

Types of Burglary

Burglaries, like robberies, occur in different types of buildings and can be classified according to the type of structure. Burglaries may happen in residential dwellings and commercial buildings. Churches are also common targets. In addition to these sites, burglaries may occur in outbuildings, such as sheds. Some jurisdictions classify the breaking and entering of an automobile as a burglary according to the prevailing law; however, these technically do not meet the FBI's Uniform Crime Reporting definition.

Investigation

The investigation of a burglary differs from the investigation of a robbery chiefly because no one usually witnesses a burglary. A typical burglar does not want to confront anyone upon entry into the structure, so the victim does not normally come into contact with the suspect. A neighborhood or area canvass may unearth some witnesses who believed a stranger's presence was innocent at the time.

Without such witnesses, testimonial evidence may of little assistance in a burglary case.

Due to the lack of testimonial evidence, burglary investigations may rely more upon physical evidence. Tool marks are common items of physical evidence important in a criminal case. A burglar may use a pry tool to defeat door or window locks to gain entry into the structure. The use of such tools may leave a mark in the wood or other material that makes up the door and window. A casting of the tool mark, or the entire item that holds the mark, may be collected for possible comparison to tools recovered from a suspect.

Tool mark evidence is often left behind at the scene of a burglary as a result of the suspect's attempt to force entry.

Fingerprints are another commonly helpful piece of physical evidence in a burglary. Investigators check the apparent entry points, the areas where property has been removed, and any other parts of the scene that may have been touched by the suspect for possible fingerprints. Another common method to gain entry into a building is through forcefully kicking the door near handles and locking mechanisms. It may be possible to locate a shoeprint from forcibly kicked-in doors or windows for comparison as well.

CASE STUDY

A series of commercial burglaries in Auburn, Washington, had investigators searching for suspects. After nine months and 100 offenses, a single latent fingerprint was recovered from one of the crime scenes and submitted for comparison. "The latent print was searched against the newly implemented Regional AFIS Database, and a match was made to a juvenile fingerprint card" (King County Sheriff's Office 2006, 42). Surveillance was set up on the juvenile, and he was caught in the act of committing another commercial burglary. The juvenile confessed to 75 of the previous cases.

The actual property that was taken from the burglary may be important in tying a suspect to the crime scene. The investigating officer inquires about the property to obtain as exact a description as possible. Burglary suspects often seek valuable property, and costly property is usually marked with serial numbers. Serial numbers may not be the only identifying marks; the owner of the property may have marked it with initials, or he may be able to report damage or unique attributes of the property that could help locate it.

Burglary suspects often sell items taken in the crimes to pawn shops. Investigators frequently check these shops in an attempt to locate stolen property. Many state laws stipulate that pawn shops must provide law enforcement agencies with a list of property with serial numbers on a regular basis to cross-check with stolen property databases. The majority of property that a pawn shop deals with is from honest customers and legitimate sources, but occasionally a criminal will attempt to trade stolen property for money through a business.

Burglars often develop a unique modus operandi based upon successful crimes in the past. The characteristic of a burglar's crime may be how she enters a house. For example, the burglar may always enter through a rear basement window. A burglary suspect may also concentrate on taking a specific type of property, for example taking tools from the victim's garage to pawn.

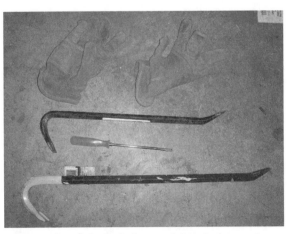

Items used to defeat window and door locks may be considered "burglar tools."

During routine encounters, such as vehicle stops and pedestrian checks, police officers may encounter individuals whom they suspect of being involved in burglaries. Property in the subject's possession may appear suspicious; for example, there may be a large number of home stereos in the car. The person may also have tools that appear to be useful for defeating doors and windows to gain entry into a structure, such as pry bars, screwdrivers, lock picks, or small explosives. Many jurisdictions have an ordinance or statute prohibiting the possession of *burglar's tools* with which to charge such individuals.

Motivations for Burglary

Individuals who commit burglary have a wide range of experience and motivations. Young people may commit burglaries to take small items, such as electronic equipment, for their personal use. These burglaries may begin mostly as a thrill-seeking undertaking but evolve into a way to make money illegally or to support a drug problem. Certain individuals fit the category of professional burglars. Professionals target specific residences based upon a carefully selected profile. A professional often works with a fence, or a person who specializes in the sale and distribution of stolen goods.

False Burglary

As with some reported robbery crimes, investigators consider the possibility of whether a burglary report is true or if it may have been falsified. Home and business owners may attempt to report a fictitious burglary to collect insurance money for stolen goods. An examination of the physical evidence may indicate that the burglary report is not valid. For example, the homeowner may claim that a broken window allowed the suspect access into the house, but the broken glass lies outside of the house instead of inside the room. Inconsistencies in the victim's statement may also be an indicator of falsehood.

LARCENY

Larceny is defined as "the unlawful taking, carrying, leading, or riding away of property from the possession or constructive possession of another" (FBI 2004, 152). Larceny differs from burglary in that a person may be in an area lawfully yet secrete and steal an item without owner's permission (breaking and entering is not necessary). Larceny is unlike robbery because force is not required in the theft.

There are many types of larceny. A larceny shoplift is the theft of an item from a retail business establishment. When an employee takes goods or cash from his employer, this is classified as *embezzlement*. A pickpocket larceny occurs when a suspect steals a wallet, purse, or some other item directly from a person. Construction sites are frequent targets for theft. Other types of theft committed by means of deceit are addressed later in this book under the category of fraud.

Some jurisdictions further classify larcenies by the value of the property or cash that was taken. A set dollar amount determines whether the crime is charged as a felony, punishable by over a year in jail, or a misdemeanor, punishable by less than a year of incarceration. In a grand larceny, for instance, property valued at more than $1,000 may have been taken. When property valued at less than this amount has been taken, the crime may be classified as a petty larceny.

Motivations for Larceny

Individuals commit larceny for different reasons. Some suffer an error in judgment and take a chance when an opportunity presents itself (e.g., a juvenile taking a piece of candy). For others, committing larceny is a business. Professional "boosters," as they are called, work with fences to trade property for cash or narcotics in a similar fashion as burglars. Individuals who are addicted to the feelings associated with shoplifting may be clinically diagnosed with a *kleptomaniac disorder* (although this doesn't change how the crime is investigated).

Investigation

Private employees who work for "loss prevention" departments at retail businesses are often involved in the initial investigation of larceny shoplifts. Loss prevention officers work in an undercover capacity, posing as customers, to attempt to catch shoplifters in the act. Many stores also have sophisticated surveillance systems to capture crimes on video. These recordings become physical evidence for the police and can be presented at trial. If a shoplifter is apprehended, the private loss prevention officer will work with police officials in reporting the steps taken during the investigation.

An embezzlement investigation is conducted in a similar fashion. A supervisor or private security officer for the company may be the first to investigate an employee theft. In other cases, a business may report a loss to the police agency and identify the employees who had access to the property or money that was taken. Physical evidence is often lacking in embezzlement cases. Fingerprints are not useful if the employee in question had legitimate access to the area where the missing items were located . Video surveillance may be helpful in this case; however, employees often are aware of these systems. Embezzlement cases may depend upon interviews and interrogations of suspected employees.

Pickpocket suspects may craft their crimes to avoid detection, making such cases difficult to solve. Pickpockets thrive in crowded environments, such as concerts, public gatherings, or busy subway terminals. If the suspect uses credit cards or other identification belonging to the victim after the theft, it may be possible to work the case based upon tracking the victim's property. A police department may also use an undercover sting operation to lure pickpocket thieves by having officers pose as potential victims.

Construction sites are targets for thieves because they are often unattended and expensive building materials and construction equipment may be accessible. The recovery of stolen construction equipment may yield clues as to the identity of those involved in a criminal operation. Another common tactic is the use of human or video surveillance to catch perpetrators in the act of theft.

Construction sites are often targeted for theft due to the fact that expensive materials and equipment are frequently left unattended.

False Larceny

As with burglaries and robberies, a larceny report may be made under false pretenses. An employee may report a larceny by a fictitious stranger to cover up embezzlement or the accidental loss of company property. Bogus larceny reports may be made to collect an insurance settlement as well. Again, inconsistencies in testimonial or physical evidence can serve as an indicator of a falsely reported crime.

MOTOR VEHICLE THEFT

The theft or attempted theft of a motor vehicle requires special techniques to investigate. The definition of a *motor vehicle*, according to the Uniform Crime Report, is

> a self-propelled vehicle that runs on land surface and not on rails; for example, sport utility vehicles, automobiles, trucks, buses, motorcycles, motor scooters, all-terrain vehicles, and snowmobiles....This category does not include farm equipment, bulldozers, airplanes, construction equipment, or water craft (motorboats, sailboats, houseboats, or jet skis). (FBI 2004, 35–36)

Motor Vehicle Theft Motivation

Individuals commit motor vehicle theft for a variety of reasons. Young people may steal a car for "joyriding" purposes, which involves using it for a short time and then abandoning it. An automobile may be stolen for use in another crime, such as a getaway car in a robbery. Professional motor vehicle thieves steal cars to resell either in their entirety or dismantled for parts.

Investigation

Motor vehicle theft investigation differs from the investigation of other types of theft because physical evidence may be more readily available. If recovered, the vehicle itself may contain fingerprints and trace evidence to compare to that from possible suspects. Quick recovery of a stolen automobile greatly aids the investigation. An important initial step in the investigation of an auto theft is to broadcast a description of the car as soon as practicable. Officers may identify stolen automobiles on the roadway and apprehend the thieves in possession of the car.

Advances in technology have helped increase the quick recovery of stolen motor vehicles. Tracking systems can be installed into automobiles to help police agencies recover them when they are stolen. The LoJack security tracking system transmits a radio signal to law enforcement receivers to help locate freshly stolen vehicles (City of Fresno n.d.). The OnStar system locates a stolen vehicle through the use of satellite tracking (OnStar 2006).

Criminal enterprises may use motor vehicle theft as a source of income. Automobiles, complete or in parts, may be stolen for resale. While vehicles carry identifying numbers, some parts of cars cannot be individually identified. These parts may be removed from a stolen vehicle and sold through fences, through salvage yards, or even as part of an Internet auction. A garage set up for the dismantling and sale of stolen vehicle parts is often called a *chop shop*. Instead of parting out a vehicle, the entire car may be resold to individuals who know the car is stolen or to unsuspecting secondary victims who believe the sale is legitimate. To circumvent the chance of tracing a vehicle as being stolen, a professional auto thief takes steps to remove or alter the serial numbers on the car.

CASE STUDY

A Pennsylvania couple pled guilty in federal court to operating a stolen motorcycle fencing operation and money laundering. According to U.S. Attorney Mary Beth Buchanan, David and Linda Gebert

> stole numerous Harley-Davidson motorcycles at motorcycle rallies in Florida, Georgia and South Dakota. The indictment specifically identified at least eighteen motorcycles stolen...during that time frame. After stealing the bikes, [the couple] took them back home to their chop shop in Sarver, where they would remove the parts from the stolen bikes. The

[couple] then purchased motorcycle frames from frame manufacturers and from businesses which sold wrecked Harley Davidson frames, all of which frames had legitimate Vehicle Identification Numbers ("VINs") on them. After purchasing the legitimate frames, [the husband] placed all the parts from the stolen motorcycles onto the legitimate frames and sold the re-constructed Harley-Davidsons to persons who believed that the bikes were legitimate. (U.S. Attorney's Office 2007, ¶ 3)

Vehicle Identification Numbers

Motor vehicles can be identified through *vehicle identification numbers* (VINs). Modern VINs are coded numbers, 17 digits in length, which can reveal characteristics of the car's make, model, features, and place of manufacture. If a number's sequence of digits is altered to prevent the detection of the car as being stolen, the investigator can identify the alteration based upon "check digits" within the numbering scheme that will not conform to the original VIN coding format. Other criminals will attempt to remove the entire VIN plate from a vehicle's dashboard (the most common mounting location) and either leave it blank or replace it with a salvaged car's VIN plate. Federal and state laws make the alteration, removal, or switching of identifying VIN codes illegal.

Vehicle Identification Numbers (VINs) are identified by plates and other placards in various places on a vehicle, including the dashboard.

To combat the crime of VIN removal and alteration, automobile manufacturers place hidden identification numbers on different parts of the vehicle. Investigators may receive training in locating these numbers on suspected stolen vehicles. Many auto thieves will recognize the common VIN plates attached to a vehicle, such as the dashboard and door jamb markers, but neglect to alter or remove the hidden numbers.

False Motor Vehicle Theft Reports

False motor vehicle theft reports may be filed for an assortment of reasons. An individual may have allowed a person to "borrow" her car in exchange for drugs, often leading to the subject's not bringing the vehicle back. Others may fall behind on vehicle payments and report the car stolen, secretly keeping the automobile. A common reason for a false auto theft report is that the driver has been involved in a hit-and-run accident and wishes to claim someone else was the driver at the time. Individuals may report a car as stolen, then damage or burn a car beyond repair in an effort to gain an insurance settlement. In a sophisticated scheme, the car may be reported stolen and then sold to individuals in a foreign country.

In investigating a possible false stolen vehicle report, detectives will examine the history of the vehicle and the victim's financial situation. Was the reported victim behind on payments? Suspicion may be raised if the car was found at an accident scene. The investigator may look into the owner's driving history to check for past convictions of driving while intoxicated.

SUMMARY

The crime of robbery involves theft through the use or threatened use of force. Robberies may be residential, commercial, or street robberies or carjackings. Robbery investigation benefits from the availability of a witness to interview. Robbery suspects often develop a modus operandi. Surveillance video is frequently present at robbery crime scenes. It is not uncommon for a robbery to be reported falsely.

The crime of burglary involves the unlawful entry of a structure to commit a felony or theft. Burglary investigations are usually complicated by a lack of witnesses. Physical evidence, including a detailed description of the property that was stolen, is often extremely important in burglary investigations. Burglary suspects also may develop a modus operandi. Burglary reports may be falsified for a variety of reasons, including to profit from insurance claims.

There are several subclassifications of larceny crime, including shoplifts, embezzlements, pick pocketing, and construction site theft. Private businesses often employ loss prevention personnel to combat larceny.

Individuals commit motor vehicle theft for joyriding, to use the car in other crimes, or to profit from the sale of the stolen vehicle or its parts. The successful investigation of motor vehicle theft depends greatly upon the recovery of the stolen car. Chop shops are garages run by criminal organizations specializing in the sale of parts stripped from stolen vehicles. Vehicles and some vehicle parts are identifiable by vehicle identification numbers (VINs). Similar to other crimes, false motor vehicles thefts may be reported for illegal profit or to cover up hit-and-run accidents involving the owner.

Key Terms

Burglar's tools: Instruments used to defeat latching and locking mechanisms on doors or windows to facilitate the crime of burglary (e.g., lock picks, pry bars, small explosives)

Burglary: The unlawful entry of a structure to commit a felony or a theft (FBI 2004, 28)

Carjacking: A robbery crime in which the principal material target is a motor vehicle

Chop shop: A clandestine facility where stolen motor vehicles are dismantled and the parts are sold

Commercial robbery: A robbery crime occurring within a business

Embezzlement: The theft of property or proceeds from a business by an employee

Kleptomania: A clinical diagnosis of an individual who is addicted to the feelings associated with stealing property

Larceny: The unlawful taking, carrying, leading, or riding away of property from the possession or constructive possession of another (FBI 2004, 152)

Modus operandi: Latin for "method of operation"; the repetitive behavioral characteristics a subject uses during a criminal act

Residential robbery: A robbery crime occurring in a dwelling

Robbery: The taking or attempting to take anything of value from the care, custody, or control of a person or persons by force or threat of force or violence and/or by putting the victim in fear (FBI 2004, 21)

Street robbery: A robbery crime occurring in an open-air environment, such as in a parking lot or on a street corner

Vehicle identification number (VIN): The unique serial number of a motor vehicle that is coded to reveal characteristics of the vehicle

Discussion Questions

1. What factors make robberies difficult to investigate? What evidence aids investigators attempting to solve robbery crimes?

2. What steps might an investigator take in attempting to solve a series of burglaries in a particular area?

3. Of the listed types of larceny, which type do you feel presents the most difficulties to investigators? Why?

4. Why is the recovery of a stolen motor vehicle essential to solving the investigation of its theft?

Exploration

1. Explore the Federal Bureau of Investigation's website listing of unknown bank robbers and view how surveillance systems can aid in the investigation of robbery: *www.fbi.gov/wanted/unkn/unkn.htm.*

2. View the website of the International Association of Auto Theft Investigators and review how coordinated efforts can combat this crime: *www.iaati.org.*

References

City of Fresno. n.d. *LoJack information.* Retrieved September 17, 2007, from www.fresno.gov/Government/DepartmentDirectory/ Police/CrimePrevention/Lo-JackInformation.htm.

City of Fresno. 2007. *Robbery suspect arrested,* January 9. Retrieved September 15, 2007, from www.fresno.gov/Government/ DepartmentDirectory/Police/NewsMedia/2007/ RobberySuspectArrested.htm.

Federal Bureau of Investigation (FBI). 2004. *Uniform crime reporting handbook.* Clarksburg, WV: U.S. Department of Justice.

Federal Bureau of Investigation (FBI). 2006. *Crime in the United States.* Quantico, VA.

King County Sheriff's Office. 2006. *The future of AFIS.* Seattle: King County.

OnStar. 2006. *Press release: OnStar wins* Popular Science's *2006 Best of What's New award,* November 17. Available at http:// 209.235.195.221/releases_detail.php?ItemID=345.

U.S. Attorney's Office, Western District of Pennsylvania. 2007. *Press release: Couple ran chop-shop for stolen Harley-Davidson motorcycles,* June 4. Retrieved September 17, 2007, from www.usdoj .gov/usao/paw/pr/2007_june/2007_06_04_1.html.

CHAPTER 10

DEATH AND ASSAULT INVESTIGATION

CHAPTER OBJECTIVES

By the end of this chapter, the reader will be able to do the following:

- Define the crime of assault.

- Define the crime of aggravated *assault.*

- Define the crime of *simple assault.*

- List and describe the common types of injuries in assaults.

- Describe approaches used to investigate assault.

- List and describe manners of death.

- Describe the certain signs of death, including *rigor mortis, livor mortis, algor mortis,* and decomposition.

- Explain the initial stages of a death investigation.

- Describe methods used to estimate times of death.

- Describe *autopsy* procedures.

- Express the factors considered in an apparent suicide investigation.

- List common methods for committing suicide.

- List common methods of accidental death.

- Describe methods used in homicide investigation.

- Explain unique aspects of infant death investigation.

- Describe investigative techniques used in serial killings.

- Define *organized* and *disorganized offenders.*

Many investigators consider crimes during which a person is hurt or killed as the most important to solve. Assaults can lead to permanent injury or disfigurement along with psychological challenges for the victim. The crime of murder is perhaps the ultimate offense. Careful investigation is required because the victim cannot testify against the suspect.

ASSAULT

The crime of *assault* is defined as "an unlawful attack by one person upon another" (Federal Bureau of Investigation 2004, 23). Assaults occur in a variety of situations. Domestic violence crimes may involve a party related to the victim (discussed further chapter 12). An assault may be associated with another crime, such as robbery or a narcotics transaction. Stranger assaults occur when the victim does not know the suspect. Such assaults may result from arguments in public places or random acts of violence committed by dangerous criminals. The average ratio of stranger assaults to assaults where the victim knows the offender is relatively even (Pima County Prosecutor's Office 2004, 3).

Types of Assault

Assault crimes may be further classified according to the seriousness of the crime.

For example, an *aggravated assault* is

> an unlawful attack by one person upon another for the purpose of inflicting severe or aggravated bodily injury. This type of assault usually is accompanied by the use of a weapon or by means likely to produce death or great bodily harm. (FBI 2004, 23)

An aggravated assault may result in a serious or permanent injury. An example would be a stabbing or shooting. A person need not be

Aggravated assaults typically involve a weapon, such as a firearm, or a serious physical injury.

injured for a crime to be classified as an aggravated assault. Other assaults are classified as simple assaults. *Simple assaults* are "all assaults which do not involve the use of a firearm, knife, cutting instrument, or other dangerous weapon and in which the victim did not sustain serious or aggravated injuries" (FBI 2004, 26).

Types of Injuries

Assaults may cause a variety of injuries. A *contusion*, also known as a bruise, is an injury caused to skin or organs by some sort of impact. Contusions present as discoloration of the tissue. *Crushing wounds* are irregularly shaped broken-skin injuries caused by an impact near bone. A *laceration* is a slicing injury to the skin, often caused by a cutting instrument such as a knife. *Abrasions* are marks left when layers of skin are scraped off. Bone injuries are also common in assaults. Any injury caused by the victim's protecting themselves from an attack is referred to as a *defense wound*. Such wounds often occur on the victim's hands or forearms.

Stabbings and shootings cause both internal and external laceration and contusion injuries. Other injuries may be due to *blunt force trauma,* or an impact with a nonedged instrument. Blunt force trauma can be caused by weapons, such as bats or poles, or by human hand with fists.

Investigation

Physical evidence may be helpful in the investigation of an assault. Wounds may show evidence of what type of weapon was used, although the exact weapon cannot usually be determined by the wound alone. Physical evidence may be present in items left by the suspect at the scene, including the weapon itself or fingerprints on the weapon or around the scene. Other trace evidence, such as fibers or hairs, may dislodge from the suspect and remain at the scene. In shooting cases, a bullet recovered from the victim can be compared to any suspected firearm recovered during the investigation. If the victim fought back, blood or other biological material from the suspect may be present at the scene. For instance, skin cells from the suspect may be present under the fingernails of the victim if she scratched the

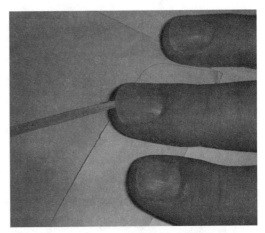

Fingernail scrapings may provide biological evidence samples for comparison to a possible suspect.

suspect in defense. Likewise, the suspect (if apprehended) may have trace or blood evidence from the victim on his person or in his vehicle or house that ties him to the crime scene.

CASE STUDY

Patricia Ann Carpenter was found strangled to death in Laguna Hills, California, in 1983. The case remained unsolved for over two decades. In 2004, police investigators re-examined the cold case and evidence collected from Carpenter's body. Investigators had originally collected skin cells from underneath Carpenter's fingernails. Modern DNA testing led to a profile that allowed for a comparison to a DNA database. The comparison revealed a match to John Laurence Whitaker, a convicted sex offender from Pasadena, California (Coleman 2007).

It is important to record the details of an assault through photography. Photographic documentation of the victim's injuries can help investigators compare wounds to weapons. Additionally, injuries heal, so photographs depict the victim's condition immediately after the assault, becoming important evidence to present during later court proceedings.

Obtaining a detailed statement from any suspects or witnesses involved in the case is necessary to procure testimonial evidence that may be beneficial to the investigation. Even if the victim or witnesses do not know the suspect, they may nonetheless have clues as to the suspect's identity. As thorough a description as possible should be gathered, including any known names, the clothing the suspect was wearing, and a physical description. Witnesses may view a lineup of suspects if individuals are identified. Every action the suspect took leading up to the incident is recorded, as each is important in determining if the elements of a crime have been met and in possibly describing the suspect's modus operandi. In stranger assaults, it is possible that the suspect may demonstrate a pattern of committing violent acts against multiple victims.

DEATH INVESTIGATION

Criminal justice professionals investigate death not only when murder is the cause but in any situation where suspicious circumstances exist. The discovery of any dead body is treated as a homicide investigation unless another cause of death is proven during the investigation. This helps ensure that all evidence is properly collected and processed.

Manners of Death

A primary determination in the early stages of a death investigation is the apparent manner of death. This determination is made after considering all of the evidence and circumstances involved. Medical *autopsies* (detailed later in this chapter) ultimately answer manner-of-death inquiries. Autopsies reveal medical causes that may not be apparent to investigators during the preliminary examination of the body. Death may occur under "natural" circumstances, which includes the loss of life due to disease or general bodily failure. Death may also be due to accidental means; that is, due to unintentional injuries. Electrocutions, motor vehicle collisions, and drowning are usually accidental deaths. A suicide, on the other hand, is a self-inflicted, intentional death. In rare instances, the investigation and the medical examination do not reveal any apparent reasons for the death. In these cases, the cause may be ruled as "undetermined."

Another manner of death is homicide. Criminal *homicide* is defined as "the willful (nonnegligent) killing of one human being by another" (FBI 2004, 15). The death in a homicide case may be immediate, or the loss of life can occur days or months after the harmful incident. While an autopsy is the only means to determine a manner of death conclusively, preliminary conclusions based upon the evidence presented at the scene may be used to start the investigation.

Initiation of the Investigation

Police officers respond to calls that may eventually become death investigations under a variety of circumstances. In some cases, the victim is still alive after an obvious assault. In these cases, it may be possible to gather testimonial evidence through a victim statement. Investigators should not interfere with any medical interventions conducted to save the victim's life; however, any possible information about the suspect is important to collect. It is not uncommon for a police officer to ride to the hospital in an ambulance in order to obtain a "dying declaration" from the victim. If the victim expires, the collection of further testimonial evidence will be limited to witnesses or other involved parties.

If a person is gravely injured, it may be possible to collect a statement during their transport to a hospital, but investigators should not interfere with medical interventions.

In other cases, the victim may be deceased upon the arrival of investigating officers. Physical characteristics may be present that indicate the victim is dead. *Rigor mortis* is the stiffening of joints that occurs after death due to chemical changes in the body. *Livor mortis* is a discoloration of the parts of the body that are lowest to the ground. Livor mortis results from blood's settling due to no longer circulating through the body and the effects of gravity. *Algor mortis* is the reduction in body temperature that occurs after death. In cases where the subject has been dead for hours, the body will be cold to the touch (depending on environmental temperature conditions). Another evident sign of death is the presence of decomposition, or the action of bacteria upon body tissues. Death is apparent if these signs exist (Indiana State Coroners Training Board 2001). Medical personnel can verify that there are no signs of life.

If death is confirmed at the scene, the body is not transported to a hospital. Investigators take steps to identify the deceased. In many cases, the calling party knows the victim. In other instances, the identity of the victim is unknown. Victims may have identification on their persons to help ascertain who they are; however, this cannot be the sole basis for a full identification. Other methods must be utilized for positive identification of the deceased. If facial features were not damaged during death, photographs may be shown to possible family members or friends. Other methods of identification are noted in chapter 11.

The Role of the Medical Examiner

The police agency controls the perimeter of the crime scene at a death investigation; however, the body is under the control of a medical examiner or coroner. The medical examiner or an investigative representative from her office may respond to the crime scene to conduct her own initial investigation. The body, as physical evidence, is recovered and examined by a medical examiner because of her unique medical training. Manner and cause of death determinations must be made by a doctor, not a layperson. These determinations are listed in a *death certificate,* which serves as legal proof of death and lists the accepted medical finding for manner and cause.

In cases where no sign of foul play is apparent and a medical history exists for the victim, the victim's medical doctor may elect to sign a death certificate in lieu of conducting a full investigation into the circumstances of the death. In arriving at this decision, the doctor may collaborate with the medical examiner. For example, if a 95-year-old male with a history of heart problems is found with no apparent external wounds, the body may not compel a criminal investigation.

In instances where foul play is more apparent, a representative of the medical examiner's office may examine the condition of the body and advise the investigators of possible contributing circumstances involved in the death. The actual manner of death cannot be determined with certainty until a full medical examination (autopsy) is performed; however, initial findings may be helpful in the early investigation. For instance, signs of struggle, including defense wounds, would indicate that the case may be a homicide and not a suicide. If a firearm is involved and present at the scene, its position in relation to the body may be important in making a suicide/homicide determination. The presence of petechial hemorrhage, or tiny red dots that show up in the whites of the victim's eyes, are a visible indicator that oxygen flow was cut off to the victim, suggesting strangulation (National Institutes of Health, U.S. National Library of Medicine, 2006). In reviewing these initial determinations, an investigator should keep an open mind as to what caused the death, as these preliminary findings are not conclusive.

Time of Death

The time that a death occurred is important to determine. Possible future suspects may offer alibis regarding their whereabouts during the time of the crime, so narrowing down the period in which the offense occurred can exclude individuals from suspicion or cast doubt upon their claims of innocence. The exact time of death cannot be established with certainty without a witness or some sort of video surveillance; however, the time frame can be shortened based upon certain physical indicators.

Lividity (livor mortis) becomes visible from a half-hour to 3 hours after death and is fixed after 6 to 18 hours. Rigor mortis generally begins within 2 to 7 hours, is fully set between 11 and 13 hours, and starts to dissipate between 12 and 48 hours. Putrefaction, or decomposition, generally becomes visible within 24 to 27 hours after death. Body temperature typically drops after death; however, various factors influence how quickly the temperature falls. *Forensic entomology,* or the study of how insects infest a dead body, can determine an approximate time of death. A trained entomologist examines the insect manifestation. The stomach contents may also indicate a time frame. A stomach typically empties in 2 to 4 hours, while the small intestine empties in between 10 to 12 hours. Stomach content evaluation is one of the more unreliable methods of determining time of death due to the number of variables that affect digestion (Indiana State Coroners Training Board 2001).

Autopsy

A full medical examination of a deceased victim is conducted via an autopsy. A medical examiner or coroner conducts the autopsy. During the autopsy, a medical examiner's assistant and/or a police investigator takes photographs documenting the procedure. The body is initially examined for apparent injuries. While it is important to note the characteristics of these visible injuries, much can be hidden below the surface. An internal examination reveals underlying injuries. The medical examiner surgically opens the individual's chest and brain cavities for close examination. The doctor takes detailed notes during the process, noting any irregularities in the subject that may have contributed to the death (American Academy of Family Physicians, n.d.). Samples of blood and tissue are collected during the autopsy to examine the possibility that the subject may have died due to poisoning. A *toxicology* examination explores what substances were present in the victim's system.

The medical examiner reviews the findings of the autopsy, the investigative reports collected by both his staff and the police, and the family and medical history of the victim to determine the manner and cause of death. The manner of death, discussed earlier, may be natural, accidental, suicidal, undetermined, or homicidal. The cause of death is "the injury, disease, or combination of the two that was responsible for initiating the train of physiological disturbances (brief or prolonged), which produced the fatal termination" (Elbert County n.d.). Examples of manners of death include gunshot wounds, oxygen deprivation, and cancer.

Scenario

A subject is found deceased in an alleyway with a puncture wound to his chest. An investigation begins. The county medical examiner conducts an autopsy and finds a bullet in the subject's lung cavity. No other medical reasons are found that may have contributed to the person's death. The medical examiner completes a death certificate listing the manner of death as homicide, with the cause of death a gunshot wound to the chest.

MANNERS OF DEATH INVESTIGATION

Suicide

A person may take his own life through a variety of means. Factors that play a role in the individual's decision of a method for committing suicide include the person's background, family, religion, and resolve.

Suicide by firearm is a common method. The most frequently used means of suicide by firearm include shots to the temple, upward through the mouth, upward through the chin, or to the chest. If an individual's religion favors an open-casket funeral, it is not uncommon for that person to choose a method that does not damage the head or face. Multiple gunshot wounds do not necessarily rule out the possibility of a suicide. It is possible for a victim to survive a bullet wound to the head and to make a second attempt.

An important consideration in a possible suicide-by-firearm investigation is the position of the weapon relative to the body. If the firearm appears to be too far from the body or if it is missing altogether, suspicion of homicide is raised. It is not uncommon for witnesses, family members, medical personnel, or even police officers to move a gun found at a suicide scene, however. Testimonial statements can clarify the positioning of a firearm if doubt exists. Crime scene investigators may examine the area directly underneath the body for marks on the floor where the firearm may have been dropped immediately

The position of a firearm relative to a body is important in analyzing evidence to determine if a death was a suicide.

after a fatal shot. Gunshot residue analysis may be warranted. Certain semi-automatic firearms cause what are referred to as *recoil marks* to the victim's hand due to the loading mechanism of the gun. Gunshot deaths may be homicidal and accidental causes as well: firearm accidents may appear on the surface to be suicides, and murderers may pose a scene to make the death appear to be a suicide.

CASE STUDY

Deputies in Littleton, Colorado, responded to the scene of an apparent homicide/suicide in December of 1978. A woman and her two teenage children were found shot dead within their home. An apparent typewritten suicide note was found still lodged within the typewriter.

The woman's husband, Robert Spangler, was interviewed and claimed he was not home during the incident.

> Spangler's original story changed significantly in a subsequent interview. Two separate, private polygraph examiners found his answers inconclusive to questions about his role in the deaths. The .38-caliber weapon used in all three shootings belonged to Spangler, and evidence of gunshot residue was found on his right palm. On January 3, 1979, the Arapahoe County coroner closed the case as a double homicide/suicide. (Johns, Downes, and Bibles 2005, 2)

The Spangler case was re-examined in 1999 with the assistance of the FBI's National Center for the Analysis of Violent Crime. Spangler had remarried twice, and his third wife also died under suspicious circumstances. A plan was developed to interview Spangler, who had been diagnosed with terminal cancer. Spangler subsequently confessed to killing both his second and third wives and his two children.

Another common method used to commit suicide is through the use of cutting instruments. Victims may cut their wrists, neck, or legs to sever arteries and veins. The loss of blood eventually causes death. Similar to a firearm death, the positioning of the knife may be important; however, a significant difference is that stabbing or cutting wounds may not cause death as immediately.

Suicide is also committed through hanging. Hanging cuts off the oxygen supply and may break the victim's neck. Medical examiners request that the investigator leave the noose affixed to the victim's neck so that they can compare the actual injuries to the apparent killing device. In some cases, suspects have posed a homicide victim in a hanging noose to make the death appear to be a suicide.

Carbon monoxide poisoning is accomplished through the ingestion of the gas, which replaces the victim's oxygen supply. The human body requires oxygen, so the removal of oxygen from the environment causes death. Motor vehicles in confined spaces, such as garages, can be used to fill the air with carbon monoxide gas. Many houses are sealed tightly enough that the victim need not be within the garage to succumb to the poisoning of the air. The vehicle used for this purpose may eventually stall or run out of gas, so the lack of a running automobile does not rule out this type of death. Carbon monoxide poisoning presents in a victim as a cherry-reddening of the skin (State of Alaska Epidemiology 1993). While many suicides are committed using carbon monoxide, it is also possible that the death is accidental; the victim may have warmed up the car or failed to shut it off upon returning home. Homicides have also been known to be committed using this method.

Empty pill containers at a crime scene may indicate a possible death by overdose.

An individual may also commit suicide by taking a lethal dosage of prescription or over-the-counter medication. Death by overdose may or may not be apparent to the investigators. Empty pill containers or vomit may indicate the ingestion of drugs. A toxicology examination of the victim's blood is performed to check for the presence of substances. The toxicologist can determine whether the amount of each substance present was lethal or not.

Death by jumping is often quite apparent based upon the positioning of the victim, unless she has been moved. Internal examination can verify damage that occurred during the fall. A thorough investigation is warranted to rule out homicide or accidental death through the fall.

One important determinant in a suicide investigation is the presence or absence of a suicide message from the victim. Many victims leave a final note behind for loved ones. If the note is written by the victim and not typed, a comparison may be performed by a handwriting recognition expert to determine if the writing is consistent with the victim's writing style and characteristics. Other victims elect to not leave a note, so the absence of a message does not necessarily indicate foul play.

Testimonial evidence plays an important role in suicide investigations. Investigators question the victim's family members and friends to ascertain the person's frame of mind prior to death. Monetary debts, the loss of a job, divorce, and the death of a loved one can be triggers for deep depression leading to suicide. The study of the victim's life is often referred to as "victimology." Compiling this type of information gives the investigators insight into the victim's personal life prior to death.

Accidental

As noted previously, accidental deaths may occur under many of the same circumstances as suicides. Gunshot wounds can happen during gun-cleaning or hunting accidents. Carbon monoxide poisoning has occurred when victims have forgotten to shut off their vehicles. An individual may unintentionally take too much of a particular drug, causing an overdose. A fall from height may be accidental as well.

Certain causes of death are more typically due to an accident than a suicide or homicide. For instance, death by drowning is most commonly an accidental death. The body's natural reaction is to avoid the ingestion of water (displacing oxygen), so it is very difficult to commit suicide by this means. Murder by drowning is possible (particularly for young or elderly victims) but difficult. Most drowning deaths occur in individuals who cannot swim or who lose consciousness in water for various reasons.

Electrocution is usually accidental in nature. Electrocution may occur due to household appliance failure, faulty wiring, work on electrical projects, or lightning strikes. Electricity causes burn injuries to the skin and malfunctions in internal organs, which often do not kill the victim. Electrocution may cause death when the current interrupts brain or cardiac activity. An important determination to make during an electrocution investigation is what caused the problem. Building inspectors, electricians, electrical engineers, or even officials from the Occupational Safety and Health Administration (OSHA) may be helpful in such investigations.

A cause of death that is often wrongfully categorized as suicide is autoerotic asphyxiation. *Autoerotic asphyxia* is the use of strangulation during masturbation in an attempt to enhance sexual pleasure (Garza-Leal and Landron 1991). The individual may devise a device to restrict the flow of oxygen during masturbation. Often a simple noose is used, and the subject bends at the knees to tighten the hold of the noose. Victims do not intend to cut off oxygen to the point where they fall unconscious; however, unconsciousness may occur accidentally. If consciousness is lost, the victim is unable to release the pressure, and death may occur. In such cases, it is important to look for physical evidence to support the theory of accidental death, such as pornographic materials or diaries describing the person's fascination with asphyxia.

Testimonial evidence may be important if a witness was present at the accident. Otherwise, it is important to interview those close to the victim to rule out suicide as the manner of death.

Homicide

Many causes of death that can result from suicides or accidental death can also be a means to commit murder. A gunshot wound may be self-inflicted or inflicted by someone else. In many cases, the involvement of another person is apparent due to the absence of a firearm at the crime scene. In other cases, the wound may be examined to determine the distance the shot was taken from. The presence or absence of soot emitted from the firearm's barrel can indicate whether the shot was from close range or from a distance. If a bullet is recovered from the victim's body or from the scene (if the bullet exited the body), it can be compared to firearms belonging to the victim or those recovered from possible suspects to determine if a match exists. Finally, an examination of how bloodstains lodged on the victim, or on a possible suspect, may indicate whether a gunshot death was homicidal or suicidal.

Ammunition shell casings recovered at the crime scene can be compared to firearms belonging to potential suspects.

Investigations involving direct-contact injuries involving a weapon (such as a club or knife) can be investigated in a similar fashion as gunshot injuries. If a weapon is recovered, the medical examiner may be able to offer an opinion about the likelihood that that particular instrument is consistent with the victim's injuries. The weapon is also examined for trace evidence, including blood, hair, fibers, or tissue that matches that of the victim. Some investigators are trained in "blood-spatter interpretation" techniques. By examining the shape of droplets of blood, these investigators may be able to discern the sequence of blows, the number of offenders, and the positioning of the victim and suspect during the assault. Blood-spatter interpretation is also helpful in fire-arm investigations.

CASE STUDY

On March 29, 2000, Sandra Duyst was found dead in her home. Duyst had been killed by two gunshot wounds to her head. Her husband advised the police that she had been severely depressed and had committed suicide. Further investigation of blood spatter patterns revealed that the death was a homicide. Duyst had also hidden a note within her residence that advised that she would never commit suicide and, if her body was found, her husband should be suspected. The husband, David Duyst, was later convicted of first-degree murder (Michigan Domestic Violence Prevention & Treatment Board 2000).

Strangulation may cause death without the use of a weapon, so a match is more unlikely. If the suspect is apprehended quickly, it may be possible to recover trace evidence from the victim through scrapings of the suspect's fingernail beds. Obtaining fingerprints from the victim's skin through the use of chemical processes is not impossible; however, it is quite difficult.

Poisoning investigations rely heavily upon medical records and the toxicology tests performed after autopsy. Depending upon the substance used, the death may be immediate, or illness may develop over time leading to the fatality. If the victim made repeated trips to the doctor or emergency room with complaints of illness, the findings of medical personnel may be important in the investigation.

Infant Death

The investigation of the death of an infant may be handled similarly to the death of any other individual; however, certain causes of death are unique to babies. It is not uncommon for a parent to find an infant deceased in his crib after a nap with no outward signs of injury. In such cases, the medical examiner may find the cause of death to be *sudden infant death syndrome* (SIDS). Medical officials do not know the exact cause of SIDS; however, some studies have suggested that positioning a baby on his back during sleep may help lessen the chance for SIDS (NIH 2007). A SIDS death is classified as accidental.

Shaken baby syndrome (SBS) is a form of child abuse that causes internal injuries that may not be readily apparent to investigators. A parent may shake a baby out of anger or frustration. An autopsy will reveal the effects of SBS, including trauma to the brain. The manner of an SBS death is classified as homicide. Of all infants who initially survive SBS and are treated, 25–30 percent eventually die (California Department of Social Services n.d.).

A child may suffer serious injury that eventually leads to death due to repeated abuse on the part of a parent. This type of abuse may be due to the mental condition *Munchausen by proxy* (MBP). MBP is "a form of child abuse in which a parent, nearly always a mother, over-reports symptoms or illness or cause unnecessary medical procedures to be performed on the child" (State of Michigan Governor's Task Force on Children's Justice 2007, 1). The injuries inflicted can range from physical abuse to poisoning of the child. Hospital personnel may be trained in recognizing a case of MBP. In other cases, where signs of abuse are discovered during autopsy, the investigators may review the medical records of the child to demonstrate a pattern of injury and illness.

Serial Murder

A serial killer is generally defined as a person who kills three or more people in a certain period of time. Serial killings are much rarer than individual murders; however, a string of killings can panic citizens, who fear the random nature of such offenses.

Serial murders are investigated through means that are similar to those used in other death investigations. In addition to standard procedures, investigators examining apparent serial killings may employ the services of a criminal investigative analyst. In the past, criminal investigative analysts were referred to as "profilers." This term was changed, because a profile of a suspect's likely characteristics is only one portion of the analysis (FBI 1990). In cases that lack direction, an analyst can give an educated opinion about leads to pursue. Included in these leads are characteristics of offenders who have committed similar offenses in the past. These characteristics are based upon careful scientific studies of prior offenses, including interviews of the criminals themselves and a close examination of the physical appearance of a crime scene.

Serial murderers have been categorized into two broad categories: organized offenders and disorganized offenders. An analysis of the offense and the crime scene evidence reveals that *organized offenders* are more likely to "plan, use restraints, commit sexual acts with live victims, show or display control of [the] victim...and use a vehicle" (Ressler, Burgess, Douglas, Hartman, and D'Agostino 1986, 66). *Disorganized offenders,* on the other hand, are likely to "leave a weapon at the scene, position [the] dead body, perform sexual acts on the [the] dead body, keep [the] dead body, try to depersonalize the body, and not use a vehicle" (Ressler et al., 66). If an analysis of the crime and scene reveals a likely organized offender, the probable characteristics of that individual are that he is "intelligent, skilled in [an] occupation, likely to think out an plan the crime...be angry and depressed at the time of the murder...have a precipitating stress...have a car in decent condition...follow [the] crime events in [the] media, and change jobs or leave town" (Ressler et al., 70 & 73).

The typical characteristics of disorganized offenders are that they are "low birth order children, come from a home with unstable work for the father, have been treated with hostility as a child, [are] sexually inhibited and sexually ignorant...have parents with histories of sexual problems, have been frightened and confused at the time of the crime, know who the victim is, [and] live alone" (Ressler et al. 1986, 73).

After a crime and its scene have been evaluated, a trained analyst can determine the category that most closely resembles the characteristics noted. Detectives can then gear their investigation accordingly. It should be noted that criminal investigative analyses are not 100 percent accurate, so investigators should keep an open mind despite the scientific evaluation of the characteristics of a crime.

SUMMARY

Assaults may happen in connection with another crime or as a specific crime. Aggravated assaults typically involve a weapon or injury; simple assaults do not. Physical evidence, including the documentation of wounds, trace evidence, blood evidence, and weapon evidence is important in investigating assaults. Photography helps document wounds immediately after the assault for jurors to consider during later judicial proceedings. Statements from victims and witnesses help in the identification of possible suspects.

Deaths are investigated not only in murder cases but also in suicides, accidental deaths, and natural deaths. Investigators proceed after a preliminary judgment of the probable cause of death. The actual cause of death cannot be determined without the aid of a full medical autopsy. If a victim is still alive upon police arrival, efforts should be made to gain a statement if this can be done without interfering with medical interventions. Certain signs distinguish death from unconsciousness, including rigor morgis, algor mortis, livor mortis, and decomposition. Once death is confirmed, if a doctor does not sign a death certificate based upon a natural cause of death, a medical examiner will start an investigation along with police investigators.

The general time of death is an important determination in a death investigation. While an exact time usually cannot be determined, rigor mortis, livor mortis, algor mortis, insect manifestation, and an examination of stomach contents may indicate a range of time. A medical autopsy can help determine the approximate time of death and the actual cause of death. The manner of death (homicide, suicide, natural, accidental, or undetermined) is established in an autopsy and included on a death certificate.

Suicide may be committed through a variety of means, including by firearm, cutting, carbon monoxide poisoning, overdose, hanging, and jumping from a tall structure.

Accidental death may happen for methods that resemble suicide and homicide; a thorough investigation is required to rule that a death was accidental. Certain causes of death, such as electrocution and drowning, are more typically accidental than suicidal or homicidal.

Any death that occurred under suspicious circumstances should be investigated as a homicide until proven otherwise. A homicide may be indicated by the physical evidence present, including the positioning of a gun or other weapon, the appearance of wounds, and the examination of blood evidence. Strangulation death and poisoning may be indicated through autopsy and toxicology tests.

Infant deaths may occur due to circumstances that are distinct from those of adult deaths. Sudden infant death syndrome (SIDS) is an unexplained accidental mode of death that may be determined through autopsy. Shaken baby syndrome (SBS) is a form of child abuse involving the violent shaking of a child or infant that leads to internal injuries and possible death by homicide. Munchausen by proxy is a psychological disorder in parents where the child is repeatedly abused in order to gain attention for the parent from medical personnel.

Serial murder investigations may require assistance from criminal investigative analysts. Serial killers may be classified as organized offenders or disorganized offenders based upon how they have left evidence at the scene. This classification may help narrow down possible suspects during the investigation.

Key Terms

Abrasion: Injury caused by the scraping off of layers of skin

Aggravated assault: An unlawful attack by one person upon another for the purpose of inflicting severe or aggravated bodily injury

Algor mortis: The loss of body temperature after death

Assault: An unlawful attack by one person upon another

Autopsy: A medical examination of a dead body to aid in determining the cause of death

Blunt-force trauma: Injuries that result from an impact with a non-edged instrument

Contusion: Injury caused to the skin or organs by an impact, usually presented by a discoloration of tissue

Crushing wound: Irregularly shaped broken-skin injury caused by an impact near a bone

Death certificate: A legal document pronouncing the cause of an individual's death.

Defense wound: A term used to describe a variety of injuries to a victim that result from the attempted warding off of an attack

Disorganized offender: A classification of a serial killer who tends not to plan a crime and leads an unusual lifestyle by most accounts

Forensic entomology: The study of insects and how they infest a dead body that is useful in determining an approximate time of death

Homicide: The willful (nonnegligent) killing of one human being by another

Laceration: A slicing injury to the skin, usually caused by a knife or other cutting instrument

Livor mortis: The discoloration of the lowest portions of a body after death due to the settling of blood after a loss of blood pressure

Munchausen by proxy: A form of child abuse where a caregiver injures a child repeatedly due to an irrational fascination with medical attention for the child

Organized offender: A classification of a serial killer who carefully plans a murder and leads a life considered "normal" by most accounts

Recoil marks: Marks on the hand of a shooter caused by the reloading mechanism of a semi-automatic weapon

Rigor mortis: The stiffening of joints that occurs after death due to chemical changes in the body

Sexual asphyxiation: The cutting off of oxygen during sexual activity intended to enhance sexual pleasure

Shaken baby syndrome (SBS): A form of child abuse where an infant suffers internal injuries due to violent shaking

Simple assault: An unlawful attack by one person upon another "which [does] not involve the use of a firearm, knife, cutting instrument, or other dangerous weapon and in which the victim did not sustain serious or aggravated injuries" (FBI 2004, 26)

Sudden infant death syndrome (SIDS): A common yet medically unexplained cause of death in infants

Toxicology: The study of poisons

Discussion Questions

1. Why is a medical autopsy needed to determine a person's actual cause of death?

2. Why is it important for the medical examiner to conduct an examination of a dead body before police investigators?

3. What types of information are important to collect in a "victimology" examination in a case?

Exploration

1. Search through news stories to locate a homicide investigation where the time of death was an important consideration in the case.

2. Search for information about two common causes of infant death, SIDS and SBS, and read about the medical findings about the causes of each.

References

American Academy of Family Physicians. n.d. *Autopsy: Questions and answers*. Retrieved December 28, 2007, from http://familydoctor .org/online/famdocen/home/pat-advocacy/endoflife/149.html.

California Department of Social Services. n.d. *Shaken baby syndrome*. Retrieved September 24, 2007, from www.ccld.ca.gov/PG550 .htm.

Coleman, Andre. 2007. Time to kill. *Pasadena Weekly*, July 12. Retrieved December 29, 2007, from www.pasadenaweekly.com/ article.php?id=4855&IssueNum=80.

Elbert County. n.d. *Office of the coroner*. Retrieved September 22, 2007, from www.elbertcounty-co.gov/dept_coroner.php

Federal Bureau of Investigation (FBI). 1990. *Criminal investigative analysis: Sexual homicide*. Quantico, VA: Federal Bureau of Investigation, National Center for the Analysis of Violent Crime.

Federal Bureau of Investigation (FBI). 2004. *Uniform crime reporting handbook*. Clarksburg, WV: U.S. Department of Justice.

Garza-Leal, J., and F. Landron. 1991. Autoerotic asphyxia death initially interpreted as suicide and a review of the literature. *Journal of Forensic Sciences* 36, no. 6 (November): 1753–1759.

Indiana State Coroners Training Board. 2001. *Guidebook for Indiana coroners*. Romney, IN: Skelton and Marsh.

Johns, Leonard, Gerard Downes, and Camille Bibles. 2005. Resurrecting cold case serial homicide investigations. *FBI Law Enforcement Bulletin* 74, no. 8 (August): 1–6.

Michigan Domestic Violence Prevention and Treatment Board. 2001. *Michigan domestic violence and sexual violence homicides*. Lansing, Michigan: Michigan Department of Health and Human Services.

National Institutes of Health (NIH), U.S. National Library of Medicine. 2006. *Visible proofs: Forensic view of the body; medical views,* July 11. Retrieved September 22, 2007, from www.nlm.nih.gov/visibleproofs/education/medical/index.html.

National Institutes of Health (NIH), U.S. National Library of Medicine. 2007. *MedlinePlus: Sudden infant death syndrome,* October 18. Retrieved February 22, 2008, from www.nlm.nih.gov/medlineplus/suddeninfantdeathsyndrome.html.

Pima County Prosecutor's Office, Victim Witness Program. 2004. *After an assault.* Tucson, AZ: Pima County Attorney.

Ressler, Robert, Ann Burgess, John Douglas, Carol Hartman, and Ralph D'Agostino. 1986. Sexual killers and their victims. *Journal of Interpersonal Violence* 1, no. 3 (September): 61–81.

State of Alaska Epidemiology. 1993. *Bulletin: Carbon monoxide: Stay aware—stay alive,* August 10. Anchorage, AK: Johnson and Bledsoe.

State of Michigan Governor's Task Force on Children's Justice. 2007. *Munchausen by proxy: A collaborative approach to investigation, assessment, and treatment,* June. Lansing: Michigan Department of Human Services.

CHAPTER 11

MISSING, KIDNAPPED, AND UNIDENTIFIED PERSONS

CHAPTER OBJECTIVES

By the end of this chapter, the reader will be able to do the following:

- Describe common methods used in investigating missing persons cases.

- Explain information that is contained in the *National Crime Information Center's Missing Persons File*.

- Describe common methods used in investigating missing child cases.

- Explain the differences between *custodial disputes* and *parental kidnappings*.

- Describe the *AMBER Alert* program.

- List investigative resources offered by the National Center for Missing and Exploited Children.

- Describe common methods used in investigating *kidnapping* cases.

- Define the crime of *human trafficking*.

- Describe common methods used in the investigation of unidentified bodies.

Crimes such as homicide are difficult for the family or loved ones of the victims to cope with. Perhaps the only type of investigation that is more difficult to deal with is a missing person case. In these investigations, a lack of closure frustrates families, as they wonder if the missing party is endangered. Kidnapping cases are also disturbing, as the well-being of the missing person is in doubt. This chapter will further explore unidentified death investigations. In tragic instances, missing persons cases can be solved through the examination of unidentified remains (although the majority of missing persons cases are resolved by finding the party alive). Finally, mass casualty cases will be examined in this chapter. Mass casualty scenes cause significant issues with victim identification.

MISSING PERSONS

Missing persons cases may or may not involve a crime. Investigators must approach missing persons reports with the worst-case scenario in mind until this theory is proven false so that the appropriate resources are dedicated to the investigation. While most cases do not end in finding the person injured or deceased (Centrex 2005), this possibility is usually on the mind of the reporting party. Families are put at ease when they observe police taking their reports seriously. Missing persons cases may also be considered in terms of the age of the individual who is lost. In this section, adult missing persons will be explored first, followed by missing children cases.

Adults

A person may be reported as missing by an acquaintance or family member after his location has been unknown for as little as a few hours to as long as several months. Police agencies do not delay a missing person investigation based upon a time factor. If a person has disappeared, there is a chance that foul play is involved. If a person has been hurt, killed, or abducted, the passage of time hinders any investigative efforts toward helping that person or solving a crime that may be involved. While the case likely will be resolved by the person's safe return, it is erroneous to assume that this will be the outcome and suggest to a concerned party that she wait to file a police report.

The initial report should describe the circumstances of the disappearance in a detailed and accurate fashion. It is important to trace the steps of the person to provide possible clues about his whereabouts. A comprehensive description of the missing party is collected, including the clothing he was last seen wearing and any unique characteristics of the person's appearance (such as scars and tattoos). This description is broadcast on police radio channels to alert field officers so the search can begin. It is helpful to collect photographs of the person to aid investigators in their search and for possible news releases or posters.

The initial search for the individual is conducted by officers immediately upon receipt of the report. Locations that the victim frequents are checked. Even if the reporting party claims to have looked in these areas, a secondary check often results in the discovery of the person. Any checks made by field personnel are noted in reports, as these sites are important to monitor on a continual basis.

The description of the individual may be entered in the *National Crime Information Center's (NCIC) Missing Persons File*. The Missing Persons File is a nationwide computerized database used by law enforcement. The Missing Persons File can help locate an individual well outside of the original investigating jurisdiction's boundaries (Federal Bureau of Investigation 1996–1997). Missing individuals are maintained in the NCIC file if they have a physical or mental disability or are possibly in physical danger, missing from a catastrophe, possibly missing involuntarily, are under 21, or are over 21 but are missing under criteria that indicate a concern for their safety (FBI n.d.c.). In addition to physical characteristics, medical and dental records may be included in the NCIC file.

Upon receipt of the initial report, the investigator will begin with a detailed study of the missing person (referred to as "victimology"). Included in this analysis of the subject is a risk assessment profile. Based upon the circumstances involved in the case and a study of the victim's characteristics, the investigator determines whether the person is at low, medium, or high risk (Centrex 2005). For example, if the person frequently leaves town without telling anyone only to return later, her case may be classified as low-risk. Conversely, if a subject always follows a certain routine and tells family and friends where she is, the case may be considered high-risk.

In cases where the disappearance is prolonged and concerns about the person's well-being escalate, further steps are taken to prepare for the possibility that foul play may have been involved. Clothing items belonging to the missing subject may be collected to give search dogs a scent for tracking. The investigator may work with family members to collect the person's medical and dental records in case the subject is found deceased (National Center for Missing and Exploited Children 2006). It is also important to collect control samples for possible physical evidence comparison, including fingerprints and DNA sources (Centrex 2005). Fingerprints, if not on file with law enforcement or elsewhere, may be collected from the individual's residence or vehicle in latent form. DNA may be collected from sources such as combs, hairbrushes, or toothbrushes.

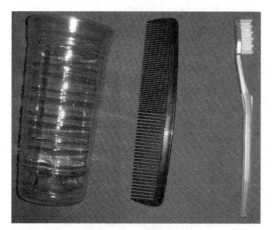

During the investigation of prolonged missing persons cases, household items that may contain biological samples are recovered for future forensic comparison to unidentified bodies.

CASE STUDY

Dru Sjodin, a 22-year-old college student, was abducted in North Dakota in November 2003. In April 2004, an unidentified body was found in Minnesota. DNA samples were collected from the body and compared to samples obtained from Sjodin's toothbrush. The body was conclusively identified as Sjodin (Timpe 2004). After a thorough investigation, a convicted sex offender was found to have abducted, assaulted, and murdered Sjodin. As a result of this case, the Dru Sjodin National Sex Offender Registry was created.

It may be helpful in missing persons cases to develop "locator" advertisements. Law enforcement can assist the family in publicizing the case. Television and print news media sources may aid in notifying the public of the disappearance. The individual's picture, along with identifying characteristics and information about his last known whereabouts, can be published in poster or flier format and distributed throughout the community. Billboards with this information have also been known to be beneficial. Some families have sought assistance from the public through the Internet. Whatever approach is utilized, a telephone number should be provided for the reporting of tips.

Locator posters and advertisements can be helpful in finding missing persons.

Sightings are investigated by evaluating the veracity of the lead and proceeding accordingly. The party collecting information from the tipster should collect as much information about the location of the sighting and the description of the person sighted as possible. If the sighting is several days old and the individual is likely no longer present, it may be helpful to post fliers in that area to see if further sightings happen. Investigators may also check for video surveillance if the sighting was at a place that has security systems in place. If the sighting is a significant distance from the original investigating jurisdiction, it is common for investigators to work with other agencies in outside jurisdictions to check on possible leads.

Missing adults raise concern in family members and friends; however, some individuals choose to withdraw from their lives and move somewhere new without telling others of their plans. A person may be fleeing an abusive relationship, leaving town due to debts owed to others, or simply starting life fresh in a new area. The job of law enforcement is to locate that individual and ensure that she is safe. The person may not want her new location described to the person who filed the original police report; the police agency must respect these wishes. The police may advise the reporting party that the individual was located unharmed and the case has been closed, but nothing further.

Missing persons cases remain open or inactive until the individual is located. In some cases, the person is never located. There are many reasons for this, including the person's being killed and the body hidden or destroyed, the person's leaving the country, or the person's simply avoiding contact with law enforcement. The case is not closed unless a verified identification is made.

Children

Missing child cases are investigated in a similar fashion to cases concerning missing adults. Missing child cases are of particular concern for several reasons. Children are usually more defenseless than adults. Children may be more easily abducted. Children are potential targets for sex offenders, or they can be subjected to parental kidnapping. While adults can choose to be missing from friends and family, children cannot legally make the same choice. These characteristics of missing child cases require some additional investigative approaches.

When a missing child is reported, the search begins immediately. A description of the child is obtained and broadcast to officers within the jurisdiction and to agencies surrounding the area. Typically, the child's home is searched first. While the parent or guardian may report that she has searched the house completely, it is not uncommon to find the child asleep or hiding in a closet or basement. Officers will check with nearby friends to see if the child is at someone's house and forgot to report home or if the friends have any information regarding the child's whereabouts (NCMEC 2006).

In some cases, the child has left indications or has shown signs that his intention is to run away. Runaway juveniles are at a high risk for becoming victims of sexual assault, violence, or other crimes. Because of this fact, every effort must be extended toward finding the child. The use of family members and friends to search for the child is encouraged. Photographs may be obtained and released to the media in an effort to locate the child.

One of the first places investigators check during a missing child investigation is the child's room; often there are many places to hide.

If there is a shared custody of the child between two parents, the case may involve a custodial dispute or a parental kidnapping. *Custodial disputes* arise when the custodial parent is not clearly legally determined. A dispute may also result from a difference of opinion regarding the language of legal documents establishing custody of the child. Custodial disputes must be sorted out based upon the circumstances and may require interpretation from a prosecuting attorney, civil lawyers, or a judge.

Parental kidnapping cases result from clear violations of legal custody determinations. Investigators must rule out that the child has not been abducted or run away prior to assuming that the noncustodial parent has taken the child. If it is verified that the child is with the noncustodial parent against court orders, the investigator will collect legal documents pertaining to the custody agreement and submit the case through the prosecuting attorney (NCMEC 2006). A warrant may be issued for the violating parent, and an attempt will be made to locate the subject and the child. Investigators may utilize law enforcement databases, civil records, mail records, and cell phone records in an effort to find the wanted parent.

CASE STUDY

In February of 2007, a 38-year-old Utah man fled the country with his two children against court orders. The man's visitation with his children had been restricted due to claims of domestic abuse. When suspicions arose that the man might have left the United States, the Federal Bureau of Investigation became involved.

FBI agents and members of Immigration and Customs Enforcement (ICE) tracked the suspect's passport records from Los Angeles to Australia. A witness advised law enforcement that the man intended to fly to his home country of Macedonia. The man was apprehended during a layover in Vienna, Austria, with his two children. The man was charged with international parental kidnapping (Rydalch 2007).

In any missing child case, the juvenile is immediately entered in the National Crime Information Center (NCIC) database. This database is accessible by law enforcement nationwide. The disappearance of the child may also be publicized through the use of the *AMBER Alert* Program, established nationwide by Congress through the PRO-TECT Act in 1993. An AMBER Alert is a cooperative effort between law enforcement and the media in publicizing a suspected child abduction as quickly as possible (Allender 2007). The rapid issuance of an AMBER Alert is a key component of the program, because the longer a child is missing, the more likely she may come to harm.

Law enforcement agencies can receive assistance in missing children investigations from the National Center for Missing and Exploited Children. This federally funded organization can provide the following services to police departments: training for police personnel, an analysis of the case, forensic assistance

AMBER Alerts are distributed through media outlets, Internet sources, and even highway information signs.

(including age-progression pictures), advocacy for families, assistance with travel to reunite families, a missing children hotline (800-THE-LOST), assistance with international abduction cases, nationwide distribution of locator posters, and direct manpower assistance with investigations through the "Team Adam" program (NCMEC n.d.).

KIDNAPPING

Kidnapping involves the taking and carrying away of a person against his will or unlawfully restricting his liberties. Kidnapping may occur for a variety of reasons. A person may be kidnapped and held for a cash ransom. An individual may be held for political reasons. Sexual offenders have been known to hold victims against their will after the commission of the crime. In other cases, an individual may hold people hostage during the commission of a crime, such as a bank robbery.

A kidnapping offense may not be discovered until the offender gives notice that he is holding the victim captive. Until that point, the case may be considered a missing person investigation. The notification is often made via a written document or by telephone. Both methods of communication offer a chance to examine physical evidence. Documents may provide sources for fingerprint examination or writing comparison to possible suspects. A telephone may be traced or provide audio evidence for voice comparison.

A local police agency usually is involved in a kidnapping investigation first. The Federal Bureau of Investigation has authorization to investigate kidnapping cases based upon congressional mandate. Federal involvement in kidnapping investigations has its origins with a famous case from the early 20th century.

CASE STUDY

On March 1, 1932, the infant son of famous aviator Charles Lindbergh was kidnapped from his nursery in New Jersey. A ransom note was left demanding $50,000. Local police responded to the call and requested the assistance of the New Jersey State Police. Little physical evidence of value was left at the scene of the crime. Three additional ransom notes were sent to the Lindberghs, increasing the demand to $70,000.

A retired Bronx, New York, school principal offered to act an intermediary for the Lindberghs with the kidnappers. The money was raised, and the intermediary received a series of phone calls and notes arranging to transfer the ransom payment. The kidnappers delivered the baby's sleeping clothes to the intermediary as a sign that they were the true suspects. Eventually, a reduced ransom of $50,000 was delivered to an unknown subject, who related that the baby could be found near Martha's Vineyard, Massachusetts. A search was conducted, but the child was not found. Slightly over two months after the child had been kidnapped, the Lindberghs's baby was found deceased approximately 4.5 miles from their home.

During the kidnapping, President Herbert Hoover directed the FBI to assist the New Jersey State Police in the investigation. The FBI served only as a support organization until May of 1932, when the president advised all federal agencies to use all resources at their disposal to solve the kidnapping.

The investigation focused upon tracking the ransom money, which had been paid in gold certificates. The serial numbers from the certificates had been recorded prior to the payoff. A gas station attendant discovered one of the certificates after it was passed from a customer. A license plate from the customer was tracked to Bruno Hauptman of the Bronx, New York. Subsequent examinations of Hauptman's handwriting found similarities to writing on the ransom notes. Hauptman was arrested, tried, convicted, and executed for the kidnapping of the Lindbergh infant (FBI, n.d.).

As a result of the Lindbergh case, Congress passed legislation authorizing the FBI to investigate any kidnapping case of a child under 12.

A quick response is needed in a kidnapping investigation, as the victim is at great risk. Descriptions of the victim and the suspect, if known, are distributed immediately. If a child is involved, an AMBER Alert is broadcast. Physical evidence examination is given priority with the hopes of identifying a suspect through fingerprints or other means. If a telephone was used to deliver demands, an attempt will be made to track the suspect's movements.

The possibility that the kidnapping may be sexually motivated is considered. Sex offender registries can be examined to identify any previously convicted individuals living in the area (NCMEC 2006). Every state in the United States requires sex offenders to register with the police. Investigators may attempt to check the homes of listed offenders, either eliminating them as suspects or perhaps locating the victim or evidence.

Kidnapping cases may develop into a process of negotiating for the exchange of the victim for a ransom or other demand. Intermediaries are no longer used as they were in the Lindbergh case; trained law enforcement officers are preferred. It is suggested that crisis negotiators be utilized to attempt to recover the victim.

Human Trafficking

Human trafficking is a particular type of prolonged kidnapping, where the victim becomes indebted to someone (or has a perceived, but not actual, indebtedness). Human trafficking is often an international issue, where immigrants from other countries are brought to the United States and promised a new life (Bales and Lize 2007). The victims are charged a "fee" for entry into the country, and they are often forced to work off the fee. Usually the work is illegal; common examples are prostitution or drug transportation. The victims often feel helpless to seek law enforcement assistance because they know they are committing illegal acts. Specifically trained victim advocates can be helpful in overcoming victims' resistance to cooperation with law enforcement.

UNIDENTIFIED BODIES

Death investigations, explored in chapter 10, are complicated when the identity of the victim cannot be established. Interviews of associates and family members cannot be conducted to attempt to determine how the death occurred. In fact, one of the most troubling aspects of unidentified bodies is that the family cannot be notified of the death. On average, over 4,000 bodies are found each year that cannot be identified (Hickman, Hughes, Strom, and Ropero-Miller 2007, 5). Of these cases, approximately 1,000 remain unidentified after one year.

Attempts to identify unknown bodies are made through a variety of means. If the unidentified body possesses characteristics similar to those of a missing person, it may be possible to have family members of missing persons view photos of the subject. Fingerprint comparison is possible if the hands of the body are not damaged. If the body is suspected to be that of a certain person but attempts to identify the subject visually are thwarted by excessive decomposition or other bodily damage, investigators may work with a medical examiner to compare the remains to the known missing person.

One method used to identify remains is the comparison of the body's teeth to known dental records. A forensic dentist, or odontologist, can perform this comparison and determine if a match exists. Forensic odontologists typically do not work for the medical examiner or coroner's office but are dental professionals trained in the field by the American Board of Forensic Odontology (National Institute of Justice 2004). The ability to determine a match depends upon the condition of the remains and the quality of the dental records. The condition of the teeth can also provide clues for estimating the victim's age and socioeconomic group. Unidentified remains with quality dental characteristics can be uploaded into the Federal Bureau of Investigation's National Dental Image Repository for comparison to dental records of missing persons (FBI 2007).

When decomposition has reduced the body to bones, certain determinations can be made from the remains. A forensic anthropologist can first determine whether the bones are human or animal. The recovery of DNA may be possible, depending upon the condition of the bones. Depending upon the number of bones located and their condition, an anthropologist can also determine the sex of the individual, an approximate age and height, and perhaps an opinion about the cause of death. Bone remains can also contribute to facial reconstruction, molds, and sketches by forensic artists.

Forensic artistry is the process of evaluating human skull remains to reconstruct the predeath features of the individual to aid in identification. Forensic artists can also modify images as an investigative aid (e.g., age progression pictures) and create demonstration pieces for evidence in court (Michigan State Police n.d.). Agencies are now publishing forensic sketches or photos of unidentified victims on the Internet in hopes of generating leads (Heinecke 2007).

If all efforts fail at identifying the victim, information about the victim can be entered into two criminal justice databases and cross-referenced. The National Crime Information Center (NCIC) Un-identified Persons File is accessible by law enforcement professionals nationwide. If the victim appears to have died due to a violent act, investigative information may also be entered into the FBI's Violent Crime Apprehension Program (VICAP). VICAP works to "combine investigative and operational support functions, research, and training in order to provide assistance, without charge, to federal, state, local, and foreign law enforcement agencies investigating unusual or repetitive violent crimes" (FBI n.d.b.). The information is analyzed and checked against existing crimes throughout the world.

The most difficult death investigations that involve unidentified bodies are mass casualty incidents. Aircraft disasters, collapsed buildings, tornados, floods, hurricanes, and large-scale terrorist events present significant difficulties to investigating officials. A crime scene is processed with large teams of individuals who carefully document the location of evidence and remains, typically spread over large areas. A processing area is set up for medical specialists to evaluate bodily tissues in an effort to identify individuals through any of the variety of methods previously mentioned. The evidence at the scene can be graphic and disturbing; it is advisable to keep trained psychologists on the scene to aid the rescue workers.

SUMMARY

Individuals may become missing due to personal choice or involvement as a crime victim. The investigation of a missing person should not be delayed due to time factors, as each passing minute may be important to coming to the missing individual's aid. A detailed report and description are required to start a missing person investigation. Descriptions may be entered in the NCIC Missing Persons File to help find the individual nationwide. A study of the circumstances of the case may determine whether or not foul play is suspected. Physical evidence, such as DNA and fingerprints, is important to collect to compare to individuals or unidentified bodies. Publicity may help locate the missing individual. If a missing person is located but advises that he is missing by choice, the reporting party should only be told that the individual was located in a safe condition.

Missing children are investigated similarly but with the understanding that they are more defenseless than adults and are thus more prone to danger. An immediate search is conducted in areas the child frequents (even if these areas have reportedly already been checked). Parental kidnapping and custodial dispute cases may require the review of an attorney as part of the investigation. An AMBER Alert is a cooperative effort between the media and law enforcement to publicize missing children cases quickly. Investigative resources are available from the National Center for Missing and Exploited Children in missing children cases.

Kidnapping may occur for ransom, political, sexual, or hostage motivations. The method the suspect uses to communicate in a kidnapping case often becomes a central component of the investigation. According to congressional mandate, the FBI may assist in kidnapping investigations. Known sex offenders may be questioned in kidnapping investigations due to the possible link between the two crimes.

Human trafficking is a particular type of kidnapping where a person is made to pay a debt through forced servitude.

When a body is discovered and its identity is unknown, various steps may be taken to identify it. Physical evidence may offer DNA or fingerprint samples for comparison to missing individuals. Family members may be able to view photos of the body to determine if it is that of their loved one. Forensic odontology, or the study of the teeth in the body, may offer the ability to compare dental records to the actual teeth in the skull of the body. Forensic artistry allows a reconstruction of facial features based upon the skull shape.

Key Terms

AMBER Alert: A cooperative effort between media outlets and law enforcement to publicize the disappearance of a child quickly

Custodial dispute: Different interpretations of a judicially determined custody plan between parents that may require investigation

Human trafficking: A form of kidnapping that involves requiring an individual to repay a debt of some type through forced servitude

Kidnapping: The taking and carrying away of a person against her will or unlawfully restricting a person's liberties

National Crime Information Center (NCIC) Missing Persons File: A computerized database containing physical characteristic information of missing individuals

Parental kidnapping: The deliberate retention of a child by a parent who is allowed temporary custody of a child outside of the parameters of the judicially determined custody plan; the taking of a child out of a jurisdiction in violation of a judicially determined custody plan

Discussion Questions

1. What factors make a missing persons case more difficult to investigate than other types of crimes?

2. What locations do you believe are important to search for a missing child?

3. Why are victims reluctant to cooperate with law enforcement in human trafficking cases? What steps can be taken to overcome this resistance?

Exploration

1. Explore the AMBER Alert website: *www.amberalert.gov*. Examine successful cases to see how the program aids victims and law enforcement.

2. View the website for the Doe Network, an online listing of missing adults: *www.doenetwork.org*. Examine the cases and the difficulties presented in solving them.

References

Allender, David. 2007. Child abductions: nightmares in progress. *FBI Law Enforcement Bulletin* 76, no. 7 (July): 1–7.

Bales, Kevin, and Steven Lize. 2007. Investigating Human Trafficking. *FBI Law Enforcement Bulletin* 76, no. 4 (April): 24–32.

Centrex. 2005. *Guidance on the management, recording, and investigation of missing persons.* Bramshill, England: Centrex.

Federal Bureau of Investigation (FBI). n.d.a. *Famous cases: The Lindbergh kidnapping.* Retrieved September 28, 2007 from www.fbi.gov/libref/historic/famcases/lindber/lindbernew.htm.

Federal Bureau of Investigation (FBI). n.d.b. *Investigative Programs Critical Incident Response Group: National Center for the Analysis of Violent Crime.* Retrieved September 28, 2007, from www.fbi.gov/hq/isd/cirg/ncavc.htm.

Federal Bureau of Investigation (FBI). n.d.c. *NCIC missing person and unidentified person statistics for 2006.* Retrieved September 27, 2007, from www.fbi.gov/hq/cjisd/missingpersons.htm.

Federal Bureau of Investigation (FBI). 1996–1997. National Crime Information Center: 30 years on the beat. *The Investigator,* December–January. Retrieved September 27, 2007, from http://permanent.access.gpo.gov/lps3213/ncicinv.htm.

Federal Bureau of Investigation (FBI). 2007. Technology update: National Dental Image Repository. *FBI Law Enforcement Bulletin* 76, no. 2 (February): 21.

Heinecke, Jeannine. 2007. Identifying the unknown. *Law Enforcement Technology* 34, no. 8 (August): 46–53.

Hickman, Matthew, Kristen Hughes, Kevin Strom, and Jeri Ropero-Miller. 2007. *Medical examiners and coroners' offices, 2004,* June. Washington, DC: Bureau of Justice Statistics.

Michigan State Police. n.d. *Forensic art 101.* Retrieved September 29, 2007, from www.michigan.gov/msp/0,1607,7-123-1589_3493_22454-59999--,00.html.

National Center for Missing and Exploited Children (NCMEC). n.d. *Assistance with missing children cases.* Retrieved September 28, 2007, from www.missingkids.com/missingkids/servlet/PageServlet?LanguageCountry=en_US&PageId=3283.

National Center for Missing and Exploited Children (NCMEC). 2006. *Missing and abducted children: A law-enforcement guide to case investigation and program management.* Alexandria, VA.

National Institute of Justice (NIJ). 2004. *Education and training in forensic science: A guide for forensic science laboratories, educational institutions, and students,* June. Washington, DC.

Rydalch, Melodie. 2007. *Press release: Arrest made in international parental kidnapping case; Children to be returned to Utah,* March 9. Salt Lake City, UT: U.S. Department of Justice.

Timpe, Brenden. 2004. A bittersweet ending. *The Dakota Student,* April 20. Retrieved January 3, 2008, from www.dakotastudent.com/home/index.cfm?event=displayArticlePrinterFriendly&uStory_id=a554d078-30f1-4196-87a3-7a84f41115e2.

CHAPTER 12

SEX OFFENSES, CHILD ABUSE, AND DOMESTIC VIOLENCE

CHAPTER OBJECTIVES

By the end of this chapter, the reader will be able to do the following:

- List and define the various types of sex crimes.

- Describe common methods used in the investigation of *forcible rape* and other sex crimes.

- Explain how physical evidence is collected in sex offense cases.

- Describe methods used to investigate serial rape.

- Describe methods used to investigate *acquaintance rape.*

- List common narcotics used in drug-facilitated rape.

- Describe methods used to investigate child abuse crimes.

- Explain the forensic interview process used with child crime victims.

- Define *domestic violence.*

- Describe methods used to investigate domestic violence, including steps taken to overcome victim resistance to cooperation.

- Describe methods used to investigate stalking.

Sex offenses, child abuse, and domestic violence cases are crimes against persons that are of particular concern to law enforcement. Sex offenders tend to repeat their offenses more than people who have been jailed for other crimes. Sex crimes and child abuse cases often involve victims who do not have the capability to defend themselves. Domestic violence incidents tend to become repetitive, and the situation can degrade further over time until the victim may be seriously injured or killed. Intervention in each of these types of cases can help victims whom society views as essential to protect.

SEX OFFENSES

A variety of crimes falls under the category of sex offenses. *Forcible rape* is defined as "the carnal knowledge (the slightest penetration of the female [vagina] by the male [penis]) of a female forcibly and against her will" (Federal Bureau of Investigation 2004, 19).

Forcible sodomy involves the forced contact of the genitalia between the victim and the suspect, including oral and anal sex. *Sexual assault* is any sexual contact without the consent of the victim. Child sex crimes are addressed later in the chapter as a form of child abuse. Other sex crimes include *voyeurism* (unlawfully viewing another while they are unclothed) and *exhibitionism* (exposing oneself to others).

Sex-related crimes receive significant attention from law enforcement for several reasons. The victims of such crimes are often preyed upon because the suspect sees them as vulnerable. Women and children are the typical targets of sex offenders. Citizens and criminal justice investigators alike see a need to protect this population from victimization. Another reason for a heightened investigative interest is that sexual offenders have shown a tendency to repeat their crimes despite efforts to punish or treat them to deter them from this behavior. Sex offenders have been found to be four times more likely to commit another sex crime than non–sex offenders (Langan, Schmitt, and Durose 2003, 1). Child molesters are even more likely to recommit. Police agencies devote substantial resources toward investigating sex crimes to address these issues.

Forcible Rape

Criminal investigators face sizeable challenges in the investigation of rape. Victims are often embarrassed about the event, and they may be reluctant to report the crime and proceed through the difficult steps involved with investigation and prosecution. The story may be difficult to relate to a stranger (the investigator); graphic details are required for a proper statement. In some cases, the question of consent arises and a testimonial evidence dispute develops about whether or not force was involved. These issues are constant challenges as the case proceeds.

Interviewing the victim is the first hurdle to overcome. The victim goes through many feelings as a result of the horrific experience, including a loss of self-worth, helplessness, a sense of blame against themselves, fear, embarrassment and rage. Rape victims are often hesitant to report the offense to the police. According to one study, only 16 percent of victims report the crime. Reasons for not reporting a rape include "not wanting others to know about the rape, fear of retaliation, perception of insufficient evidence, uncertainty about how to report, and uncertainty about whether a crime was committed or whether harm was intended" (Kilpatrick, Resnick, Ruggiero, Conoscenti, and McCauley 2007, 2).

To ensure that the victim is treated with compassion, the investigator may be carefully selected. An investigator should be able to be nonjudgmental during the interview to allow the victim to discuss the incident freely. Victims may be from a variety of socioeconomic backgrounds, so the investigator must be prepared to relate well to individuals from different walks of life. The quality of the interviewer should be the most important determinant in the selection of the investigator; however, consideration may be given toward selecting a female interviewer if this makes the victim more comfortable. Trained victim advocates can also overcome hesitancy barriers. Once the victim is able to relate freely what occurred, it is vital that every detail of the crime (no matter how graphic) is recorded in the statement.

Physical evidence is extremely important in a rape investigation. A primary type of physical evidence in rape investigations is DNA material, typically in the form of semen or blood. These biological materials may be recovered from the crime scene from bedding or other fabric near where the offense occurred. The victim is asked to provide the investigators with the clothing she had on during the offense (changing clothes if necessary), as this may provide samples for comparison. *Ultraviolet (U/V) lighting* is often used to help locate biological stains at a crime scene, because it makes stains appear more readily. A search for biological evidence should be conducted even if it appears that the suspect has attempted to thwart the transfer of DNA through the use of a condom. Often the suspect carelessly discards a condom near the crime scene; this is important evidence to collect.

An ultraviolet (UV) light may help reveal physical evidence at a sexual assault crime scene.

CASE STUDY

In November 1998, a man broke into a female U.S. Navy petty officer's quarters and brutally attacked and raped her. Although the assailant wore a ski mask, the victim thought she recognized him. A condom was left on the floor of her room after the suspect fled. The condom was collected and subjected to DNA testing. A match was made to the man the victim identified: a mess management specialist also in the Navy who claimed that it was a case of mistaken identity. The man was convicted of rape (*United States v. Allison* 2006).

Other types of trace evidence, such as fibers and hair, may be important pieces of a rape investigation. Ultraviolet lighting may help locate this type of evidence. Also, *oblique lighting,* or holding a light at an angle to a surface, often makes this type of trace evidence more apparent to the naked eye. Investigators may also utilize a hinge lift (a large, sticky pad) or forensic vacuum to search for trace evidence. Even the smallest of fibers may tie a suspect to a crime scene.

The victim's body actually serves as one of the most significant sources of physical evidence. For many of the same reasons that testimonial evidence is difficult in rape investigations, physical evidence may be hindered due to the victim's uncertainty in reporting the incident. Delays in reporting can lead to a deterioration of trace evidence that was transferred to the victim during the incident. The victim may shower and clean herself due to feelings of embarrassment and of being violated. While this action is understandable, it also serves to destroy physical evidence that could help identify an offender.

The collection of physical evidence from a victim's body is facilitated through the use of medical personnel because of the sensitive nature of such examinations. Specially trained doctors and nurses are often utilized to conduct the forensic examination and collection of evidence. *Sexual Assault Nurse Examiners,* or SANE nurses, are trained not only in the collection of physical evidence but also in how to help the victim through the psychological trauma associated with rape (Yost and Burke 2006). Medical personnel use a standardized *sexual assault kit* to collect urine samples, vaginal swabs, and hair samples from the victim's body. The victim is also tested for sexually transmitted diseases during the examination.

Photography documents any injuries the victim may have sustained in the assault. In cases where the suspect claims that the victim consented to intercourse, injuries can prove that consent was not given. Bruising or lacerations are common and can be documented through close-up photos. Internal injuries may also occur and may be documented in medical reports after an examination. These medical reports become part of the investigative case file.

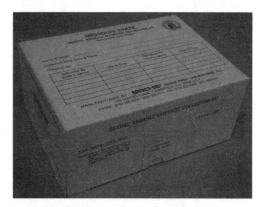

A standardized sexual assault evidence kit is utilized by medical personnel to collect evidence from a victim.

If a suspect is apprehended soon after a rape offense, it is also possible to collect physical evidence from his body to compare to that from the victim. A sexual assault kit may be collected from the suspect, including swabs of his genitals for biological evidence. Combings of the suspect's pubic hair area may reveal trace evidence matching the victim. The arrested party may also have injuries that were inflicted by the victim's attempts to defend herself. These injuries are documented through photography. DNA samples may be collected through a blood draw performed by medical personnel. A swab of a subject's mouth for skin cells, known as a *buccal swab,* may also be used to collect DNA samples.

The interrogation of a rape suspect may reveal facts about the case without, or in conjunction with, physical evidence. Common defenses that individuals offer to a rape accusation are denying any involvement, claiming that their identity has been mistaken, or claiming that the sexual contact was consensual. A denial of being involved with the victim or a claim of mistaken identity may conflict with physical evidence that proves otherwise. Suspicion is raised if physical evidence collected from the victim matches the suspect or vice versa. Consent disputes may be called into question if injuries are present on the victim, indicating that a struggle occurred.

Just as with other types of criminal investigations, the detective must keep an open mind when investigating rape cases. Studies regarding false allegations of rape vary widely, with some indicating that as many as 85 percent of reports are false while others claiming that only 9 percent are not founded (Hinojosa 2003, 70). No matter what the true figure, it is possible that the veracity of the complaint is questionable. Investigators must remain mindful that their goal is to collect facts for presentation to a prosecuting attorney, while still ensuring that victims are approached with concern and compassion and given appropriate assistance.

Serial Rape

Criminal intelligence efforts may be able to identify serial rapists operating in a certain area. Rapists often base their methods upon past successful crimes. The suspect may develop a modus operandi, selecting victims that fit a certain profile. It may be possible to determine what area the rapist is targeting and employ tactical surveillance to catch him loitering or peeping into windows. If a case lacks any leads, DNA profiles from physical evidence can be entered into the Federal Bureau of Investigation's Combined DNA Index System (CODIS) for comparison to known sex offenders (FBI n.d.). If no match is found, the profile may be kept on file for comparison to future offenses or new offenders added to the system.

CASE STUDY

Police in Cape Girardeau, Missouri, were unable to solve a violent rape and sodomy case that occurred in 2001. The investigation was abandoned due to a lack of leads. A DNA profile was developed from physical evidence and was eventually entered into the CODIS database.

Five years later, an individual incarcerated for an unrelated robbery charge was found to be a match to the evidence sample through the CODIS system. The match was made possible by a Missouri law that required all felony offenders to surrender a DNA sample for entry into CODIS (Crowell 2006).

Acquaintance Rape

In certain instances, the victim may know who the suspect in a rape is. *Acquaintance rape* is the term used to describe a rape where the victim and the suspect know each other but the suspect has not obtained consent from the victim for sexual activity. This term is preferred over "date rape," as it describes the relationship rather than a situation. The mere existence of a relationship does not provide automatic consent for sexual contact, making forcible rape possible even among married couples.

Acquaintance rape is often facilitated through the use of drugs to reduce the victim's resistance. Studies have indicated that over 3 million women have been raped after the suspect used drugs to overcome the victim's opposition (Kilpatrick et al. 2007, 2). The substance may range from legal alcoholic beverages to dangerous controlled narcotics. Marijuana, cocaine, and amphetamines are common illegal drugs used to facilitate rape. Rohypnol (flunitrazepam) and GHB (gamma hydroxybutyrate) are two colorless, odorless drugs that can easily be added to a beverage (National Institute of Drug Abuse 2006). These drugs cause unconsciousness and can lead to coma and death. Another common incapacitating drug is ketamine, an animal tranquilizer that is often stolen from veterinarian offices (Drug Enforcement Administration n.d.). In addition to standard physical evidence collection procedures, a toxicology test of the victim's blood or urine should be performed to check for these substances in a drug-facilitated rape.

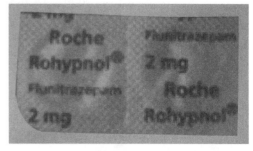

Drugs such as Rohypnol are used to reduce a victim's resistance in acquaintance rape.

Sex Offenses

Other types of sex offenses are investigated in a fashion similar to rape cases with regard to physical and testimonial evidence. Sexual assault victims may carry similar physical evidence, including biological evidence and injuries. Voyeurism investigations often rely upon an analysis of geographic and time patterns of incidents and surveillance in an attempt to catch the offender. Exhibitionist cases may also be handled through surveillance or rapid response to victim complaints.

Child Abuse

Child abuse encompasses a variety of crimes against children, ranging from sex-related crimes to assault. Law enforcement takes a special interest in the protection of children from abuse by caregivers, relatives, or strangers due to the fact that children often are more vulnerable than adults. Crimes against children may be investigated in a similar fashion as adult-involved crimes with some supplemental steps.

Each state regulates the age at which at which a person can consent to sexual activity. An individual cannot claim that a juvenile under a certain age consented to intercourse or any other sexual activity as a defense to a crime. Sexual activity with a juvenile in these cases is often defined as "statutory rape," meaning that the activity is illegal according to state statute.

Investigations of illegal sex acts with a minor are sometimes made more difficult by the juvenile's reluctance to cooperate in the investigation. The detectives may be able to overcome this hesitation by working closely with the family and victim advocates.

Sexual activity between an adult and a minor falls under the broad category of child molestation. The suspect in such cases is often a parent or caregiver or someone else who has frequent access to the victim. Police detectives coordinate child molestation investigations with social service agencies to ensure that the safety of the child is considered. A social service agency will follow the investigation and conduct a parallel review of the circumstances to consider whether or not the child should be taken into protective custody. This decision may also be based upon the facts unearthed in the police investigation.

Testimonial evidence is collected carefully in child molestation and abuse investigations. In many cases, witnesses are not present, so the case depends upon the victim's statement. Children are extremely impressionable, and the most subtle indication of judgment on the part of the interviewer can influence the victim's account of what occurred. For this reason, forensic interviews are used to collect a child's statement. A *forensic interview* is conducted by individuals trained in methods to control verbal and nonverbal cues that can alter the victim's testimony. The interview is designed to withstand judicial scrutiny (North Carolina Division of Social Services 2002). Questions are open-ended and are phrased to avoid "leading" the victim to an answer, allowing the victim to choose the right wording to describe the incident.

Domestic Violence

"*Domestic violence* is a pattern of physically, sexually, and/or emotionally abusive behaviors used by one individual to assert power or maintain control over another in the context of an intimate or family relationship" (Department of Criminal Justice Services, Victims Services Section 2004, 3). Domestic violence may include assaults, sexual abuse, verbal abuse, threats, and stalking. The definition of a family member varies from state to state; usually it includes persons related by blood, marriage, or intimate relationships. These cases are of particular concern to law enforcement and social service workers, as violent relationships may tend to worsen, leading to progressively more harmful acts. Studies indicate that 22 percent of individuals murdered in the United States in 2002 were killed by family members (Durose et al. 2005, 1).

A significant challenge in the investigation of domestic violence is gaining cooperation from the victim. Victims may be unwilling to assist for several reasons. Some see the offense as a private and personal matter between the two parties. Others feel that the issue is not important enough to merit law enforcement involvement. A fear that the offender will punish the victim for cooperating with law enforcement may keep the case from proceeding further. The relationship between the victim and offender can hinder investigative efforts; many seek to protect the suspect despite the wrongful act (Durose et al. 2005).

Domestic violence produces problems not only for the victim but for every member of the family. Approximately two-thirds of men who abuse women were subjected to abuse or witnessed abuse as a child (Governor's Commission on Domestic and Sexual Violence 1999, i). A "cycle of violence" may be created by children witnessing continual abuse within their household. Intervention and proactive steps to end violence within families can help break this cycle.

Difficulties in gaining victim cooperation thwart law enforcement efforts to intervene. Physical evidence may indicate that an assault occurred, but without testimonial evidence, investigators are left guessing about what happened. In response to this issue, states throughout the country have implemented laws mandating arrest when probable cause exists to believe an assault has occurred. The victim is no longer required to press charges against the suspect; a law enforcement officer can pursue the case without initial victim cooperation (Lane,

Lucera, and Boba 2003). Without testimony from the victim, prosecution relies upon the careful documentation and collection of physical evidence. This approach is termed *evidence-based prosecution,* (National Advisory Committee on Violence Against Women 2005, 4) referring to physical evidence.

To overcome the victim's hesitancy to cooperate with law enforcement, agencies often utilize the skills of victim advocates. Advocates from women's shelters can give a victim options for escaping an abusive relationship. Barriers, such as worries about where the victim will live during the investigative and court processes, can be overcome through shelters and by assisting the victim with orders of protection (also known as restraining orders). Advocates can help the victim with financial assistance, day care needs, and psychological support.

Stalking

In cases where the victim has separated from the offender, domestic violence can continue through the crime of stalking.

> Stalking generally refers to harassing or threatening behavior that an individual engages in repeatedly, such as following a person, appearing at a person's home or place of business, making harassing phone calls, leaving written messages or objects, or vandalizing a person's property. (Tjaden and Thoennes 1998, 1)

Several issues complicate stalking investigations. Stalking is often a repeated series of events instead of a single occurrence. Jurisdictional boundaries may be traversed to commit stalking; the crime may include the use of email, telephone, and text messages. In most cases, it is difficult to predict when the offender will commit an act of stalking again (National Center for Victims of Crime 2004).

Victims in stalking cases are encouraged to document each instance of harassment carefully. A log of incidents can serve as notes to provide testimonial evidence to investigators. Because stalking cases often boil down to the victim's testimony versus the suspect's, any physical evidence to support the victim is helpful. If state laws allow an individual to record telephone conversations, the victim should be encouraged to record any harassing phone calls received. Video surveillance systems may be set up around the victim's residence and place of employment. Neighbors may also be encouraged to keep watch on the victim's residence to provide additional, unbiased eyewitness accounts of any harassing activity.

Telephone recording devices are helpful in collecting evidence in stalking cases.

SUMMARY

Sex offenses receive considerable attention from law enforcement because the victims are often vulnerable individuals. A challenge for investigators is gathering a statement from the victim, as recounting the story can be painful and embarrassing. Physical evidence is often important in sex offense investigations. Biological evidence, such as blood or semen, may reveal DNA profiles to match to potential suspects. This evidence may be recovered from the crime scene, the victim's clothes and body, or the suspect. Medical personnel are used to collect physical evidence from the victim's body during an examination.

Serial sex offenders may develop a traceable modus operandi. It may be possible to match physical evidence to potential suspects through the CODIS database.

When a victim is forced to have intercourse by a suspect with whom the victim has a relationship, this may be classified as an acquaintance rape. Suspects often facilitate this type of crime by giving the victim different types of narcotics.

Child abuse cases are carefully investigated due to the relative defenselessness of the victim. Juveniles cannot consent to sexual activity, so claims of consent by adult suspects are not valid. Social service agencies conduct corresponding investigations to determine the safety of the child's custodial circumstances. Testimonial evidence must be collected carefully, as children are susceptible to influence that may alter their statement about the sequence of events. Specially trained forensic interviewers can overcome these barriers.

Domestic violence cases often involve unwilling victims who fear cooperating with the police for a variety of reasons. Prosecution may be based upon physical evidence alone, so the proper documentation of statements and injuries is vital.

Key Terms

Acquaintance rape: The forcible rape of a person by someone with whom she has a relationship

Buccal swab: A swab used to collect skin cells for DNA comparison from a subject's mouth

Domestic violence: "A pattern of physically, sexually, and/or emotionally abusive behaviors used by one individual to assert power or maintain control over another in the context of an intimate or family relationship" (Victim Services Section 2004, p. 30).

Evidence-based prosecution: An approach to the prosecution of a crime that relies heavily upon physical evidence

Exhibitionism: Exposing one's naked body to another

Forcible rape: The carnal knowledge (the slightest penetration of the female [vagina] by the male [penis]) of a female forcibly and against her will

Forcible sodomy: The forced contact of genitalia between a victim and the suspect

Forensic interview: A specifically structured interview intended for use with child crime victims to avoid influencing their statements

Oblique lighting: Lighting held at an angle that helps expose trace evidence at crime scenes

Sexual assault: Any sexual contact without the consent of the victim

Sexual assault kit: A standardized kit used by medical personnel to identify and collect physical evidence in sexual assault cases

Sexual Assault Nurse Examiners (SANE): Nurses specially trained in the identification and collection of physical evidence in sex offenses

Ultraviolet lighting: An alternative lighting that helps expose trace evidence at crime scenes

Voyeurism: Unlawfully viewing another while the victim is unclothed

Discussion Questions

1. The question of whether or not a victim consented to sexual activity is often a point of contention in forcible rape trials. What steps can be taken in the investigation to prove that consent was not given?

2. Explain why it is important for law enforcement to work closely with medical professionals in the investigation of sex-related offenses.

3. What type of evidence is important to collect in domestic violence cases to overcome a lack of cooperation from the victim?

4. Why are victims hesitant to cooperate with investigators in domestic violence cases? What can be done to help the victims overcome their fears?

Exploration

1. Search the Internet for information about Sexual Assault Nurse Examiners. Examine the training requirements for this specialization.

2. Explore the U.S. Department of Justice's website for the Office of Violence Against Women. Read about the challenges and dangers associated with domestic violence: *www.ovw.usdoj.gov.*

References

Crowell, Jason. 2006. *DNA testing update: Making our communities safer/solving cold cases,* September 22. Jefferson City: Missouri State Senate.

Department of Criminal Justice Services, Victims Services Section. 2004. *An information guide for domestic violence victims in Virginia,* June. Richmond, VA: Department of Criminal Justice Services.

Drug Enforcement Administration (DEA). n.d. *Ketamine.* Retrieved October 1, 2007, from www.dea.gov/concern/ketamine_factsheet.html.

Durose, Matthew, Caroline Harlow, Patrick Langan, Mark Motivans, Ramona Rantala, and Eric Smith. 2005. *Family violence statistics,* June. Washington, DC: U.S. Department of Justice, Office of Justice Programs.

Federal Bureau of Investigation (FBI). n.d. *Brochure: Combined DNA index system.* Quantico, VA.

Federal Bureau of Investigation (FBI). 2004. *Uniform crime reporting handbook.* Clarksburg, WV: U.S. Department of Justice.

Governor's Commission on Domestic and Sexual Violence. 1999. *In-home providers: Domestic violence protocol,* June. Concord: State of New Hampshire.

Hinojosa, Juan. 2003. *House committee on criminal jurisprudence, Texas House of Representatives: Interim report 2002,* February 18. Austin: Texas House of Representatives Committee on Criminal Jurisprudence.

Kilpatrick, Dean, Heidi Resnick, Kenneth Rugiero, Lauren Conoscenti, and Jenna McCauley. 2007. *Drug-facilitated, incapacitated, and forcible rape: A national study,* July. Charleston, SD: National Crime Victims Research & Treatment Center.

Lane, Erin, Joan Lucera, and Rachel Boba. 2003. *Inter-agency response to domestic violence in a mid-size city*, June. Washington, DC: U.S. Department of Justice Office of Community-Oriented Policing Services.

Langan, Patrick, Erica Schmitt, and Matthew Durose. 2003. *Recidivism of sex offenders released from prison in 1994*, November. Washington, DC: Bureau of Justice Statistics.

National Advisory Committee on Violence Against Women. 2005. *Response to the charge*. Washington, DC: U.S. Department of Justice, Office of Violence Against Women.

National Center for Victims of Crime. 2004. *Stalking*, January. Washington, DC: U.S. Department of Justice, Office of Community-Oriented Policing Services.

National Institute of Drug Abuse. 2006. *Rohypnol and GHB*, May. Bethesda, MD.

North Carolina Division of Social Services. 2002. What is forensic interviewing? *Children's Services Practice Notes* 8, no. 1 (December): 2-8.

Tjaden, Patricia, and Nancy Thoennes. 1998. *Stalking in America: Findings from the national violence against women survey*, April. Washington, DC: U.S. Department of Justice, National Institute of Justice.

United States v. Allison. 2006. U.S. Court of Appeals for the Armed Forces: No. 05-0235. Criminal Appeal Number 200000637.

Yost, Joseph, and Tod Burke. 2006. Forensic nursing: An aid to law enforcement. *FBI Law Enforcement Bulletin* 75, no. 2 (February): 7–12.

CHAPTER 13

NARCOTICS

CHAPTER OBJECTIVES

By the end of this chapter, the reader will be able to do the following:

- Explain the difference between controlled and noncontrolled substances.

- Describe the federal schedules used to classify drugs.

- Describe the different types of commonly used illicit drugs.

- List and describe the three types of drug investigations.

- Describe procedures used in a consent to search a residence (*knock-and-talk* operation).

- Describe procedures used to collect information about illicit drug distributors.

- Describe controlled and undercover drug purchase operations.

- Explain the dangers associated with investigating illicit drug-manufacturing operations.

The investigation of the use, manufacture, and distribution of illegal narcotics involves not only the criminal laws relating to the drug trade but other crimes related to narcotics. Drug usage and criminal activity seem to be highly related. Studies indicate that approximately 67 percent of arrestees in select cities in the United States tested positive for one of five illicit drugs (Zhang 2004, 7). It is felt that through a reduction in the sale, usage, and manufacture of narcotics, other crime may be impacted as well. Narcotics investigations require a distinctive approach, as the common victim/suspect relationship does not exist. This chapter will explore customary methods involved in illicit drug investigation.

CONTROLLED SUBSTANCES

Drugs are used in society for both legitimate and illicit reasons. Drugs may be prescribed by doctors for patients with a valid, legal, medical reason to take the substances. In other instances, drugs may be illegally used, distributed, or manufactured by individuals without the authorization of a doctor. Whether or not drug possession or sale is illegal is determined by the classification of the drug in question and laws pertaining to the substance.

Many substances can be described as drugs. To alleviate confusion over whether or not a particular substance is illegal for certain persons to possess or sell, the Controlled Substances Act was created. Under this law, the U.S. Drug Enforcement Administration and Department of Health and Human Services can classify drugs in five categories. Any drug placed into these schedules is considered a "controlled substance" and is regulated by law. Whether a substance is placed into a schedule depends upon "the substance's medical use, potential for abuse, and safety or dependence liability" (Drug Enforcement Administration 2005a). Of the five categories, Schedule I–controlled substances may be the most concerning. These drugs have a high potential for abuse and no accepted, safe use in medicine. A Schedule V–controlled substance has a low potential for abuse and a widely accepted use in the medical field. Other drugs fall within the remaining schedules based upon their varying characteristics. New drugs may be added, or a substance may be removed

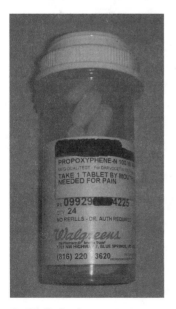

Controlled substances may only be obtained through a doctor's prescription.

as technology and research develop. A controlled substance cannot be obtained without a doctor's permission. Noncontrolled substances can be purchased over-the-counter at retail stores without a prescription. Common controlled substances are explored in the following sections.

Cocaine

Cocaine is a powerful stimulant derived from the leaf of the coca bush (National Institute of Drug Abuse 2004). Cocaine is highly addictive. This plant is primarily grown in Bolivia, Peru, and other countries throughout Central and South America. The drug has legitimate medical uses in surgical procedures and is classified as a Schedule II–controlled substance. Cocaine is primarily found in white powder and an off-white rocklike form (known as "crack" cocaine). It is most commonly ingested through the nose, by use of an intravenous needle, or by smoking it.

Crack cocaine has been processed into a form that can be smoked by the user. The cocaine is "processed with ammonia or sodium bicarbonate (baking soda) and water, and heated to remove the hydrochloride" (National Institute of Drug Abuse 2004, 2). Smoking crack cocaine tends to offer a quicker high for the user. Because the process yields small but powerful quantities of cocaine, crack is offered at a lower price than powder cocaine, making it more appealing to low-income users.

Cocaine is harvested in South American countries and often processed in large, clandestine facilities. It is then transported into the United States through Central American countries into Mexican border states or through channels in the Caribbean. Once in the United States, cocaine is transported by both commercial and private vehicles. Organized criminal operations in the United States and Central and South America control the large-scale distribution of cocaine (National Drug Intelligence Center 2005). Once cocaine is funneled down to neighborhood-level distribution points, the sale of powder or crack cocaine is sold by individual dealers or street gangs.

Methamphetamine

Methamphetamine is a central nervous system stimulant synthetically produced in *clandestine laboratory* operations (National Institute of Drug Abuse 2006b). Methamphetamine is extremely addictive for users. Methamphetamine is commonly known as "meth," "ice," "crystal," "speed," and "crank." The drug is used legitimately for the treatment of sleep disorders and attention deficit hyperactivity disorder and was formerly used as an appetite suppressant. Because of these

medical applications, methamphetamine is classified as a Schedule II–controlled substance. Methamphetamine is normally found in powder form in a variety of colors, or it may be found in liquids that are injected.

Methamphetamine in liquid form is injected by the user.

Methamphetamine is produced in Latin American countries in large laboratories and in smaller production facilities within the United States. The drug is commonly transported into the United States through southwestern border states (NDIC 2005). Imported methamphetamine distribution is often controlled by Latin American criminal organizations. Domestically produced methamphetamine may be transported from rural drug laboratories into more densely populated areas, or it may be sold directly from where it was produced. Criminal street gangs and outlaw motorcycle gangs have been involved in the distribution of both foreign and domestically produced methamphetamine.

Marijuana

Marijuana is a drug produced from the plant *Cannabis sativa* (National Institute of Drug Abuse 2005b). Marijuana is typically smoked in self-made cigarettes (joints) and cigars (blunts) or in large apparatuses called bongs. The chemical delta-9-tetrahydrocannainol (THC) affects users' decision-making processes, reaction times, and thoughts.

Marijuana is currently a Schedule I–controlled substance. It is the most widely used illegal drug in the United States.

Marijuana is produced within the United States in interior growing facilities or in rural farm fields. It is also produced in Latin American countries for transport into the United States through southwestern border states and though Canada. The drug is transported

Marijuana may be cultivated in indoor growing facilities.

around the country through commercial and individual vehicles. Drug-trafficking organizations based in Latin American and Asian countries, criminal street gangs, and outlaw motorcycle gangs have been involved in the distribution of marijuana (NDIC 2005). Marijuana is also produced and sold by individuals who operate greenhouse-type marijuana farms within their homes.

Heroin

Heroin is a highly addictive drug created through processing the drug morphine (National Institute of Drug Abuse 2005a). Morphine is extracted from the naturally occurring poppy plant. While morphine is commonly used as a pain reliever and is classified as a Schedule II–controlled substance, heroin is more potent and is classified as Schedule I. Heroin may be found in white or brown powders or in a black gel-like form known as "black tar heroin." Heroin may be smoked or snorted. It is often converted into a liquid form to be injected with needles.

Heroin is produced in Middle Eastern countries, such as Afghanistan, and South American and Southeast Asian countries (NDIC 2005). The drug arrives in the United States through southwest border states, through shipping port states such as New Jersey, and through airports. Criminal drug-trafficking organizations from Latin America, the Middle East, Asia, and the United States have played a role in the distribution of heroin.

MDMA and Club Drugs

MDMA (3,4-methylenedioxy-N-methylamphetamine) is also known by the street name "ecstasy." This drug is commonly found in tablet form and acts as a stimulant and hallucinogen (NDIC n.d.). MDMA is often classified, along with other synthetic drugs, as a "club drug" due to the fact that it is associated with use at dance clubs and parties, where individuals enjoy the hallucinations and increased energy caused by the drug. MDMA can cause an increased body temperature, dehydration, and a rapid heart rate, among other effects. MDMA is physically addictive. Because MDMA does not have an accepted medical use, it is classified as a Schedule I–controlled substance.

Most of the MDMA available in the United States is produced in European countries (NDIC 2005). However, clandestine MDMA laboratories have been discovered in the United States as well. MDMA tablets are smuggled into the United States through air and marine shipping ports. The distribution of MDMA has been controlled by drug-trafficking organizations in Europe and Asia. MDMA is frequently sold in night clubs, at private parties, and in residential neighborhoods.

The term "club drugs" refers to a grouping of drugs associated with nightclubs and "rave" parties. Rave parties are gatherings where the hallucinogenic properties of illicit drugs are heightened through the use of laser lighting, intense music, and other sensory stimulation. Along with MDMA, Rohypnol, GHB, LSD, and ketamine are commonly used club drugs. While not typically categorized as club drugs, other common narcotics, such as cocaine and methamphetamine, are used within the rave scene.

The liquid drugs Rohypnol and GHB were mentioned in chapter 12, as they are commonly used to facilitate sexual assault by incapacitating the victim. Both can be "colorless, tasteless, and odorless, [allowing them to be] added to beverages and ingested unknowingly" (National

Institute of Drug Abuse 2006a, 1). Both drugs are used for legitimate medical purposes in other countries, although they are Schedule I–controlled substances in the United States. They are smuggled into the United States through border countries and Europe (NDIC 2005). Ketamine is a Schedule III–controlled substance used as a dissociative anesthetic primarily in animals but to a lesser extent in humans (NDIC). Ketamine, also a liquid, may incapacitate an individual and cause hallucinations. The drug is smuggled into the United States from Latin American countries, and it is also acquired through burglaries of veterinary offices. Lysergic acid diethylamide (LSD) is a Schedule I–controlled substance that causes powerful hallucinations in the user (NDIC). LSD is commonly found in liquid form or dried on small pieces of paper or stamps. LSD is typically ingested orally. The drug is produced in clandestine laboratories in the United States by experienced chemists; the production process is very complicated (NDIC). Club drugs are commonly distributed by younger individuals at parties and night clubs.

CASE STUDY

The Drug Enforcement Administration and New Orleans Police Department conducted a joint investigation into The State Palace Theater in New Orleans in the late 1990s.

> During the course of this investigation, DEA agents learned that over the past two years 400 to 500 teenagers and young adults had been treated at local emergency rooms for overdose-related illnesses following their participation in rave events hosted by the [theater]." (Hutchison 2001, "The State Palace Theater Investigation")

Undercover operations were held at the theater. Parties within the theater were filmed, showing blatant drug use among partygoers. Undercover agents also purchased quantities of narcotics from several individuals.

Theater officials were charged with crimes for allowing the activity, and the corporation was levied a $100,000 fine in 2001.

PCP

Phencyclidine, or PCP, is a dissociative anesthetic listed as a Schedule II–controlled substance. Side effects of the drug are "delirium, visual disturbances, and psychotic behaviors" (NDIC 2005, 118), so it is not used in medical practice. Individuals who have taken PCP are often said to have seemingly superhuman strength. In reality, this strength is due to the fact that one may actually injure oneself through exertion but not recognize the associated pain. PCP is commonly found in powder, pill, and liquid forms and may be ingested orally, through injection, and by smoking. PCP is produced in clandestine laboratories in the United States and distributed most commonly through criminal street gangs.

Prescription Medications

Tablets and pills used for legitimate medical purposes are sold illegally by individuals who have acquired them through legitimate or criminal means. Prescription drugs that are commonly diverted from legitimate use are pain-relieving medications, such as oxycodone and hydrocodone. Medicines may be acquired by an individual through "doctor shopping," or continually seeking medical care and pain medicine prescriptions from different physicians. Prescription fraud, theft, unscrupulous physicians, and illegal Internet-based pharmacies are also used to distribute illicit pharmaceuticals (NDIC 2005). The drugs are distributed by a variety of individuals and drug-trafficking organizations.

INVESTIGATION

Narcotics investigations may be based upon one of three crimes: possession, manufacture, and distribution. The crime of possession typically applies to drug users holding narcotics for personal use. Manufacturers of narcotics operate *clandestine drug laboratory* operations that develop synthetic drugs or alter existing drugs into a different form. Distributors may operate large-scale drug-trafficking organizations or participate in street-level, hand-to-hand sales.

Possession

Law enforcement organizations most commonly target manufacturers and distributors of narcotics with long-term investigations to stem the flow of drugs into the general public. Smaller-scale investigations may focus upon those who possess narcotics, or those who possess illicit drugs may be encountered during normal police operations.

Possession cases are typically developed through tip calls or informants. For example, a neighbor may call to report the smell of narcotics use coming from a nearby residence. In other cases, a regular police informant may give information regarding a known narcotics user in possession of a large quantity of drugs. Investigators will take this testimonial evidence and either attempt to develop probable cause for a search warrant or approach the suspected drug offender and ask for consent to search for narcotics. Probable cause can be established through the testimony of the informant as long as that individual has proven reliable and has timely and accurate information.

The term knock-and-talk describes an operation where narcotics investigators approach the owner of a residence and request consent to search for drugs. A small group of investigators will approach and attempt contact; larger contingents of police officers may be considered to be coercive to the homeowner. Typically, the investigators will explain that a complaint of drug use at the residence has been received. The detective will explain that it is incumbent upon the police department to check on these complaints and that the officers are seeking the cooperation of the homeowner. Prior to asking for consent, the investigator will relate that the subject does not have to allow the police to enter and search. Any indication that coercion was used in

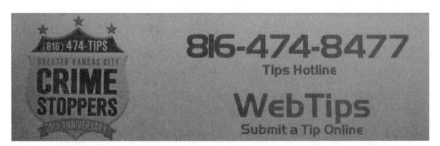

Information about drug possession may be obtained through crime hotlines.

gaining consent from the homeowner will nullify the use of evidence found in later court proceedings.

Drug evidence may include: the drugs themselves, items used to ingest drugs, and biological evidence samples proving that an individual has used narcotics. Depending upon the applicable state law, a small amount of certain controlled substances may present enough evidence to warrant a felony case. Other types of drugs may require larger quantities to distinguish a felony from a misdemeanor. Drug paraphernalia refers to items used in the preparation and ingestion of controlled substances, such as smoking pipes, hypodermic needles, and snorting straws. Drug evidence may also be collected from samples of blood, urine, or hair prove that a person was under the influence of a narcotic. In certain cases, proof that the individual has used drugs is sufficient to charge an individual with possession.

Distribution

Drug possession cases are important to investigate; however, law enforcement tends to concentrate on drug dealers to reduce the availability of narcotics. While those who distribute drugs can be charged with possession if they are found to have narcotics, the penalties for drug distribution are typically more severe than for possession. Proving that an individual is involved in drug distribution is more difficult than proving that he was in possession of a controlled substance. A more proactive approach is usually required to solidify a distribution case.

CASE STUDY

The Oklahoma Bureau of Narcotics (OBN) has ended a month-long undercover drug sting in Bartlesville resulting in numerous arrests and search warrants. OBN Spokesman Mark Woodward says agents and officers from several departments fanned out just after noon today armed with arrest warrants for nearly 50 defendants accused of selling drugs to undercover OBN agents.

OBN Director Darrell Weaver said that a Mobile Operations Team was created by the agency consisting of "a group of highly covert, veteran undercover agents strategically deployed into an area local law enforcement have identified as troubled spots within their communities. The Bureau agents go undercover and secure the evidence themselves rather than utilizing confidential informants thus making cases that have an extremely high conviction rate." (Woodward 2007, 1)

Drug distribution cases originate with information that a person or organization is involved in narcotics sales. This information may come from an informant or though citizen tips. Many jurisdictions have drug hotlines for people to call with this information. In most cases, the receipt of this information is not sufficient to provide probable cause of drug distribution; further verification and investigation is necessary.

Verification that a subject is involved in drug sales often begins with surveillance. Drug distribution may be conducted from individual residences. In some cases, good Samaritans who report drug complaints may be encouraged to watch the house for indicators of drug trafficking. As long as it is safe to do so, neighbors may collect license plate descriptions of vehicles that frequent the house, for instance. Otherwise, surveillance may be conducted by police personnel. Investigators may keep a watch on the residence from vehicles or fixed locations. It is also common to employ video technology to monitor a location.

Certain indicators can help verify that a particular residential location deserves further investigation. The resident may show a prior history of drug trafficking. Police investigators may check the vehicle registration information of frequent visitors to the house against records of known drug users and dealers. Residences involved in drug sales often have heavy vehicle traffic bringing short-term visitors. Drug houses are often the center of an increase in disturbances, graffiti, and criminal activity, including prostitution and drug use, in a neighborhood.

Informants, addressed in chapter 7, play a significant role in drug investigations. Not only do they provide information to the police, they also may become active participants in the investigation through controlled drug purchases. A *controlled drug purchase* is an operation where an informant serves as an undercover operative to buy narcotics. The key to such an operation is control—the informant does not work without direct supervision from a police investigator. The informant must be approved and registered according to agency protocols. Prior to each operation, investigators meet to plan and develop contingency strategies in case the operation strays from the original design.

Once the plan is in place, a pre-operational meeting is held among all of the investigators who will be involved in the drug purchase. The plan is related to each investigator. The primary investigator then meets with the informant. During this meeting, the investigator carefully places a transmitting device on or near the informant to allow the investigators to monitor conversations and activity between the informant and the suspect, primarily for the informant's safety. The transmitted conversations can also be recorded for possible use as evidence. The informant will be supplied with a code phrase that he can use if his life is in danger. If the phrase is heard over the transmission, police investigators waiting in the area can respond to extract the informant and end the operation. The safety of everyone involved supersedes the need to complete an investigation.

The informant is also searched to ensure that she does not have any narcotics in her possession prior to entering the residence. If the informant uses a car to get to the drug house, her car will also be thoroughly searched. The informant is given cash from a police investigative fund to make the purchase. The serial numbers on the bills are recorded, as they may be recovered during subsequent search warrants. The informant is then followed to the drug purchase site. Investigators use care before, during, and after the operation to ensure that the drug dealers are not using human or video camera "countersurveillance" to spot police investigators. Once the informant has procured the narcotics, she meets investigators at a prearranged spot to give the investigators the drugs that were purchased. The informant is searched again to ensure that she does not have any leftover funds or hidden narcotics in her possession.

A drug purchase made by an undercover officer is handled in a similar fashion as one by an informant. A primary difference is that a purchase by a police officer is more controllable. Also, utilizing the officer instead of a citizen as a witness in later court proceedings may be easier, as informants may be reluctant to appear in court. Undercover police officers are also more used to using electronic surveillance devices and at sensing when their safety is compromised.

In some cases, only one drug purchase will be conducted. In other cases, several purchases will be made to develop a strong case against the individual or to prove that she is capable of distributing larger amounts of controlled substances. Single purchases are called "buy-bust" operations. The purchase is made, and the suspect is immediately apprehended. Buy-bust operations may be beneficial when the identity of the suspect is not known.

Drug purchase operations are conducted with the goal of establishing probable cause for an arrest and/or search warrant. Search warrants are carried out at the conclusion of drug purchase investigations to recover any further narcotics the suspect may have in his possession and possibly recover evidence indicating the scope of the distribution network. The suspect may keep informal records of drug transactions. Large amounts of cash may be located, serving to indicate the profits the drug dealer has made over time. The investigative funds used by the police during undercover drug buys might also be located. Search

Special tactical teams are used to serve high-risk search warrants during drug investigations.

Photo courtesy of the Independence (Missouri) Police Department

warrants of drug houses are often conducted as high-risk entries by trained special weapons and tactics (SWAT) teams. To reduce danger, investigators relay any known threats or challenges to the officers serving the search warrants, such as the presence of guns, surveillance cameras, children, or large dogs. The investigators may learn of these factors during the course of their investigation.

Manufacture

Drug investigations may also focus upon those who manufacture controlled substances. Manufacture may be in conjunction with street-level sales. A manufacturing process is involved with the conversion of powder cocaine to crack and in the production of methamphetamine, LSD, and MDMA. Each process utilizes different steps, but most involve dangerous chemicals. Elements of the investigation, such as the use of informants and undercover officers, are often the same as those of other drug investigations; however, the recovery of physical evidence in manufacturing cases must be handled with extreme care.

CASE STUDY

Six pounds of methamphetamine were recovered from a residence after an explosion in Fishtown, Pennsylvania, in 2003. DEA Special Agent in Charge James Kasson advised that on February 16, an explosion "blew the roof off of a garage" at a residence.

> The second floor of the building was being used for the production of methamphetamine. The drug was being manufactured in a large room and vented through the bathroom on the same floor. At the time of the explosion, the roof blew off the joist and then landed back on the building at an angle moving part of one wall of the building. (Vaira 2003, ¶ 2)

The term clandestine drug laboratory may conjure an image of a clean, organized scientific lab. These illicit manufacturing facilities are usually quite the opposite. Clandestine drug labs are typically operated by individuals who have learned rudimentary procedures from equally untrained individuals and through trial and error.

Their practices often have disastrous consequences, including explosions, chemical burns, and poisoning. In recognition of the dangers associated with processing clandestine drug labs, federal regulations for processing hazardous waste apply to the cleanup of these crime scenes. The Standards for Generators of Hazardous Waste listed under the Resource Conservation and Recovery Act (RCRA), published by the U.S. Environmental Protection Agency, are applicable to law enforcement recovery, disposal, and storage of clandestine laboratory evidence (DEA 2005b). Regulations address how hazardous materials should be

Various chemicals and supplies found in clandestine drug labs are recovered by trained investigators.

handled, what protective equipment should be worn by those who enter laboratory scenes, and how materials should be transported.

SUMMARY

Drugs are classified in the United States according to the Controlled Substances Act set forth by the Drug Enforcement Administration and the U.S. Department of Health and Human Services. A controlled substance must be prescribed by a doctor. Noncontrolled substances are available over-the-counter.

Common controlled substances sold illegally in the United States are cocaine, methamphetamine, marijuana, heroin, MDMA, PCP, and diverted prescription painkillers. Methamphetamine, MDMA, and PCP are produced in dangerous clandestine drug labs.

Drug crimes that are investigated include possession, distribution, and manufacture. Informant or citizen tips are sources of information about drug users and sellers. Consent searches, called knock-and-talks, are conducted to investigate drug cases. Surveillance also may be conducted to develop intelligence about a possible drug house. Undercover operatives and informants may attempt carefully controlled drug purchases to establish probable cause that drugs are being sold from a residence. Drug evidence also includes records of drug use and sale and drug use and manufacturing paraphernalia.

Key Terms

Clandestine drug laboratories: An illegal manufacturing facility dedicated to producing controlled substances

Controlled drug purchase: A planned investigative operation involving surveillance and the utilization of an informant to purchase narcotics from a source

Knock-and-talk: An organized search of a residence with the consent of the owner

Discussion Questions

1. Why do law enforcement agencies concentrate on those who manufacture and distribute controlled substances? Do you agree with this approach? Why or why not?

2. What types of evidence would tend to prove an individual is involved in narcotics distribution as opposed to mere possession?

3. Why is it important to closely control and document controlled drug purchase operations?

Exploration

1. View the Drug Enforcement Administration (DEA) website at *www.usdoj.gov/dea/index.htm.* Read the agency's mission and evaluate how it relates to addressing drug crimes in America.

References

Drug Enforcement Administration (DEA). 2005a. *Drugs of abuse: Chapter 1—The controlled substances act.* Retrieved October 6, 2007, from www.usdoj.gov/dea/pubs/abuse/1-csa.htm.

Drug Enforcement Administration (DEA). 2005b. *Guidelines for law enforcement for the cleanup of clandestine drug laboratories.* Washington, DC.

Hutchison, Asa. 2001. *DEA congressional testimony,* December 4. Retrieved January 5, 2007, from the Drug Enforcement Administration website at www.usdoj.gov/dea/pubs/cngrtest/ct120401 .html.

National Drug Intelligence Center (NDIC). n.d. *MDMD (ecstasy) fast facts.* Johnstown, PA.

National Drug Intelligence Center (NDIC). 2005. *National drug threat assessment, 2005,* February. Johnstown, PA: U.S. Department of Justice.

National Institute of Drug Abuse. 2004. *Cocaine abuse and addiction,* November. Washington, DC: U.S. Department of Health and Human Services, National Institutes of Health.

National Institute of Drug Abuse. 2005a. *Heroin abuse and addiction,* May. Washington, DC: U.S. Department of Health and Human Services, National Institutes of Health.

National Institute of Drug Abuse. 2005b. *Marijuana abuse,* July. Washington, DC: U.S. Department of Health and Human Services, National Institutes of Health.

National Institute of Drug Abuse. 2006a. *Info facts: Rohypnol and GHB,* May. Washington, DC: U.S. Department of Health and Human Services, National Institutes of Health.

National Institute of Drug Abuse. 2006b. *Methamphetamine abuse and addiction,* September. Washington, DC: U.S. Department of Health and Human Services, National Institutes of Health.

Vaira, Mary. 2003. *News release: Explosion leads to seizure of meth-amphetamine laboratory,* February 19. Available from the Drug Enforcement Administration website at www.justice.gov/dea/pubs/states/newsrel/2003/phila021903.html.

Woodward, Mark. 2007. *Press release: Mobile operations team deployed to halt Bartlesville drug dealers,* January 25. Available from the Oklahoma Bureau of Narcotics and Dangerous Drug Control website at www.ok.gov/obndd/documents/Clinton%20Oklahoma%20%20MOT%20Operation.doc.

Zhang, Zhiwei. 2004. *Drug and alcohol use and related matters among arrestees.* Washington, DC: National Institute of Justice, Arrestee Drug Abuse Monitoring Program.

CHAPTER 14

TERRORISM, ORGANIZED CRIME, AND GANGS

CHAPTER OBJECTIVES

By the end of this chapter, the reader will be able to do the following:

- Define the term *organized crime*.
- Describe the differences among criminal organizations, gangs, and terrorist groups.
- List some of the culturally based criminal organizations.
- Define the term *gang*.
- Define *hate crime*.
- Describe common methods used in the investigation of criminal groups.
- Explain some ways to identify members of organized crime groups, gangs, or terrorist organizations.
- Describe three common communication-intercept techniques.
- Define the term *money laundering*.
- List and describe the laws commonly utilized in organized crime investigations, with particular emphasis on the Racketeering Influenced and Corrupt Organizations (RICO) Act.

- Define *terrorism*.

- List and describe typical motivations for terrorism.

The elements of crimes committed by members of criminal organizations do not differ from those perpetrated by individuals on their own; however, criminal justice professionals have found that the approach to these investigations must be different to ensure effectiveness. While an individual's criminal activity may be stopped after a successful investigation and trial, a criminal organization may continue through its other members. Specific strategies are employed to address criminal and terrorist organizations, gangs, and hate groups. These techniques will be explored further in this chapter.

ORGANIZED CRIME

The term *organized crime* refers to a variety of groups, all focused upon furthering their profitability through criminal activity. Most people immediately conjure images of the Italian Mafia; however, organized crime includes individuals from many different cultures and walks of life. The phrase *organized crime* can be defined as

> a structured group of three or more persons existing for a period of time and acting in concert with the aim of committing one or more serious crimes or offense(s) in order to obtain, directly or indirectly, a financial or other material benefit. (National Institute of Justice 2007, 1)

Based upon this definition, a criminal organization can range from a small group of individuals committing crimes within a single community to a large, internationally based syndicate with a complex structure.

The definition of *organized crime* can be interpreted to include other criminal groups, such as terrorist regimes and street gangs. There are generally accepted differences between these two despite the technical match between the terms. Criminal organizations typically have a stricter structure than street gangs, where membership may be less formalized and more dynamic. Terrorist organizations may also possess a sophisticated structure; however, the goals of terrorists are not material in nature (terrorism goals are discussed later in the chapter). Members of organized crime are also secretive about their memberships, while street, motorcycle, and hate-based gang members often flaunt their associations.

The crimes in which an organized group may participate are varied. Recalling the definition of *organized crime,* it is noted that a financial or material goal is usually involved in these groups' criminal activity. Typical organized crime endeavors include narcotics trafficking, prostitution, gambling, extortion, loan sharking, fraud, fencing of stolen property, money laundering, and corruption. Each of these crimes focuses upon furthering the organization financially.

The activities of criminal organizations are typically focused upon material gain.

In addition to materially motivated crimes, the organization may also perpetrate offenses geared toward maintaining the status and organization of the group. The cohesiveness of the organization is ensured through discipline and intimidation. "Customers" of the organization (drug buyers, prostitution patrons, illicit loan recipients, etc.) are also held in check through the threatened or actual use of physical force. Criminal organizations also frequently attempt to maintain their influence by corrupting public officials.

Criminal organizations may be based in a particular community or region, or they may conduct operations internationally. Organized crime is a concern to law enforcement no matter where the group's activities are conducted. Internationally operated organizations are a significant challenge, though, due to the jurisdictional boundaries the outfit may traverse during the course of its crimes. The term *transnational organized crime* refers to groups that conduct operations across national borders (NIJ 2007). Transnational investigations are complicated by matters of jurisdictional authority and differences in laws between nations, although many countries have stiffened laws targeting criminal organizations.

Culturally Based Criminal Organizations

Persons involved in organized crime often mature within a common culture. Many grow up in foreign countries and immigrate or conduct operations in the United States. An example familiar to most is La Cosa Nostra (LCN), commonly known as the Italian Mafia. *La Cosa Nostra*

> is a collection of Italian-American organized crime "families" that has been operating in the United States since the 1920s. For nearly three quarters of a century, beginning during the time of Prohibition and extending into the 1990s, the LCN was clearly the most prominent criminal organization in the U.S. (Finkenauer n.d.)

This organization is certainly not the first criminal group in the United States or the most powerful at present; however, popular media has glamorized the Mafia and ensured its place in infamy. La Cosa Nostra was very powerful in the early to mid-20th century, but its influence has declined considerably due to advancements in criminal investigation. La Cosa Nostra exhibits a sophisticated level of organization, ranging from senior advisors to captains to soldiers who conduct the business of the group (Finkenauer n.d.). This structure is maintained through violence and intimidation. La Cosa Nostra is also noted as being entrepreneurial in its operations, exhibiting a dynamic ability to adjust to criminal markets.

Organized crime has also surfaced within Asian cultures, spanning across the Pacific to reach the United States. The Triad from China, Yakuza from Japan, and groups from Vietnam have become a concern to law enforcement globally. Asian criminal organizations are involved in many of the same activities as similar groups; they are often associated with the sex trade, human trafficking, human smuggling, and narcotics sales.

Criminal organizations originating in Eastern Europe and Russia expanded due to the fall of the Soviet Union in the late 20th century (Finckenauer and Voronin 2001). Commonly known as the "Russian Mafia," it is involved in narcotics, arms and human trafficking, and money-laundering operations.

Organized crime has also been an issue in Latin and South American countries. Drug cultivation in the region has led to complex narco-trafficking organizations, including the Colombian drug cartels. Joint efforts between national governments have been targeted at reducing the efforts of these organizations.

While criminal organizations often develop along cultural lines, investigators are cautioned to avoid stereotyping all members of that culture as being involved in gangs. Some members of every culture possess questionable ethics and become involved in crime; however, a person's culture is not an indicator of involvement in criminal activity. The majority of people in every culture are law-abiding citizens who wish to see criminal elements addressed.

Investigative methods for organized crime are similar in many respects to those used in gang and hate group investigations. These techniques will be explored after a discussion of these other types of criminal enterprises.

GANGS

"*Gangs* can be said to be a group of three or more individuals bonded together by race, national origin, culture, or territory, who associate on a continual basis for the purpose of committing criminal acts" (Brantley and DiRosa 1994, 2). Gang members may commit crimes for financial reasons, similar to members of organized crime groups, or for other reasons, such as bravado, to prove themselves to other members, as part of an initiation, or for no particular reason. Gangs are more loosely structured than criminal organizations. However, in some instances, a low-level street gang may develop into a sophisticated criminal organization. Gangs are further categorized into subtypes, including street gangs, outlaw motorcycle gangs, and hate groups.

Street Gangs

Street gangs are most often composed of juveniles or young adults (both male and female). In many cases, the gangs develop along cultural lines, although multicultural street gangs also exist. While street gangs have existed in the United States for decades, they increased exponentially in the late 20th century.

> In the 1980s, a combination of factors fueled a dramatic increase in gangs and gang affiliation among the Nation's youth. Gang violence grew to unprecedented levels as an expanded number of groups battled for control of turf and profits from drug distribution. (Brantley and DiRosa 1994, 1)

Members of street gangs hold the geographical boundary of their "turf," or territory, in reverence. The gang's territory is important for both symbolic and economic reasons. Symbolically, the area represents its perceived zone of control. Economically, it serves as the gang's base for the furtherance of its pursuits.

> Gangs claim territory to create a safe haven for drug sales. The more territory they claim, the safer they feel, and the more street corners they can utilize for drug sales. The more drugs they sell, the more money they generate. (Jackson 2004, 17)

These boundaries can become the basis for battles between rival gangs involving multiple violent crimes.

Gangs mark their territory of control through graffiti.

CASE STUDY

Steve L. "Moody" Wright was convicted in 2006 for a variety of crimes, including three counts of using a firearm for murder. Wright was a member of the 51st Street Crips of Kansas City, Missouri. "Wright and other gang members engaged in turf wars with rival groups over areas in which drugs were illegally sold" (Schlozman 2006, 1). During gang battles, Wright and fellow gang members also shot several others who survived the assaults.

Street gangs participate in crimes similar to those perpetrated by organized crime groups but typically at a lower level of sophistication. Street gangs are heavily involved in neighborhood-level drug sales. Gang members also conduct burglaries, auto thefts, and larcenies to fence stolen property. During turf wars with other gangs or as part of enforcement and intimidation, street gangs may commit assaults and homicides. Membership in a gang can help prove a motive for these types of cases during trial (Jackson 2004). Drive-by shootings became a popular method for assaulting rival gang members in the 1980s. Gangs also vandalize property with graffiti to mark their territories.

Outlaw Motorcycle Gangs

Another type of gang is the outlaw motorcycle gang. *"Outlaw motorcycle gangs* (OMG) began forming shortly after World War II, when disgruntled former Armed Forces personnel established groups based on common philosophies and a mutual passion for motorcycles" (Brantley and DiRosa 1994, 2). These gangs have continued worldwide. OMGs divide up areas geographically but usually on a larger scale than street gangs. An entire state may be "claimed" by an OMG, with

Outlaw motorcycle groups wear patches identifying their membership.

Photo courtesy of Steve Cook and the Independence (Missouri) Police Department enforcement through intimidation and violence against any rival gang that enters the area.

Outlaw motorcycle gangs also are involved with narcotics trafficking. OMG members frequently specialize in the theft of motorcycles and motorcycle parts. OMGs use violence as an enforcement and intimidation tool.

The majority of motorcycle-rider clubs are not criminal in nature. The dress and motorcycles of these groups may resemble those of outlaw gangs, but law enforcement should recognize the distinctions between the two.

Hate Groups

Hate crimes "manifest evidence of prejudice based on race, religion, sexual orientation, or ethnicity, including where appropriate the crimes of murder, non-negligent manslaughter, forcible rape, aggravated assault, simple assault, intimidation, arson, and destruction, damage or vandalism of property" (Bureau of Justice Assistance 1999, 2). These crimes may be perpetrated by individuals or groups of people who may be classified as "hate groups." They are held together by a common bias against a certain culture.

Individuals or groups that speak of biases they hold against others aren't necessarily committing a hate crime. The First Amendment protects a person's right to free speech, even if that speech espouses hatred toward another. A hate crime is committed when these biases are reflected in discriminatory, illegal actions against others. Hate crimes may be acts of violence, such as assault or homicide, or property crimes, such as graffiti or vandalism (where messages of hatred are left).

The line between hate crimes and terrorism is somewhat unclear (Bureau of Justice Assistance 1999). Terrorism is influenced by political beliefs; however, religion also has been known to play a role in terrorism. The two are investigated similarly, and the distinction may be important only for sentencing purposes.

Investigation of Criminal Groups

The investigation of criminal organizations, including gangs and hate groups, begins with identification. The group itself must be identified as an organization, and the individual members have to be identified as well. Members of organized crime groups are reluctant to identify themselves and often do so only to become informants under duress. Gangs members, on the other hand, often display their membership openly. Street gang members frequently wear specific colors or a certain sport team's clothing to identify themselves as belonging to a particular gang, or "set." Outlaw motorcycle gang members wear leather or denim jackets with patches indicating the gang's name and territory. Hate group members often wear clothing with symbols indicating their affiliation, such as swastikas for neo-Nazi groups. Gangs and hate group members may also have tattoos indicating membership. The documentation of these identifying symbols may be helpful in prosecuting an individual or group during gang-related cases (it is unlikely that such gang-related clothing will be worn in court). In some states, gang involvement in a crime results in an enhancement to a person's prison sentence upon conviction.

The gathering and analysis of information as intelligence is important in the investigation of criminal groups. One form of analysis, termed *link analysis,* is graphically displaying the relationships among individuals involved in a criminal enterprise. Link analysis is important in determining the rank structure of a criminal organization, gang, or terrorist group. Intelligence such as link analysis can help determine which individuals are important to include in an investigation; for instance, one might want to prosecute a gang leader in an effort to topple the entire organization. "Once crime problems are identified and quantified through intelligence assessments, key criminals can be targeted for investigation and prosecution" (Peterson 2005, 9).

The names of gangs, locations of operations, the crimes committed, symbols and colors indicative of gang membership, rival and enemy factions, and vehicles are all helpful to collect as intelligence for investigations related to gangs and organized crimes. Monikers can help tie a certain person to a crime, as witnesses may often only know a person by his nickname (Wilson 1997). This information may be provided by informants or gang members who are open to talking about their membership. Disenchanted gang members, neighborhood residents, community activists, and school teachers may be sources of information about gangs.

Gangs may also be monitored through the recording and interpretation of graffiti. Informants may be able to describe what various symbols mean. It is not uncommon for threats to other gangs to be delivered through graffiti. Police officers photograph all gang graffiti that is discovered for collection as potential intelligence. After the marks have been photographed, the home or shop owner is encouraged (or required by law) to remove the graffiti, as it may invite retaliatory graffiti or further vandalism.

Organized crime and gang investigations may also be aided by the interception of communications. By virtue of the fact that the group must communicate to conduct operations, a weakness is exposed. A *wire tap* allows investigators to monitor word-for-word telephone conversations between individuals. A *pen register* is a device that captures all numbers dialed on a certain phone. A *trap-and-trace device* records both incoming and outgoing numbers from a phone. All three telephone communication capture devices require a court order to use.

Investigators also target the proceeds of criminal activity that contribute to the organization's strength. During the course of materially motivated criminal activity, an enterprise may amass significant cash resources. The crime of money laundering involves converting proceeds from criminal activities into funds that seem to have been acquired legally. For instance, organized crime figures may have a legitimate business, such as a waste-hauling service, which they use to funnel cash acquired through the sale of drugs and give the appearance that their wealth has been acquired legally. These individuals may come under scrutiny from law enforcement or the Internal Revenue Service for evading the payment of taxes. Money laundering is a crime at both the state and federal level. Criminal justice agencies request, through court proceedings, that a criminal organization forfeit any assets acquired with illegal funds (Naylor 1999). Asset forfeiture and money-laundering prosecution have become important tools for dismantling a criminal organization.

CASE STUDY

In 2006, Cheng Chui Ping was sentenced to 35 years in prison as a result of a human-smuggling operation in New York. Ping worked in cooperation with the Chinatown Fuk Ching gang to ensure that the victims she trafficked into the United States from China paid their fees; they were held hostage by the gang until they did so. Many of the immigrants smuggled into the United States by Ping died while sailing on the makeshift transport vessels used in the operation. Among the charges levied against Ping was the crime of money laundering. Ping laundered the proceeds from the trafficking case through her Chinatown variety store (Hadad and Gaffney 2006, 10).

A significant issue with the investigation of organized crime is witness intimidation (Burns 2003). It is common for gangs and organized crime figures to threaten a potential witness during an investigation or prior to a trial. "[A citizen] witness's fear is legitimate, and the prosecutor will have a difficult time assuaging that fear" (Jackson 2004, 19). Law enforcement may address this problem through thorough investigations of witness-tampering reports. In extreme cases, it may become necessary to protect a witness through security programs, such as the U.S. Marshals Service Witness Security (WITSEC) program.

In recognition of the difficulties and complexities associated with organized crime and gang investigations, many agencies have formed specialized units to investigate these crimes. These units may be multijurisdictional task forces comprised of individuals from several different local, state, and federal agencies. In the San Diego County, California, area, criminal justice agencies have united to form the Jurisdiction United for Drug and Gang Enforcement (JUDGE) task force. JUDGE is a cooperative effort among prosecutors, the probation department, and special operations units in local police departments (Reed and Decker 2002).

> These collaborative efforts are designed to increase the gathering of intelligence on gang activity and gang membership, develop key community informants, and promote greater cooperation between crime witnesses and law enforcement in prosecuting gang members. Rigorous, successful prosecution of these offenders is especially important in overcoming the strong feelings of invulnerability and immunity to prosecution many gang members hold. (Reed and Decker, 173)

Organized Crime Laws

Law enforcement is aided by special laws used to address organized crime entities. The Hobbs Anti-Racketeering Act, passed in 1946, prescribes heavy penalties for those who use extortion, robbery, or other criminal means to disrupt interstate commerce. In 1968, Congress passed the Omnibus Crime Control and Safe Streets Act, which allows for the expanded use of wire taps in the investigation of organized crime due to its inherent threat to the country. The Organized Crime Control Act of 1979 prohibits the creation of illegal gambling organizations, gives grand juries more powers of investigation, and provides measures for the protection of witnesses. One of the most significant organized crime laws is the *Racketeering Influenced and Corrupt Organizations Act* (RICO) of 1970.

RICO provided for enhanced penalties for those committing criminal activities as part of an ongoing criminal organization. RICO enables law enforcement to attack the organizational structure of organized crime and to levy severe criminal and civil penalties, including forfeitures. It is the threat of these penalties that has convinced many made members of the LCN to become informants and/or to seek immunity from prosecution in return for becoming a cooperating witness. (Finckenauer n.d.)

Criminal organizations may be prosecuted effectively through RICO statutes in federal court.

TERRORISM

Terrorism is defined in the U.S. Code of Federal Regulations as "the unlawful use of force and violence against persons or property to intimidate or coerce a government, the civilian population, or any segment thereof, in furtherance of political or social objectives" (28 C.F.R. Section 0.85). A key difference between terrorism and street or organized crime is the goal of the criminal action. A "political or social" message is conveyed through the terrorist act, which normally involves a violent activity. The message a terrorist act intends to convey varies according to the organization or individual. The message may be political/religious, such as militant Muslim or right-wing, radical Christian attacks against a government. The message may also be political/social, such as a bombing of an abortion clinic or vandalism of an animal-testing facility. In addition to message-motivated crimes, terrorist organizations may conduct illegal activities for monetary gain (e.g., narcotics sales) to fund their activities.

Terrorism may be further classified as either international or domestic terrorism. Domestic terrorism is generally considered to be a terrorist action taken by an individual or group whose country of origin is the United States (or relevant country). International terrorism is committed by individuals or groups from a foreign country.

Terrorism investigations are similar to those conducted of other criminal organizations. Intelligence analysis is crucial in identifying organizations and their members. Because the membership of terrorist organizations often spans jurisdictions and even national borders, cooperation among law enforcement agencies at all levels of government is important. The Federal Bureau of Investigation has created Field Intelligence Groups (FIG) and Joint Terrorism Task Forces (JTTF) to ensure this cooperation (Spiller 2006). "JTTFs team up police officers, FBI agents, and officials from over 20 federal law enforcement agencies to investigate terrorism cases (Federal Bureau of Investigation 2004, 38). The agency has also created partnerships with private sector businesses to help in the investigative process through the Infragard program (FBI).

Intelligence in terrorism cases involves collecting information through informants and physical and electronic surveillance activities. Terrorists are identified through a variety of means. The National Media Exploitation Center reviews video, audio, Internet, and documents to find claims of responsibility for terrorist attacks to identify members (FBI 2004). Once a terrorist is identified, she is entered into criminal justice databases so her activities can be tracked or so she can be captured. The FBI's Terrorism Screening Center is a resource for investigators to use to identify possible terrorists (FBI).

Collected information is processed by intelligence analysts to produce meaningful facts for investigators. Intelligence products such as link analysis charts must be disseminated in a timely fashion to the appropriate investigators to be of value. "Dissemination requires getting intelligence to those who have the need and the right to use it in whatever form is deemed most appropriate" (Peterson 2005, 7).

Terrorist operations are also thwarted through the investigation and prosecution of the crimes used to fund the organization.

> Terrorist organizations must develop and maintain robust and low-key funding sources to survive. Domestic and international terrorist groups raise money in the United States to exploit the nation's market-based economy and democratic freedoms for profits that they send overseas or use locally to finance sleeper cells." (Olson 2007, 1)

Narcotics violations, fraud, and theft are common crimes used to fund terrorism. Like organized crime groups, terrorist organizations launder money through legitimate businesses. In recognition of these funding issues, the FBI has created a Terrorism Financing Operations Section (FBI 2004).

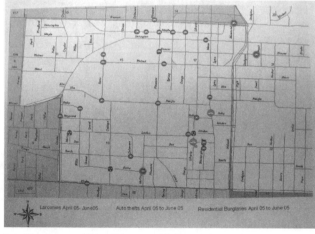

Intelligence provides important information to investigators to help prevent or reduce crime.

SUMMARY

Organized crime refers to highly organized criminal groups that typically focus upon economic gain. Intimidation is a tool used by organized crime groups to control both members and customers. It is common for criminal organizations to form along cultural lines. One of the most well-known organized crime groups is La Cosa Nostra. A common error is to stereotype all members of a culture as belonging to an organized crime group.

Gangs are usually more loosely formed groups, often committing crime for monetary gain but also to intimidate their own members or others. Some gangs develop into well-organized groups similar to criminal organizations. Common types of gangs are street and outlaw motorcycle gangs. The territory claimed by a gang becomes important to its members for economic and symbolic reasons.

Hate groups are motivated by prejudice against specific cultures or groups. Hate groups participate in legal speech that espouses their beliefs and may commit hate crimes.

Identification is the first important component of investigating criminal groups. The group itself must be identified as an organization, and then each member must be identified. Gangs and hate groups may wear observable indicators that they are members, while organized crime members and terrorists are typically more covert. Intelligence is important to collect about all criminal groups. Link analysis shows the relationships among members of the organizations. For gangs, the interpretation of graffiti may be an important way to track their activities. Communication interception, including the use of wire taps, pen registers, and trap-and-trace devices, helps follow or intercede in the operations of criminal groups. Because most criminal groups rely upon illicit funding sources, investigations targeting criminally gotten profits, including money laundering, are used.

In recognition of the difficulties associated with investigating organized crime, laws have been passed to aid law enforcement. The most significant law is the Racketeering Influence and Corrupt Organizations (RICO) Act, which provides for enhanced penalties for members of criminal organizations operating on their behalf.

Terrorist groups differ from others in their motivations, which are political, religious, or social in nature. Intelligence is important in combating terrorism, and several criminal justice agencies aid in the collection and dissemination of intelligence.

Key Terms

Gang: A group of three or more individuals, bonded by race, national origin, culture, or territory, who associate on a continual basis for the purpose of committing criminal acts

Hate crime: Crimes that manifest prejudice based on race, religion, sexual orientation, or ethnicity

La Cosa Nostra: An organized crime group originating in Italy that rose to prominence in 1920's America

Link analysis: A graphical representation of a group that displays its hierarchy and other information about the relationships among its members

Organized crime: A structured group of three or more persons existing for a period of time and acting in concert with the aim of committing one or more serious crimes or offenses to obtain, directly or indirectly, a financial or other material benefit

Outlaw motorcycle gang: A group of individuals involved in organized criminal activity who share a devotion to motorcycle riding

Pen register: A device that captures all numbers dialed from a telephone

Racketeering Influenced and Corrupt Organizations Act (RICO) of 1970: A law that provides for enhanced penalties for members of criminal organizations participating in criminal activity for the furtherance of those organizations

Terrorism: The unlawful use of force and violence against persons or property to intimidate or coerce a government, the civilian population, or any segment thereof in furtherance of political or social objectives

Trap-and-trace device: A device that records both incoming and outgoing calls from a telephone

Wire tap: A live audio investigative monitor of telephonic conversations allowed only by court order

Discussion Questions

1. What complicates identifying members of organized crime or terrorist groups? What steps can be taken to identify these members?

2. Why is the quick eradication of graffiti important for a community?

3. What issues might complicate the investigation of money laundering?

4. Explain why the collection of intelligence is important in combating terrorism. What information is important to collect about terrorist groups?

Exploration

1. Read through the Southern Poverty Law Center's website, which addresses hate groups. Look at the Hate Map and see what groups may be operating in your area: *www.splcenter.org/index.jsp*.

2. Explore the Joint Terrorism Task Force's website and read about how it combats terrorism: *www.usdoj.gov/jttf/*.

References

Brantley, Alan, and Andrew DiRosa. 1994. Gangs: A national perspective, May. *FBI Law Enforcement Bulletin* 63, no. 5 (May): 1–6.

Bureau of Justice Assistance. 1999. *A policymaker's guide to hate crimes,* November. Washington, DC: U.S. Department of Justice.

Burns, Edward. 2003. *Gang- and drug-related homicide: Baltimore's successful enforcement strategy,* July. Retrieved October 11, 2007, from the Bureau of Justice Assistance website at www.ncjrs.gov/html/bja/gang/.

Federal Bureau of Investigation (FBI). 2004. *The FBI's counterterrorism program since 2001,* April 14. Washington, DC.

Finckenauer, James O. n.d. *La Cosa Nostra in the United States.* Washington, DC: U.S. Department of Justice, National Institute of Justice, International Center. Retrieved September 12, 2007, from www.ncjrs.gov/pdffiles1/nij/218555.pdf.

Finckenauer, James O., and Yuri Voronin. 2001. *The threat of Russian organized crime,* June. Washington, DC: U.S. Department of Justice, National Institute of Justice.

Hadad, Herbert, and Megan Gaffney. 2006. *Press release: Sister Ping sentenced to 35 years in prison for alien smuggling, hostage taking, money laundering and ransom proceeds conspiracy,* March 16. New York: Department of Justice. Available from the Federal Bureau of Investigation, New York Field Office website at http://newyork.fbi.gov/dojpressrel/pressrel06/sispter_ping031606.htm.

Jackson, Alan. 2004. *Prosecuting gang cases: What local prosecutors need to know,* April. Alexandria, VA: American Prosecutors Research Institute.

National Institute of Justice (NIJ). 2007. *Asian transnational organized crime and its impact on the United States,* January. Washington, DC: U.S. Department of Justice.

Naylor, R. T. 1999. *Follow-the-money methods in crime control policy,* December. Retrieved October 11, 2007, from the Nathanson Centre website at www.ncjrs.gov/nathanson/washout.html.

Olson, Dean. 2007. Financing terror. *FBI Law Enforcement Bulletin* 76, no. 2 (February): 1–9.

Peterson, Marilyn. 2005. *Intelligence-led policing: The new intelligence architecture,* September. Washington, DC: U.S. Department of Justice, Bureau of Justice Assistance.

Reed, Winfred, and Scott Decker (eds.). 2002. *Responding to gangs: Evaluation and research,* July. U.S. Department of Justice, National Institute of Justice.

Schlozman, Bradley. 2007. *Press release: gang leader sentenced to life in prison for murders, drug trafficking, firearms violations.* February 9. Kansas City: Department of Justice. Available from the U.S. Department of Justice website at www.usdoj.gov/usao/mow/news2007/wright.sen.htm.

Spiller, Susan. 2006. The FBI's field intelligence groups and police. *FBI Law Enforcement Bulletin* 75, no. 5 (May): 1–6.

Wilson, Craig. 1997. What's in a name? Gang monikers. *FBI Law Enforcement Bulletin* 66, no. 5 (May): 8–13.

CHAPTER 15

ARSON AND EXPLOSIVES

CHAPTER OBJECTIVES

By the end of this chapter, the reader will be able to do the following:

- Define the crime of *arson*.

- Explain the characteristics of *accidental* and *incendiary fires*.

- List the motivations for arson.

- Describe the complications involved in arson investigation.

- Explain why interagency cooperation is required in arson investigation.

- List and describe indicators of arson at a fire scene.

- Describe common methods used in the investigation of arson.

- Explain how accelerant evidence is located.

- Describe special considerations in investigating juvenile arson crimes.

- Describe special considerations in investigating serial arsonists.

- List the fire and arson investigation computerized databases.

- Define the term *explosives*.

- List the common types of explosives.

- Describe common methods used in the investigation of explosions.

"When fire occurs, the social and economic costs to the community can be devastating: the loss of the tax base, jobs, and injury and deaths both to civilians and firefighters" (National Fire Academy 2002, SM 1–3). Fire's destructive effects make it a popular weapon for those who wish to inflict physical harm to others or damage property. The intentional setting of fire falls under the criminal category of arson. Arson losses are typically well over $3 billion annually (National Fire Data Center 1997, 14). The use of explosives to inflict harm or damage is less common but no less potentially damaging than arson. Special techniques are required to investigate both types of crimes.

ARSON

Arson is defined as "any willful or malicious burning or attempt to burn, with or without intent to defraud, a dwelling house, public building, motor vehicle or aircraft, personal property of another, etc." (Federal Bureau of Investigation 2004, 37). The intent to start a fire is required for a blaze to be considered arson. Unintended or naturally caused fires do not qualify as arson.

Because arson is targeted toward property, it is classified as a property crime. Due to the destructive and dangerous nature of fire, many argue that it should either be classified as a crime against persons or a hybrid of the two.

> As a crime, arson's long-standing definition as the willful and malicious burning of property does not do justice to the fact that today arson is usually a personal crime that is directed intentionally against specific victims. It is time for arson to be dealt with as a violent crime against persons, not just a crime against property. (U.S. Fire Administration 2004, i)

Arson is often targeted toward specific victims to intimidate or harm them and thus could be considered equal to an assault committed with a weapon.

In recognition of the fact that fire can be used as a weapon, state arson laws may vary based upon the intent of the crime. Many states categorize the deliberate burning of an occupied dwelling as a higher-level felony than the arson of an abandoned structure or automobile. If a victim suffers injuries or dies in a fire, the criminal penalties are likely to be more severe (or fall under the category of assault or homicide). Jurisdictions may also vary the charges based upon the type of property targeted (commercial buildings, residences, outbuildings, trash dumpsters, vehicles, etc.).

Fire Classifications

Fires may be classified under two primary categories: accidental and incendiary (National Fire Academy 2002). An *accidental fire* may result from natural occurrences, such as lightning strikes. Fires arising from heating and cooking equipment, the careless handling of cigarettes, and faulty electrical connections are classified as accidental.

Arsons may be classified according to the targeted property, including vehicle or residential fires.

Arson fires are classified as *incendiary fires.* Prior to determining a fire as incendiary, accidental causes should be eliminated first (National Fire Academy). The term *suspicious fire* is often used to describe a fire with no readily apparent cause where further investigation is necessary. In rare cases, the cause of a fire may be classified as unknown.

Motivations for Arson

Arson may be committed for a wide variety of reasons. Some studies indicate that revenge is the most frequent reason (U.S. Fire Administration 2004, ii). Arsons have also been committed to intimidate others or as part of a hate crime, as in the burning of culturally based churches. The damaging nature of fire makes it a common means to cover up another criminal act (e.g., a murder or burglary scene). During times of civil disorder (rioting), arson may be used as part of the destructive activities of the group. Fire and the effects of smoke can be used as a murder weapon or a means to take one's own life (National Fire Data Center 1997).

Arson is frequently used for economic motives, including defrauding insurance companies in hope that the fire will be ruled as accidental (leading to a policy payout). A property owner may have a significant level of debt and view arson as a way out of the situation. In blighted economic areas, owners may wish to sell properties but find selling difficult due to neighborhood conditions; they may use arson to destroy such properties, gaining an insurance payout. Finally, business owners have been known to eliminate competitors through arson.

CASE STUDY

A Raleigh County, West Virginia, man was arrested in 2007 for allegedly burning down his home and filing an insurance claim for the damages. The 51-year-old man faces a sentence of 2 to 20 years in prison for the arson and 1 to 10 years for the fraud. West Virginia Insurance Commissioner Jane Cline commented that "insurance fraud cases are very complex in nature and those involved in committing such illegal acts are typically involved in other types of crime as well" (Maselli 2007, ¶ 3).

Two distinct types of arson fires are those committed by juveniles and serial fire setters. Investigations of these types of fires will be addressed later in this chapter.

INVESTIGATION

Who Investigates Arson?

Arson investigation is complicated by the dual nature of responses to fires. The U.S. Fire Administration recognized this issue:

> In arson investigations ideally, an investigator would have practical experience as a firefighter and as a police officer. The investigator would be

knowledgeable about fire chemistry and behavior, construction methods and materials, and reaction of materials to fire exposure—including burn rate and heat release. Incident management investigation procedures and methods for securing and preserving evidence are essential capabilities, as are skills in questioning and interviewing, arrest, judicial procedure, criminal behavior, and psychological profiles. If an investigator also knows something about bookkeeping, forensic science, computers, and surveillance—so much the better. Since it is practically impossible for one person to possess all of these abilities and knowledge, and to remain current in these diverse fields, it is logical that a fire and police team represents the strongest capability for dealing with criminal fires. (2004, 13)

Fire department officials may be better trained in the scientific principles of fire investigation. These principles can help determine the cause and the origin (starting point) of a fire. Firefighters may also be able to testify as to how the techniques used in stopping the fire may have influenced evidence. Police officers are typically better versed in the investigation of crime and the collection of intelligence to track down arsonists. State law and individual jurisdictional preferences may determine how arsons are investigated.

CASE STUDY

The Oklahoma City Fire Investigations Unit, as it is operated today, started in 1977. Prior to that, the Arson Investigators would determine cause and origin of fires and the Police Department Detective Unit would follow up the cases. In 1977, the Fire Marshal's office took fire and arson investigation and all related responsibilities from the Police Department, recognizing that fire and arson investigation was a Fire Department concern. (City of Oklahoma City n.d.)

The agencies that investigate arson vary by jurisdiction. One way of organizing the investigation utilizes the fire department to determine cause and origin, while the police conduct the actual investigation. Another approach is to use an integrated team of fire and police investigators to work on the case together. Finally, the fire department may handle the entire investigation. Qualifications for either police or firefighter investigators are based upon training standards establishing them as Certified Fire Investigators (U.S. Fire Administration 2004). Private sector organizations, particularly insurance companies, may also be involved in a fire investigation based upon their vested interest in the cases.

Complications

Several issues cause difficulties to investigators in arson cases. A primary problem is that evidence is destroyed due to the fire itself or through firefighting efforts. Few witnesses may exist, particularly for

fires in abandoned properties. The initial fire report may be falsified, making the victim an unreliable source of information. These factors combined make it difficult to determine if a crime has been committed; classifying the fire as either accidental or incendiary is a challenge.

Arson investigations are complicated by the fact that critical evidence is destroyed during the course of the fire.

Indicators of Arson

Certain factors may help in determining whether or not a fire is in fact arson. Suspicions are raised if more than one point of origin exists for the fire. A *point of origin* is the place within the fire scene where the fire started. Burn patterns may also appear to be irregular or inconsistent with normal fire behavior, in an arson fire. "Burning in a downward direction is considered unnatural, and may have been caused when flammable liquids ran and carried flames downward" (National Fire Academy 2002, SM 4-58).

Suspicions are raised if the owner's behavior is odd, such as if he moved items out of the residence prior to a fire. Also, fires that occur on holidays and weekends, when others are not present, may indicate the need for further investigation (National Fire Academy 2002). Investigators become concerned as well if previous fires have occurred in the same structure.

The strongest indicator of an arson fire is the presence of fire-starting materials, including igniters and accelerants. *Igniters* are items used to start the fire, such as matches, electric starting devices, and fuses. *Accelerants* are highly flammable liquids used to spread a fire quickly and ensure an intense heat capable of sustaining the fire. "The successful presentation of fire scene evidence of incendiarism is often dependent upon the

Accelerant containers near a fire scene are important to document and collect.

ability to document and verify the presence of accelerant residue in debris samples" (U.S. Fire Administration 1993, 10).

Physical Evidence

Testimonial evidence is often lacking in arson investigations, making the successful collection of physical evidence even more important. Evidence is collected according to Fourth Amendment guidelines and search and seizure rules; however, fire scenes automatically draw an emergency response, which brings investigators into the scene. Evidence may be witnessed in such responses. In *Michigan v. Tyler* (1978), "the U.S. Supreme Court ruled that the fire department has the right to enter property under exigent (emergency) circumstances and to remain until the emergency is over" (National Fire Academy 2002, SM 6-5). A warrant is not necessary for fire investigators to search for origin and cause within a reasonable time during the fire response.

Fire scenes are distinguished from other crime scenes due to the inherent safety concerns that exist.

> Just because the fire is out does not mean the hazard has passed. Toxic combustion products like carbon monoxide, carbon dioxide, cyanides, sulphur dioxide, hydrogen sulfide, acrolein, nitrogen oxides, and other substances exposed by the fire, such as asbestos, are just a few of the toxic

inhalation hazards present on the fireground after a fire is extinguished. (U.S. Fire Administration 1993, 5)

The structure containing the crime scene is often unstable, exposing sharp construction materials, unsafe walls and floors, and electrical and gas lines.

To ensure safety, investigators use personal protective equipment. Safety guidelines established by the National Fire Protection Association are published in *NFPA 921: Guide for Fire and Explosion Investigations* (National Institute of Justice 2000a, 6).

Arson investigators look for particular signs within a fire scene to determine whether or not the fire is incendiary in nature. Areas where heat appears to have been more intense receive particular attention. "*Spalling* is the result of concrete or masonry being heated and rapidly cooled by water....this causes the surface to crack and loosen, and can produce a pitted appearance or large craters" (National Fire Academy 2002, SM 4-56). *Crazing* is the bending of glass material due to intense heat. Spalling and crazing are not conclusive indicators of arson, but they are cause for concern. *Depth of char* describes how deeply a material has burned. Depth of char is usually greater where accelerants may have been used. "Normally, most accidental structural fires produce very little floor charring" (National Fire Academy, SM 4-55).

Burn patterns may also indicate how a fire spreads. Irregular burn patterns may show signs of arson. A *pour pattern* is an area of fire damage that closely resembles the shape of a liquid stain. A *line of demarcation* is the line between charred and nonburned material. A *trailer* is a burn pattern that is caused by "any combustible or flammable material used to spread fire from one point or area to another" (National Fire Academy 2002, SM 4-53). Investigators look for these signs as indicators of accelerant usage. If these indicators are present, the investigator will document them through extensive photography.

Investigators search for accelerants using special detection techniques and methods based upon the principles of how flammable liquids

Irregular burn patterns provide investigators signs of arson.

tend to move. "Flammable liquids will settle to the lowest parts of the floor area" (National Fire Academy 2002, SM 4-55) and soak into absorbent materials. Canines that are specially trained in detecting the odor of flammable liquids are often used to locate accelerants. "The first accelerant detection canine program was developed in 1986 through a joint program of the Bureau of Alcohol, Tobacco, and Firearms, Connecticut State Police, Connecticut Bureau of State Fire Marshal, and New Haven (CT) State's Attorney's Office" (U.S. Fire Administration 1993, 8). Electronic "sniffing" devices also may be utilized to detect elements common in accelerants that are present at arson scenes (U.S. Fire Administration).

CASE STUDY

In December of 2006, the Montgomery County Fire and Rescue Service responded to a car fire in Rockville, Maryland. The fully engulfed vehicle was eventually extinguished and an investigation began. The fire appeared to be arson.

The fire victim and owners of the burned vehicle and others provided Montgomery County Fire and Rescue Service, Fire and Explosive Investigators with information that led to a person of interest. K-9 Mira detected evidence of ignitable liquids being used at the scene to possibly start the fire. (Piringer 2006, ¶ 3)

Officials responded to the suspect's residence and took him into custody.

___

After possible accelerant evidence is located, the material must be collected for further laboratory testing. The collection should be performed as soon as possible to prevent the loss of this fragile evidence. Common areas to collect material are near apparent pour patterns and from absorbent materials capable of retaining flammable liquids (e.g., carpet, carpet padding, wood, etc.). Evidence may also be found on the suspect himself, if she is apprehended. To facilitate the collection of any evidence, "the recommended fire scene evidence container is a clean, unused, unlined, airtight metal container (paint can)" (National Fire Academy 2002, 5). Kapak™ brand bags may also be used; these containers are specially formulated to prevent vapor leakage (U.S. Fire Administration 1993).

After arson evidence is collected, it is sent to a crime lab for further testing. Gas chromatography is used in crime laboratories to identify elements that are common in accelerants (U.S. Fire Administration 1993). With a sufficient quantity of material, a detailed analysis can indicate what liquids were present in the fire.

In addition to specialized evidence, such as accelerants and igniters, more common physical evidence may be found at an arson scene. Serological samples, such as blood and skin, may be located to use in DNA comparison tests. Fingerprints may be found in undamaged areas (U.S. Fire Administration 1993). Fingerprints on flammable liquid containers can be particularly important. Shoe prints, tire impressions, and tool and pry marks may be found in and around the scene. Fires caused by careless handling of dangerous chemicals in clandestine drug laboratories may be indicated by drug evidence within a fire scene (NIJ 2000a).

Juvenile Arson

Arsons committed by juveniles may require a special approach. Child-committed arsons are common based upon curiosity that builds into reckless behavior. "Many children display an interest in fire and a willingness to take that fascination a step further in actually playing with it" (Zipper and Wilcox 2005, 2). It has been reported that over half of all arson fires in the United States are committed by individuals under the age of 18 (U.S. Fire Administration 2004, 40).

In addition to using common investigative techniques, law enforcement agencies may approach juvenile arsons by addressing the psychological issues of offenders and potential offenders. Cobb County, Georgia, has instituted early intervention programs to emphasize responsible behavior. An education program, mental health treatment, and diversion-based approach are used in Phoenix, Arizona, to address juvenile arson (U.S. Fire Administration 2004). Arson is dangerous no matter what the age of the offender. The goal of these programs is not only to solve arson crimes but also to prevent future offenses.

Serial Arson

When numerous arsons occur in a particular area, it may be the work of a serial arsonist. Individuals who set several fires may be pyromaniacs.

> *Pyromania* is an established psychiatric diagnosis in the *Diagnostic and Statistical Manual of Mental Disorders*, fourth edition (DSM-IV). It falls into the category of "impulse control disorders," along with disorders like kleptomania (stealing), intermittent explosive disorder (violent and destructive outbursts) and pathological gambling. These disorders are characterised by a failure to resist impulses, such as the impulse to light a fire. (Australian Institute of Criminology 2005, ¶ 2)

Serial fires may also be set by those seeking to do massive damage through vandalism. In some unfortunate cases, firefighters have been known to commit a series of arsons. "The motives of firefighter arsonists often stem from a desire to experience the excitement that many firefighters feel in putting out fires" (National Fire Data Center 1997, 33).

CASE STUDY

A man from Shasta Lake City, California,

> was arrested by the California Department of Forestry and Fire Protection (CDF) Arson Investigation Unit on Monday July 24, 2006. [The 42-year-old] was arrested in connection with 16 felony counts of arson relating to fires that have occurred in northern Shasta County since 2005.
>
> Investigators continue to examine evidence relating to more than 60 fires that have occurred since 2003 to determine if [the man] can be charged with additional felony counts of arson. (Upton 2006, ¶ 1–2)

The fires set by the suspect endangered several residential neighborhoods in the Shasta County area. No indication was given as to the suspect's motive.

Special methods may be utilized to address serial arson problems. A popular approach is the use of an arson strike force. An arson strike force is defined as "a special purpose, short-term mobilization of a team (or teams) of investigators together with allied resources that applies high intensity investigative efforts to a major arson incident or series of incidents" (U.S. Fire Administration 1989, 2). Strike forces offer "greater productivity with existing resources," "better inter-agency coordination and cooperation," and "stronger prosecutions" (U.S. Fire Administration, 4–5). Strike forces may be able take investigative efforts across jurisdictional boundaries to capture a serial arsonist.

Pyromaniacs and other serial arsonists commonly feel a need to view the results of their crimes. Investigators may find success in photographing crowds of onlookers who may be present at a fire scene during the initial stages of the fire (NIJ 2000a).

Testimonial Evidence

The statements of victims and witnesses may be important in arson investigations. In suspicious cases, inconsistencies in the statements of the property owner may cast suspicion on him. Interviewing the person who reported the fire (who may be a different individual than the homeowner) may reveal new details. This person is often the first witness and was in position to see the early stages of the blaze. On some occasions, the arsonist reports the fire and poses as a helpful citizen.

A neighborhood canvass may also reveal important facts about the fire. Some individuals come forward without being contacted first, while others have to be sought out.

> Witnesses do not always perceive the value of what they know. Effective interviewers on the scene can collect a surprising amount of information about, for example, who lived in the building or owned it. They can learn where and when the first signs of smoke and flame appeared, what typical routine the neighborhood follows, and whether anything unusual occurred at about the same time as someone first shouted, "Fire!" Witnesses also prove critical for establishing motive for the blaze because of their knowledge of neighborhood residents. (Zipper and Wilcox 2005, 4)

Fire Databases

Investigators are also aided by federal government–run computerized fire databases. The Bureau of Alcohol, Tobacco, and Firearms provides the Arson and Explosives National Repository. The Bomb Data Center, administered by the Federal Bureau of Investigation, also collects some fire statistics. Both of these databases disseminate information for research and analysis, possibly leading to investigative leads or intelligence. The U.S. Fire Administration runs the National Fire Incident Reporting System, providing raw statistical fire data to investigators. State and local governments may also have fire data systems available (NIJ 2000a).

> Information in these databases helps investigators identify suspects, case-specific similarities regarding explosive and incendiary device construction, methods of initiation, types of fuels and explosives used, and methods of operation in explosives or arson cases. The databases are also designed to help investigators link thefts of explosive materials with criminal misuse of the explosives. (Office of the Inspector General 2004, 1)

EXPLOSIVES

The investigation of explosions is comparable to fire investigations, as the resultant damage is similar. The term *explosives*

> means any chemical compound, mixture or device, of which the primary purpose is to function by explosion, and includes but is not limited to dynamite and other high explosives, black powder, pellet powder, initiating explosives, detonators, safety fuses, squibs, detonating cord, igniter cord and igniters. (Office of the Kansas State Fire Marshal n.d., 96)

Explosives rapidly expand after ignition, spreading debris throughout a crime scene and damaging persons and property nearby. Explosives are thus used to vandalize property or kill or injure people.

Types of Explosives

Several different types of explosives are commonly used in crimes.

> The most common types of explosive/incendiary devices encountered by fire service and law enforcement personnel in the United States are traditionally pipe bombs, Molotov cocktails, and other improvised explosive/incendiary devices. The most common explosive materials used in these devices are flammable liquids and black and smokeless powder. (NIJ 2000b, 3)

Many of the materials used to create these devices are commonly available through retail shops. Instructions to make such explosives are widely available over the Internet and in books.

Car bombs are often used in terrorist incidents. A vehicle is capable of holding a large amount of explosive material. The mobility of a car bomb makes it extremely dangerous. A pipe bomb is a makeshift explosive device usually manufactured out of metal pipe. Molotov cocktails are flammable liquids in glass containers that ignite, shatter, and explode upon impact. Other incendiary devices are operated with timing mechanisms, allowing the suspect to be miles away when the explosion occurs.

Those who investigate explosives require specialized training. "The Hazardous Devices School (HDS), a joint effort between the FBI and the U.S. Army, represents the government's only civilian bomb school" (Jernigan 2006, 15–16). This school offers a basic, six-week course that includes training in how to disable an active device, operate robots used to handle explosive devices, and investigate blast scenes. Investigators attend this training to become Explosive Ordnance Disposal (EOD) technicians.

Explosion scenes are investigated according to National Fire Protection Association guidelines published in *NFPA 921: Guide for Fire and Explosion Investigations* (NIJ 2000a). EOD technicians are typically present to help investigate. Investigators must be cognizant of the possibility that secondary explosive devices may be present. Other hazards are similar to those at fire scenes, including damaged structural components and

Explosive ordnance technicians are trained in the operation of bomb-handling robotics.

hazardous materials (NIJ). Personal protective equipment is worn to guard against such dangers.

The point of an explosion is called the *seat*. The explosion may create a crater in and around the seat. The damage in the surrounding area is referred to as the *blast effect* (NIJ 2000b). Determining where the seat is may be important in figuring out how the explosive was delivered. The perimeter for the explosion scene should be established as the furthest identified point where material from the explosion is found. Physical evidence may be spread throughout this area and be deposited on victims, witnesses, and suspects in the zone. Canines are used to detect explosives and explosive materials similar to the way accelerant-detecting dogs are used.

Explosives may be acquired through legal purchases, but they are also obtained illegally through theft. "Stolen explosives...pose a significant threat to public safety in the United States" (NIJ 2000b, 3). Normal larceny investigative procedures are followed to capture thieves of explosive materials.

Databases

The ATF Arson and Explosives National Repository and FBI Bomb Data Center contain information about explosives in addition to the fire data mentioned previously. Information from these databases may be helpful in the investigation of explosions.

SUMMARY

Arson crimes cause over $3 billion in damages annually. The first step in an arson investigation is determining whether or not the fire was deliberately set. Fires are classified as either accidental or incendiary. The presence of igniters, accelerants, intense heat in particular areas, and irregular burn patterns indicate a possible arson. The activities of the property owner may also raise suspicion.

Arson fires may be started for revenge, to harm someone, out of curiosity, due to a psychological problem, or for economic reasons.

Both police agencies and fire departments are involved in arson investigations based upon their areas of expertise. Arson investigations are complicated by a lack of witnesses, the destruction of evidence by the fire, and the possibility of false arson reports. Scene conditions are also dangerous. Databases are maintained by the ATF and the U.S. Fire Administration to aid in the investigation of arson.

Explosion scenes are complicated by the disbursement of physical evidence from the crime. Explosive material may be purchased legitimately or stolen. Common explosives used in the United States are car bombs, Molotov cocktails, pipe bombs, and other improvised explosive devices. Specialized training is required to investigative blast crime scenes. Determining the seat of an explosion is an important first step in finding out how the explosive was delivered.

Key Terms

Accelerants: Highly flammable liquids used to spread a fire quickly and ensure an intense heat capable of sustaining the fire

Accidental fire: A fire that occurs without any malicious intent due to natural or unintentional circumstances

Arson: Any willful or malicious burning or attempt to burn, with or without intent to defraud, a dwelling house, public building, motor vehicle or aircraft, personal property of another, etc.

Blast effect: The damage surrounding the area of an explosion

Crazing: The bending of glass material due to intense heat

Depth of char: A measurement of how deeply a material has burned

Explosives: Any chemical compound, mixture, or device, of which the primary purpose is to function by explosion, and includes but is not limited to dynamite and other high explosives, black powder, pellet powder, initiating explosives, detonators, safety fuses, squibs, detonating cord, igniter cord and igniters

Igniters: Items used to start a fire, such as matches, electric starting devices, and fuses

Incendiary fire: A fire set intentionally by an individual

Line of demarcation: A line between charred and nonburned material in a fire scene

Point of origin: As it relates to fire investigation, the initial starting point of the fire, which is an important determination in an investigation

Pour pattern: An area of fire damage that closely resembles the shape of a liquid stain

Pyromania: A psychological disorder involving a fascination with fire

Seat: The point where an explosion occurs

Spalling: Damage caused to concrete or masonry due to intense heat and rapid cooling, producing a pitted appearance

Suspicious fire: A fire that has no readily apparent cause and requires further investigation

Trailer: A burn pattern that is caused by any combustible or flammable material used to spread fire from one point or area to another

Discussion Questions

1. What issues cause difficulties at arson crime scenes?

2. List some indicators of arson evidence. How would an investigator document and/or collect this evidence?

3. What hazards exist at explosion scenes? What can be done to protect investigators against these hazards?

Exploration

1. Read about the Bureau of Alcohol, Tobacco, and Firearm's investigative resources devoted to arson and explosive crimes: *www.atf.treas.gov/about/programs/proex.htm.*

2. Visit the U.S. Army's Redstone Arsenal training facility website and read about the Explosive Ordnance Disposal training programs offered there: *http://omems.redstone.army.mil/eod/eodtd.html.*

References

Australian Institute of Criminology. 2005. The arsonist's mind: Part 2—Pyromania. *BushFIRE Arson Bulletin* 9 (March 1). Available at www.aic.gov.au/topics/arson/arsonist.html.

City of Oklahoma City. n.d. *Prevention.* Oklahoma City: Author. Available at: www.okc.gov/fire/marshal/index.html.

Federal Bureau of Investigation (FBI). 2004. *Uniform crime reporting handbook.* Clarksburg, WV: U.S. Department of Justice.

Jernigan, David. 2006. Hazardous devices school. *FBI Law Enforcement Bulletin* 75, no. 8 (August): 14–19.

Maselli, Lynette. 2007. *Press release: Raleigh County man arrested on arson and insurance fraud charges*, May 8. Charleston: West Virginia Offices of the Insurance Commissioner. Available at www .wvinsurance.gov/pressrelease/pdf/pr-20070508.pdf.

Michigan v. Tyler. 436 U.S. 499. 1978.

National Fire Academy. 2002. *Arson detection for the first responder*, August. Emmitsburg, MD: U.S. Department of Homeland Security, National Fire Academy.

National Fire Data Center. 1997. *Arson in the United States*, August. Washington, DC: Federal Emergency Management Agency, National Fire Data Center.

National Institute of Justice (NIJ). 2000a. *Fire and arson scene evidence: A guide for public safety personnel*, June. Washington, DC: U.S.

National Institute of Justice (NIJ). 2000b. *A guide for explosion and bombing scene investigation*, June. Washington, DC: U.S.

Office of the Inspector General. 2004. *The Bureau of Alcohol, Tobacco, Firearms and Explosives' and Federal Bureau of Investigation's arson and explosives intelligence databases.* Washington, DC.

Office of the Kansas State Fire Marshal. n.d. *Revised statutes: K.S.A. Chapter 21.* Topeka, KS.

Piringer, Pete. 2006. *Press release: Potomac man arrested for arson*, December 29. Rockville, MD: Montgomery County Fire and Rescue Service. Available at www.montgomerycountymd.gov/ Apps/firerescue/Press/PR_details.asp?PrID=2981.

Upton, Janet. 2006. *Press release: CDF investigators arrest suspected serial arsonist*, July 24. Redding: California Department of Forestry and Fire Protection. Available at www.fire.ca.gov/newsreleases _content/downloads/2006archive/ArsonArrest_NR.pdf.

U.S. Fire Administration. 1989. *Establishing an arson strike force,* February. Emmitsburg, MD.

U.S. Fire Administration. 1993. *Basic tools and resources for fire investigators: A handbook,* September. Emmitsburg, MD.

U.S. Fire Administration. 2004. *Attacking the violent crime of arson.* Emmitsburg, MD.

Zipper, Paul, and David Wilcox. 2005. Juvenile arson. *FBI Law Enforcement Bulletin* 74, no. 4 (April): 1–8.

CHAPTER 16

FRAUD

CHAPTER OBJECTIVES

By the end of this chapter, the reader will be able to do the following:

- Define the crime of *fraud*.

- Define the term *negotiable instrument*.

- Define the various terms associated with negotiable instruments (*drawee, drawer, payee,* and *MICR*).

- List and describe the types of negotiable instrument fraud.

- Describe common methods used in investigating negotiable instrument fraud, including forensic document examination.

- Define the crime of *counterfeiting*.

- Describe different methods of counterfeiting.

- Describe common methods used to investigate counterfeiting operations.

- Describe common methods used to perpetrate credit card fraud.

- Describe common methods used to investigate credit card fraud.

- List and describe common *scams*.

- Describe common methods used to investigate scams.

- Define the term *identity theft*.

- Describe common methods used to perpetrate identity theft.

- Explain why identity theft is more complicated to investigate than other crimes.

- Describe common methods used to investigate identity theft.

Fraud is defined as "the intentional perversion of the truth for the purpose of inducing another person or other entity in reliance upon it to part with something of value or to surrender a legal right" (Federal Bureau of Investigation 2004, 140). Fraud involves obtaining something of value from another through the use of deceit. This can be accomplished through a variety of means, several of which will be explored within this chapter.

NEGOTIABLE INSTRUMENT (CHECK) FRAUD

A *negotiable instrument* is a written promise to pay for something, typically goods or services. The most common type of negotiable instrument is a personal check. Money orders, cashier's checks, and traveler's checks are also included under the category of negotiable instruments. The presentation of a negotiable instrument that is worthless may constitute the crime of fraud.

Several terms apply to the investigation of negotiable instruments. The *drawee* is the financial institution where the account is held; the drawee is required to pay the instrument once it is presented to it. The *drawer* is the subject who actually writes the check, normally a customer of the drawee. The *payee* is the individual or establishment authorized to receive payment from the drawee (bank) or to whom the drawer has written the negotiable instrument. *Magnetic Ink Character Recognition* (MICR) numbers are digits embossed on the bottom portion of a check that can be electronically read by bank equipment. "The numbers usually are encoded with the name and address of the drawee financial institution, the account number, and the check number. The dollar amount is added to the MICR line during check processing" (Check Fraud Working Group 1999, 1).

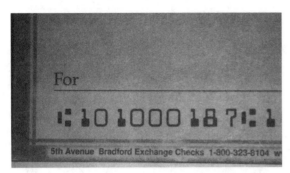

Magnetic Ink Character Recognition (MICR) allows for the faster processing of negotiable instruments.

In some instances, an individual may present a worthless check from a legitimate (but overdrawn) bank account that she is authorized to use. The passing of such a check may be without any malicious intent, as in cases where careless bookkeeping is involved. These cases may be classified as civil matters between the drawer and payee. In other cases, the individual knows that sufficient funds do not exist to cover the check but presents it as valid anyway. Insufficient fund laws vary from jurisdiction to jurisdiction. The level of criminal charges associated with such a case may vary according to the amount of the negotiable instrument.

Another type of fraud involving negotiable instruments is the use of checks drawn against closed bank accounts. "This type of fraud generally relies upon the float time involved in interfinancial institution transactions" (Check Fraud Working Group 1999, 6). The individual or retail establishment accepting the check may not know that it is valueless until the check reaches the writer's bank. At that time, the check will be returned unpaid.

Altered checks may also be used to defraud a drawee bank and payee.

> Altered checks are a common fraud that occurs after a legitimate maker creates a valid check to pay a debt. A criminal then takes the good check and uses chemicals or other means to erase the amount or the name of the payee, so that new information can be entered. (Check Fraud Working Group 1999, 2)

Alternatively, the defrauding party may have received the check under legitimate circumstances and simply increased the amount of the check through alteration. In other cases, the check may be stolen from the drawer's mailbox from a bill payment envelope or taken by an employee of the payee and subsequently altered. The alteration occurs through *check washing,* or using certain chemicals to remove ink but leave the check surface relatively undamaged.

Forgery is a form of fraud in which a person imitates the signature of another to gain something of value. Signing a personal check as the payee when an individual does not have the right to do so is an example of forgery. Forgery may also be used on other documents for material gain, such as life insurance policies and fake bills of sale.

Investigation

Electronic check-tracking measures, such as *Check 21,* have deterred negotiable instrument fraud.

> Check 21 authorizes the use of a new negotiable instrument, called a "substitute check," to facilitate the broader use of electronic check processing and sets forth requirements that affect savings associations that create or receive substitute checks, including consumer disclosures and expedited recredit procedures. (Check Fraud Working Group 2005, 2)

In other words, the payee's financial institution does not have to present the check physically to receive payment confirmation from the drawer's account. This reduces the float time that many who commit fraud count upon. Closed or insufficient accounts are also tracked by private companies who report to the payee at the point of sale; the check can be refused at that time to avoid fraud.

A benefit to investigators of negotiable instrument fraud is that witnesses typically exist who can offer testimonial evidence. A significant amount of time may be involved in the transaction process, allowing the victim or witness some time to view the perpetrator. This increases the chance that the suspect can be identified. Due to the nature of the crime, the suspect has likely given a false name during the transaction. However, the true identity of the offender may be established through capturing a subject in the act and linking him with other frauds or intelligence. Press releases of video surveillance footage may also help identify a potential suspect.

In addition to common physical evidence, such as fingerprints and video surveillance, investigators usually have the writing itself to review. Forensic document examination is the analysis of written documents, including negotiable instruments, to link a suspect to a crime. Trained investigators examine the writing on a document under different lighting sources and with specialized optical instruments. A comparison may be made between a writing example collected from a known source and a document from an unknown author (or "questioned" document). The examiner looks for internal consistencies or inconsistencies, identifying characteristics, and comparable elements in the writings (FBI 2000).

Based upon the forensic document examination, the investigator will generate a report of her findings. The findings may fall under one of several categories: that significant similarities or dissimilarities exist, that it is highly probable the person in question did write the document, that he probably wrote it, that indications exist that he wrote it, that no conclusions could be made, that indications exist that he did not write it, that he probably did not write it, that it is highly probable he did not write it, or that the person can be eliminated. These findings are based upon standards of comparability set forth by the Scientific Working Group for Forensic Document Examination (SWGDOC) (FBI 2000).

Handwriting samples are examined for unique characteristics in the writing.

COUNTERFEITING

Counterfeiting is defined as "the...copying, or imitating of something, without authority or right, with the intent to deceive or defraud by passing the copy or thing altered or imitated as that which is original or genuine." (FBI 2004, 140). Counterfeiting can be committed with any type of document, but it is most commonly done with checks and currency.

Investigation

The investigation of counterfeiting begins with detection. Retailers and individuals must recognize false notes during the initial transaction prior to passing them on to banks or others. If an individual is apprehended in the act of passing a counterfeit bill or check, follow-up investigations may reveal the source of multiple incidents. The individual may be interviewed, and searches may be conducted of her property to see if the person is involved in producing the bills or checks. Computer and copying equipment can be inspected to see if was used in counterfeiting. Additional counterfeit items may also be located.

In recognition of the overall impact that counterfeiting has on the country, the federal government has given the U.S. Secret Service responsibility for investigating counterfeit currency operations. "The Secret Service conducts investigations of counterfeiting activities and provides counterfeit-detection training" (U.S. GAO 1996, 6). The Secret Service often works in coordination with local police agencies in solving these cases.

CREDIT CARD FRAUD

Fraudulent activity also occurs through the use of credit devices. Stolen credit cards may be used at retail businesses prior to the card being reported as stolen. Credit card numbers may be obtained from written receipts, statements, the card itself, or from Internet transactions and used to purchase goods or obtain cash.

> Victims don't typically discover the crime until some time after it has occurred—in some cases, years. If a retailer has lax security, and an offender gets away with using a stolen credit card, the legitimate cardholder may not realize it until receiving the next card statement. (Newman 2004, 8)

Like other financial fraud crimes, credit card fraud involves several parties as potential victims. The holder of the credit card may be a victim, unless the credit card company covers the cost of the loss; in that case, the credit card issuer becomes the victim. Whoever sustains the loss of money is the victim of the fraud.

Investigation

Standard investigative procedures are utilized in investigating credit card fraud. As with counterfeiting, it is beneficial if an individual is caught in possession of the stolen credit card or card numbers or in the act of committing the credit card fraud. If a signature was required for the transaction, a forensic document examination may be conducted.

Investigators often work with private banks and credit-issuing companies (such as retailers and gas stations) in working on credit fraud cases. Credit company investigators are frequently able detect fraudulent transactions or attempted transactions more quickly through electronic tracking of purchases. Video surveillance from retail security camera systems may provide a picture of the perpetrator.

SCAMS

Fraud also occurs through *scams,* or ruses perpetrated to steal money from an unaware victim. Scams are conducted through a variety of means. Elderly individuals or those who are in desperate situations are often targeted in their moments of weakness. Scams tend to appeal to the victims' desire to help others or to help themselves out of rough situations. Scams may be perpetrated face-to-face, over the telephone, by mail, or over the Internet.

Common scams include the following:

- *Sweepstakes scam:* An individual is contacted and advised that he has won a contest or sweepstakes. The con artists "tell consumers that the only thing that separates them from their 'winnings' is a fee to cover the taxes or service charges" (FTC 2005b, ¶ 1). The winnings never materialize for the victims.

- *Fake accident:* The victim is told that a loved one has been involved in an accident and that money must be wired for medical treatment.

- *Bail bond:* This scam is similar to the fake accident, but the victim is told that the relative needs money to be bonded out of jail.

- *Widow scams:* Surviving spouses are contacted after an obituary is published in a newspaper. The con artist claims that the deceased person ordered goods or services and did not pay for them.

- *Repair schemes:* An individual offers to do some repair work on a victim's house, such as paving a driveway, with "leftover" materials from another job. Because of the reduced material costs, the victim is promised that the job can be completed cheaply. The victim pays for half of the work, but little to no work is done or what is completed is of no value (Office of Elder Services 1995).

- *Internet auction/classified ad scam:* "A scam artist replies to a classified ad or auction posting, offers to pay for the item with a check, and then comes up with a reason for writing the check for more than the purchase price. The scammer asks the seller to wire back the difference after depositing the check. The seller complies, and later, when the scammer's check bounces, the seller is left liable for the entire amount" (FTC 2007, "Fake Checks: Variations on a Scheme").

Investigation

Interagency cooperation is often needed to investigate scam operations successfully. These crimes frequently cross jurisdictional boundaries and may even span the globe. Perpetrators are difficult to track when scams are conducted via mail, the telephone, or the Internet. The federal government recognizes these difficulties and has established specific assistance to address these crimes.

The Internet Crime Complaint Center (IC3) was established as a partnership between the Federal Bureau of Investigation (FBI) and the National White Collar Crime Center (NW3C) to serve as a means to receive Internet related criminal complaints and to further research, develop, and refer the criminal complaints to federal, state, local, or international law enforcement and/or regulatory agencies for any investigation they deem to be appropriate. (Internet Crime Complaint Center n.d.)

The Federal Trade Commission also offers assistance in investigating scam crimes.

IDENTITY THEFT

Identity theft is a broad term that describes a situation in which one individual obtains and uses the identity of another. "Research indicates that the two dominant motives for identity theft are financial gain and concealment (either of true identity or of a crime)" (Newman 2004, 13). Identity theft is even used to conceal the identity of terrorists and illegal aliens. Identity theft is perpetrated by individuals and by groups who are skilled at stealing identifying information.

CASE STUDY

Homeland Security Secretary Michael Chertoff, Assistant Secretary for Immigration and Customs Enforcement (ICE) Julie L. Myers, Federal Trade Commission (FTC) Chairman Deborah Platt Majoras, and Cache County (UT) Attorney N. George Daines today announced that approximately 1,282 persons have been arrested as part of an ongoing worksite enforcement investigation into immigration violations and a massive identity theft scheme that has victimized large numbers of U.S. citizens and lawful U.S. residents. (U.S. Immigration and Customs Enforcement 2006, ¶ 1)

Six large meat-processing facilities were raided as part of the operation. Said Assistant Secretary Myers,

"This investigation has uncovered a disturbing front in the war against illegal immigration. We believe that the genuine identities of possibly hundreds of U.S. citizens are being stolen or hijacked by criminal organizations and sold to illegal aliens in order to gain unlawful employment in this country. Combating this burgeoning problem is one of ICE's highest priorities." (U.S. Immigration and Customs Enforcement 2006, ¶ 5)

Evidence uncovered during the investigation, which began in February 2006, indicates that hundreds of these illegal aliens may have illegally assumed the identities of U.S. citizens and improperly used their Social Security numbers and other identity documents in order to gain employment at [the meat packing] facilities. The investigation has uncovered criminal organizations around the country that traffic in genuine birth certificates and Social Security cards belonging to U.S. citizens. In other cases, they have purchased these documents from U.S. citizens willing to sell their identities for money, including homeless people and individuals in jail. (U.S. Immigration and Customs Enforcement 2006, ¶ 6)

Information may be obtained through larceny, mail theft, computer phishing, trash theft, vehicle larceny, collusion with businesses, or illicit purchases on the street (Newman 2004). Once the information is stolen, it may be used to open checking and credit card accounts, take out a loan, or sign an insurance policy to defraud the company using another's name. The losses to organizations can be staggering.

Law enforcement professionals should be aware that suspects have presented counterfeit or altered identification documents to obtain [Social Security] cards and then used them to acquire multiple credit cards, resulting in the loss of hundreds of thousands of dollars to credit card companies. (Ballezza 2007, 15)

Account statement and receipts are recovered from discarded trash by identity thieves. Shredding is recommended to protect individuals from victimization.

Identity theft is distinguished from other crimes for several reasons. Identity theft laws are often vague and the crime is more difficult to prove than related crimes, such as fraud or forgery. Identity theft is usually not a singular incident but a series and pattern of interrelated events. "A significant feature of identity theft is the offender's repeated victimization of a single person. This may include repeatedly using a stolen credit card, taking over a card account, or using stolen personal information to open new accounts" (Newman 2004, 1). The crime often takes years for the victim to clear up, as he works to repair his damaged credit.

Investigation

The deterrence of identity theft begins with the securing of data and information, keeping it out of the hands of perpetrators. This is difficult to achieve, as some information necessarily is divulged through normal business and government transactions. A study found that

> approximately one-third of offenders used their employment to carry out their crimes. These offenders included those who worked for mortgage agencies, government workers (e.g., state department of motor vehicles), or businesses that have access to credit card numbers and/or social security numbers (e.g., banks, universities, convenience stores). (Copes and Vieraitis 2007, 4)

Due to this fact, consumer education has emerged as an important strategy to combat identity theft. Consumers must also be encouraged to report identity theft when it occurs.

Like other financial crimes, identity theft is difficult to investigate as it may involve multiple victims, including individuals, financial institutions, and retail establishments. "Identity theft crimes fall under the authority of many different agencies, including the local police, Secret Service, Postal Inspection Service, FBI, Homeland Security, local government offices, and motor vehicle departments, to name just a few" (Newman 2004, 30). A task force approach is often utilized to overcome these difficulties.

Laws applicable to identity theft are becoming more common as the issue is becoming more recognized. Local, state, and federal laws prohibit the use of another person's information for one's own gain. Additionally, laws hold organizations accountable for information held in their databases. "State and/or federal laws such as GLB

(Gramm-Leach-Bliley Act), HIPAA (Health Insurance Portability and Accountability Act of 1996), and FACTA (Fair and Accurate Credit Transactions Act) require certain businesses or institutions to protect information better" (Newman 2004, 33).

To help track identity theft and aid law enforcement, the Federal Trade Commission established the Identity Theft Data Clearinghouse in 1999 (FTC 2005a). Through use of the clearinghouse, trends can be evaluated to help reduce the availability of information for identity thieves. Law enforcement may also use the database to coordinate investigations with other agencies throughout the country.

SUMMARY

Fraud is perpetrated in a number of ways. A common method is through the use of negotiable instruments. Offenders may use worthless checks drawn against closed accounts, stolen accounts, or bogus accounts. The amount listed on a valid check may also be altered. Forgery is the crime of falsifying a person's signature to commit fraud. Fraud is deterred through more rapid check processing via systems such as Check 21. Fraud investigation is aided by forensic document examination, which can help determine whether or not similarities exist in writing.

Counterfeiting is perpetrated with both negotiable instruments and currency. Various methods are used to counterfeit currency and documents, many involving the use of computer and duplication equipment. Detection of counterfeit bills is important in deterrence and has been aided by the addition of security features. The U.S. Secret Service is charged with investigating counterfeit currency due to the impact the crime has on the economy.

Fraud is perpetrated through credit cards as well. The victim of credit card fraud may be the card holder, the bank, or the business accepting the card, depending upon who suffers the loss of funds. A private business-police relationship helps in the investigation of credit card fraud, as tracking is more easily facilitated by the issuing company.

Scams are schemes to defraud an individual of money. Various types of scams play upon the weaknesses of carefully selected victims. Scams may be perpetrated face-to-face, by mail, by the Internet, or by the phone. Interagency cooperation is often necessary when investigating scams, as the crimes frequently cross jurisdictional boundaries.

Identity theft involves the use of a victim's information to open fraudulent accounts for material gain. Information is obtained through a variety of sources, including the Internet, trash dumpsters, and larceny and burglary crimes. Identity theft is difficult to investigate as it may not be restricted to a single incident; the victim may be repeatedly victimized over time. Identity theft is reduced through the securing of data. More laws have been passed in recent years to address identity theft. Federal government databases have been created to help track identity theft.

Key Terms

Check 21: An electronic check payment system that speeds the transfer of negotiable instrument funds

Check washing: The use of chemicals to remove ink from a check, leaving other characteristics relatively undamaged

Counterfeiting: "The copying or imitating of something, without authority or right, with the intent to deceive or defraud by passing the copy or thing altered or imitated as that which is original or genuine" (Federal Bureau of Investigation 2004, p. 140).

Drawee: The financial institution where an account is held that is required to pay a negotiable instrument once it is presented

Drawer: A subject who writes a negotiable instrument

Forgery: The falsification of a signature to commit fraud

Fraud: "The intentional perversion of the truth for the purpose of inducing another person or other entity...to part with something of value or to surrender a legal right" (Federal Bureau of Investigation 2004, p. 140)

Identity theft: The use of a victim's identifying information to defraud the individual

Magnetic Ink Character Recognition (MICR) numbers: Encoded magnetic digits embossed on the bottom of a check that can be read electronically by bank equipment

Negotiable instrument: A written promise to pay for a good or service

Payee: The individual or establishment authorized to receive payment from the drawee (bank) or to whom the drawer has written the negotiable instrument to

Scams: Ruses perpetrated to defraud an individual for material gain

Discussion Questions

1. Aside from checks, what documents may be evaluated through forensic document examination during the course of various investigations?

2. A search warrant is conducted on a residence that is purportedly involved in a currency-counterfeiting operation. What types of items are likely to be seized and why?

3. What steps can be taken by a criminal justice agency to deter scams within the community? What about identity theft?

Exploration

1. Explore steps that the U.S. Mint and the Secret Service have taken to deter counterfeiting: *www.ustreas.gov/usss/know_your_money .shtml*.

2. Review the FTC's suggestions for preventing identity theft: *www .ftc.gov/bcp/edu/microsites/idtheft/*.

References

Ballezza, Richard. 2007. Identity and credit card fraud issues. *FBI Law Enforcement Bulletin* 76, no. 5 (May): 11–15.

Check Fraud Working Group. 1999. *Check fraud: A guide to avoiding losses,* February. Washington, DC: U.S. Department of the Treasury.

Copes, Heith, and Lynne Vieraitis. 2007. *Identity theft: Assessing offenders' strategies and perceptions of risk,* July. Birmingham: University of Alabama.

Federal Bureau of Investigation (FBI). 2000. Guidelines for forensic document examination. *Forensic Science Communications* 2, no. 2 (April). Available at www.fbi.gov/hq/lab/fsc/backissu/april2000/swgdoc1.htm.

Federal Bureau of Investigation (FBI). 2004. *Uniform crime reporting handbook.* Clarksburg, WV: U.S. Department of Justice.

Federal Reserve Board. 2004. *U.S. unveils new $50 note with background colors,* April 26. Washington, DC.

Federal Trade Commission (FTC). 2005a. *National and state trends in fraud and identity theft, January–December 2004,* February. Washington, DC.

Federal Trade Commission (FTC). 2005b. *New spin on sweepstakes scams,* October. Washington, DC: Author. Available at www.ftc.gov/bcp/conline/pubs/alerts/sweepsalrt.shtm.

Federal Trade Commission (FTC). 2007. *Giving the bounce to counterfeit check scams,* January. Washington, DC: Author. Available at www.ftc.gov/bcp/edu/pubs/consumer/credit/cre40.shtm.

Internet Crime Complaint Center. n.d. *About us.* Retrieved November 11, 2007, from www.ic3.gov/about/.

Newman, Graeme. 2004. *Identity theft,* June. U.S. Department of Justice: Office of Community Oriented Policing Services.

Office of Elder Services. 1995. *Fighting financial exploitation.* Augusta: Maine Department of Health and Human Services.

U.S. Attorney, District of Nevada. 2005. *Press release: Leader of counterfeit check ring sentenced to 175 months in prison,* May.

Las Vegas, NV: U.S. Department of Justice. Available at www.usdoj.gov/usao/nv/home/pressrelease/may2005/leung051705.htm.

U.S. General Accounting Office. 1997. *Treasury's plan to study genuine and counterfeit U.S. currency abroad.* April. Washington, D.C.

U.S. Immigration and Customs Enforcement. 2006. *U.S. uncovers large-scale identity theft scheme used by aliens to gain employment at nationwide food processor,* December 13. Washington, DC: Author. Available at www.ice.gov/pi/news/newsreleases/articles/061213dc.htm.

CHAPTER 17

EMERGING INVESTIGATIVE CHALLENGES AND TECHNIQUES

As the political and technological landscape of the world evolves, crime transforms along with it, and investigators adapt their methods and techniques to keep up. Technology available to those involved in criminal activity is also available to law enforcement investigators working to counteract these crimes.

There are many developing trends in crime and criminal investigation. This chapter will explore some of the most significant current challenges as well as recent advancements in criminal investigation to address the growing types of crime in society.

CHALLENGES

Computer Crime

Computers have become available to individual users worldwide as technology has developed and costs have decreased. Computers have increased worldwide communication capabilities through the use of the Internet. This form of communication has amplified opportunities for criminal exploitation on a global scale. Law enforcement has struggled to keep up with the numerous challenges presented by computer crimes. Included in this category are child pornography, solicitation, exploitation crimes, and Internet fraud.

Crimes against children are of particular concern to criminal investigators. While the Internet is a great source of communication among businesses and individuals, this same pathway has provided dangerous sex offenders access to minors.

> From the safety of their homes, pedophiles can use the Internet to anonymously and simultaneously prepare numerous children for future molestations. With the click of a mouse, child pornographers easily can distribute their collections to many other offenders or even to juveniles. (Bowker and Gray 2005, 12)

Networks of sex offenders have developed, facilitating the open exchange of illicit photographs and information.

"Before the advent of the Internet, individuals with deviant tendencies usually were isolated. Today, however, offenders feel normal because they see from chat rooms and Web sites that many other individuals have the same interests" (Bowker and Gray 2005, 14). As sex offenders communicate, they help each other develop skill at gaining access to children targeted for exploitation. Offenders solicit children for sex or to pose for pornographic pictures.

Individuals also use computers to gather information about others to perpetrate fraud. The information may be identifying data, such as Social Security numbers and dates of birth, or financial account numbers. Perpetrators use this information to open new accounts or access existing accounts to steal money or goods.

Information is stolen through several approaches. Spyware programs are computer viruses surreptitiously installed on computer hard drives that give remote users access to information on a subject's computer. An individual may open an email attachment, thinking it is a picture; however, the attachment actually installs a spyware program on the computer. Another method of gaining information covertly is "phishing." Phishing involves directing a person to a fraudulent website where the individual unknowingly enters identifying information. For instance, an email that appears to be valid but is actually counterfeit may ask a person to update his account information. The email contains a link to a bogus website. The consumer may unwittingly enter his account number, Social Security number, or other information at that website, providing the offender with all the information needed to access his account fraudulently.

Fraud may also occur through the sale of goods or services via the Internet that are either never delivered or are not what they were purported to be. Internet auction sites, for instance, provide criminals the means to sell goods and accept payment without delivering the items. Others may advertise name-brand electronic items but instead deliver imitation goods that are similar in appearance.

In addition to these Internet-perpetrated crimes, criminals use computers to store records and logs of traditional criminal activity.

> Criminals keep records of transactions, document planned crimes, and communicate with their peers via personal computers. As a result, courts now are being asked to analyze searches and seizures of computer equipment, computer peripherals, and information obtained from ISPs (Internet Service Providers) based on the venerable Fourth Amendment to the U.S. Constitution. (Cogar 2003, 11)

Computer records of interest to law enforcement include financial data, chat room and instant messenger transcripts, emails, and clandestine drug recipes.

Investigations involving computers are taxing upon law enforcement because they require a specialized expertise and approach. "[The large number of computer-related crimes] puts a strain on computer forensic examiners who have the training, skills, and abilities to properly handle digital evidence" (Mercer 2004, 28). Police agencies will need to improve their capability of performing these types of investigations. Some progress has been made in computer-based investigation; this will be explored in the techniques section of this chapter.

Identity Theft

Identity theft was described in chapter 16. This particular type of criminal activity continues to grow as the market trends toward the electronic exchange of funds and goods. "Between January and December 2005, Consumer Sentinel, the complaint database developed and maintained by the FTC, received over 685,000 consumer fraud and identity theft complaints. Consumers reported losses from fraud of more than $680 million" (Federal Trade Commission 2006, 2). Particularly in large, urban areas, merchants and bankers do not know their customers as well as they did in the past. As a result, it is not difficult to assume the identity of another person.

Identity theft investigations need to be addressed through joint operations among investigative elements at different levels of government and private sector financial institutions. Local agencies are often the first to be contacted by victims of identity theft. At the federal level, the Federal Trade Commission, Federal Bureau of Investigation, and Internal Revenue Service are only a few of the many agencies that might become involved in an identity theft case. Private sector businesses and financial institutions often have their own security teams, many of which now have identity theft specialists on staff.

Terrorism

The terrorist attacks within the United States on September 11, 2001, alerted many worldwide of the dangers associated with organized terrorism. However, terrorism has existed for centuries, both within and outside of the United States. It was unfortunate that it took such a devastating attack to cause an increase in the resources available to law enforcement and improve the approaches required to investigate terrorism successfully.

Law enforcement at all levels of government will need to continue to monitor terrorist activities. An assessment of terrorist threats published in 2007 described the apparent existing and evolving concerns:

> We judge the US Homeland will face a persistent and evolving terrorist threat over the next three years. The main threat comes from Islamic terrorist groups and cells, especially al-Qa'ida, driven by their undiminished intent to attack the Homeland and a continued effort by these terrorist groups to adapt and improve their capabilities. (National Intelligence Council 2007, 6)

We assess that al-Qa'ida's Homeland plotting is likely to continue to focus on prominent political, economic, and infrastructure targets with the goal of producing mass casualties, visually dramatic destruction, significant economic aftershocks, and/or fear among the US population. The group is proficient with conventional small arms and improvised explosive devices, and is innovative in creating new capabilities and overcoming security obstacles. (National Intelligence Council 2007, 6)

Drugs

Drugs that have been the focus of law enforcement for some time, such as cocaine, heroin, and marijuana, will continue to be a concern in coming years. Methamphetamine use and production continues to spread geographically throughout the United States (National Institute on Drug Abuse 2004). In addition to the continued problem posed by these common narcotics, new trends continue to develop.

The abuse of prescription medications seems to be a developing concern. "Opiates/narcotics (excluding heroin) appear increasingly in drug indicator data, particularly hydrocodone and oxycodone products" (National Institute on Drug Abuse 2004, 2). Prescription fraud, both from the consumer and supplier side, will likely be an issue for law enforcement in coming years. Criminal investigators may find themselves working increasingly with medical professionals to decrease the illicit use and trafficking of medications.

TECHNIQUES

Some of the challenges presented by developing crime trends have been explored in the first part of this chapter. Law enforcement can address some of these challenges through the development and enhancement of investigative techniques. Two particular areas that have been improved and will continue to expand are digital evidence processing and intelligence. The investigation of each of the challenges presented previously can be aided through these techniques.

Digital Evidence Processing

The forensic investigation of digital evidence can be helpful in a variety of crimes.

CASE STUDY

Local police investigating a homicide in upstate New York during 2005 found a weird combination of evidence in the home of the chief suspect: an old, war-relic hatchet, a note written in Italian, and a personal computer. Investigators from the New York State Police (NYSP) Computer Crimes Unit (CCU) were called in to see if they could shed any light on the puzzle. Their analysis of the PC showed the online search engines Google and Ask had been used to research methods of committing a homicide. (New York State Police Department 2007, 54)

In recognition of the importance of digital evidence, police agencies are developing approaches and standards for collecting and examining electronic data.

Agencies that employ or use computer forensic laboratory resources must recognize that computer forensic examiners need to 1) adhere to a set of scientific standards that include a chain of custody policy encompassing the unique nature of digital evidence, 2) use standard operating procedures that assure known results from duplication and authentication, and 3) follow policies that meet standards of forensic science and expert witness testimony as promulgated by the courts. (Mercer 2004, 32)

Digital evidence is not limited to computer storage devices. Evidence can be contained in cell phones, pagers, digital cameras, pocket personal computers or personal digital assistants (PDAs), or any number of devices. Communication records, images, and even global positioning satellite tracking data may be available from these devices.

To meet increasing digital evidence-processing needs, Regional Computer Forensics Laboratories, or RCFLs, have been developed, chiefly through the Federal Bureau of Investigation. These laboratories specialize in examining digital evidence without destroying it. Among the cases commonly address by RCFLs are "Terrorism, Child Pornography, Crimes of Violence, Trade secret theft, Theft or destruction to intellectual property, Financial crime, Property crime, Internet crimes, [and] Fraud" (Regional Computer Forensics Laboratory n.d., ¶ 1).

In addition to the RCFLs, local and state crime labs have increased their digital evidence-processing capabilities. The training of law enforcement officers should include procedures to ensure the safe collection and storage of this type of evidence as it becomes more and more common.

Intelligence

Intelligence efforts have always existed in law enforcement, but the increasing global nature of criminal activity has necessitated the expansion of the intelligence function. In wake of the September 11 terrorist attacks, the 9/11 Commission stated that "intelligence gathered about transnational terrorism should be processed, turned into reports, and distributed according to the same quality standards, whether it is collected in Pakistan or in Texas" (National Commission on Terror Attacks Upon the United States 2004, 417). Intelligence is not related to terrorism only; it can include any type of crime that is likely to span jurisdictional borders. Such crimes include computer fraud and sex crimes, serial murders, auto theft, and a myriad of other activities.

Training in threat analysis will likely continue to increase. Agencies at the local, state, and national level will need to coordinate communication and develop conduits for the exchange of confidential information. Distribution of this information is as important as its collection. Each of these areas is important to address formally to ensure that the intelligence function works properly.

Various intelligence groups have been developed to improve operations. Terrorism Early Warning centers, or TEWs, are one approach. An example is the St. Louis, Missouri, Terrorism Early Warning Center.

The St. Louis Terrorism Early Warning (TEW) Group provides a public safety partnership consisting of local, state and federal agencies, as well as the public sector and private entities that will collect, evaluate, analyze, and disseminate information and intelligence to the agencies tasked with Homeland Security responsibilities in a timely, effective, and secure manner. (St. Louis Terrorism Early Warning Group n.d., ¶ 1)

It is likely that these multijurisdictional efforts will continue to grow. Efforts will need to be made to coordinate these groups to ensure that duplication of effort is reduced and intelligence is distributed through a focused conduit.

References

Bowker, Arthur and Michael Gray. 2005. *The cybersex offender and children. FBI Law Enforcement Bulletin.* March 74 (3): 12–17.

Cogar, Stephen. 2003. Obtaining admissible evidence from computers and Internet providers. *FBI Law Enforcement Bulletin* 72, no. 7 (July): 11–15.

Federal Trade Commission (FTC). 2006. *Consumer fraud and identity theft data, January-December 2005,* January. Washington, DC.

Mercer, Loren. 2004. Computer forensics: Characteristics and preservation of digital evidence. *FBI Law Enforcement Bulletin* 73, no. 3 (March): 28–32.

National Commission on Terror Attacks Upon the United States. 2004. *The 9/11 Commission report: Final report of the National Commission on Terrorist Attacks Upon the United States.* Washington, DC.

National Institute on Drug Abuse. 2004. *Nationwide trends,* September. Bethesda, MD: U.S. Department of Health and Human Services.

National Intelligence Council. 2007. *The terrorist threat to the US homeland,* July. Washington, DC: National Intelligence Council.

New York State Police Department. 2007. NYSP computer crimes unit: A full-service approach to fighting crime. *FBI Law Enforcement Bulletin* 76, no. 1 (January): 54–57.

Regional Computer Forensics Laboratory. n.d. *About RCFLs.* Retrieved November 24, 2007, from www.rcfl.gov/index.cfm?fuseAction=Public.P_about.

St. Louis Terrorism Early Warning Group. n.d. *What is the TEW and why is it needed?* Retrieved November 24, 2007, from www.sltew.org/index.cfm/CFID/436929/CFTOKEN/72125728/MenuItemID/103.htm.

INDEX